THE COMMODITY FUTURES MARKET GUIDE

Stanley Kroll
and
Irwin Shishko

NEW YORK, EVANSTON, SAN FRANCISCO, LONDON

1817

THE COMMODITY FUTURES MARKET GUIDE

HARPER & ROW, PUBLISHERS

A portion of this book previously appeared
in *CPA Journal* in somewhat different form.

STANDARD BOOK NUMBER: 06-033397-9

LIBRARY OF CONGRESS CATALOG CARD NUMBER: 69-15315

Designed by Sidney Feinberg

CONTENTS

v

PREFACE

In writing this book we are, first of all, mindful of the evidence that most speculators lose money trading commodities. This point merits reflection by anyone who contemplates trading. It suggests the need for a critical evaluation of the opinions and methods which have, so far, guided individuals and trade interests in their pursuit of commodity profits.

It is remarkable that so much of what passes for commodity economics on Wall Street leans more on intuition and precedent than on objective scientific method. Few commodity analysts are highly trained either in economics or statistics. Few opinions developed and disseminated by brokers or advisory services owe their origin to tested or refined methods.

One reason for the unscientific nature of most commodity research on Wall Street is the prevalent scepticism concerning "systems" in general. Sophisticated methods have not generally proven themselves in the only way that counts—making money. A second and more important reason is that, to date, Wall Street has not been prepared to invest the necessary money and effort to develop professional commodity research.

This picture is hopefully beginning to improve, in response to the demands of a computer-age public which is becoming increasingly sceptical of arbitrary methods of opinion-making, and of buy or sell recommendations which often seem more calculated to promote business than to objectively interpret the market. It is our earnest hope that this book will help to accelerate the trend towards more careful and disciplined commodity research.

A distinguishing feature of this "new commodity research" is the belief that, whenever possible, trading concepts and "decision rules" should be formulated in ways that can be tested. Sometimes this new research contradicts popular Wall Street ideas. We have not hesitated to challenge existing ideas where they seemed unsupportable, or to utilize them where they seemed sound.

Ideally, commodity research should merge the insights derived from practical trading experience with the more formal methods and standards of the academic community. Analogously, this book merges the viewpoints of two authors: one a seasoned broker in commodities and commodity futures; the other an economist with long experience as a commodity consultant to brokerage firms, commercial interests, and government organizations.

In writing this book, we have had the benefit of a number of fine popular works already published in this field. We have tried to add to this materially, particularly in our stress on systematic methods and tested decision rules. We have incorporated, on an introductory level, material on the use of the computer in commodity research, both as a tool for trend-following studies, and as an implement for economic analysis.

Other features of this book include:

1. A thorough reevaluation of technical and fundamental methods of price analysis.
2. An examination of futures' versatility as both a pricing and a marketing medium.
3. A survey of government regulations of commodity markets, both domestic and international.
4. A study of the logic of changing price differences, as they affect hedgers and straddle traders.
5. A unique chapter concerning commodity put and call options.
6. An appendix with basic trading information concerning the principal commodities traded in the United States, Canada and Great Britain.

In addition to focusing on both speculative and trade interests, one audience to which this book directs particular attention is the university or graduate school student, desirous of studying the commodity exchanges and their expanding role in the world marketing system. We have sought to provide this academic audience with a commodity book that is unique in coverage, innovative in concept and realistic in approach. It is our hope that this book will fill a pressing need for a comprehensive text in commodity courses.

Finally, we have tried to portray, as candidly as possible, the problems which face anyone who tries to "beat the commodity market." It is our intention to discourage all those who, by fortune or disposition, are ill-suited to the hazards of futures trading. At the same time, we expect our "technical" sections to be particularly helpful to all who trade commodity futures, whether producers or users, hedgers or speculators.

This book, in short, seeks to aid and instruct the speculator, the hedger, and the academic student, and to encourage the professionalization of commodity research on Wall Street.

STANLEY KROLL

IRWIN SHISHKO

PART **I**

ORGANIZED COMMODITY

MARKETS: THEIR DEVELOPMENT

AND OPERATION

CHAPTER 1 The History of Futures Markets

Commodities have been linked with organized commerce for at least 50 centuries. Ancient Sumerian documents, circa 3,000 B.C., reveal a systematic use of credit based on loans of grain by volume and loans of metal by weight.

Active markets in commodities, under rules and regulations, existed in China, Egypt, Arabia, and India 12 centuries before the coming of Christendom. In the city-states of Greece, occasionally beset by famines, laws were enacted to assure food supplies and to prevent manipulation. The specialization of markets for trade in a single commodity was accomplished in pre-Christian Rome. According to Baer and Saxon:

> In the heyday of Roman dominion and power by land and sea there were in Rome nineteen . . . trading markets, called "fora vendalia" (sales markets), which specialized in the distribution of specific commodities, many of them brought from the far corners of the earth by caravan and galley.[1]

Modern futures markets are offshoots of medieval European seasonal festivals, the most important of which took place in the county of Champagne, in central France. Typically, the locale of these fairs was the principal production or distribution center for each particular commodity. Although initially established as annual events, many of these bazaars evolved into important year-round markets, incorporating such features of present-day futures markets as self-regulation of business conduct, guarantee of contract fulfillment, and mutual trust among merchants.

As the volume of goods traded on these interregional markets expanded, the merchants became increasingly sophisticated, and began to concentrate

---

1. J. B. Baer and O. G. Saxon, *Commodity Exchanges and Futures Trading,* New York, Harper & Brothers, 1947, p. 4.

3

on particular specialized facets of marketing. The history of commerce reveals an early recognition by businessmen of the risks involved in owning goods, and a continuing attempt to either reduce or transfer these risks to others. It has been reported that the ancient Chinese and Romans formed syndicates to pool risks and share profits. But it was not until the sixteenth century that the pooling of risks of marine loss was actually documented, in northern Italian commercial centers. During the latter part of that century, a great commercial insurance dynasty was founded in the English coffee house of Edward Lloyd.

The Industrial Revolution, beginning in the late eighteenth century, witnessed an extensive replacement of hand labor by machinery for the production and processing of goods. The time required for conversion of raw into finished products was telescoped, and the demand for commodities multiplied manyfold. To supply this growing demand, an enormous volume of commodities poured into the channels of world trade. For example, British imports of raw cotton soared from an estimated 11 million pounds in 1785 to approximately 588 million pounds in 1850.

The profits of the world's merchants swelled, but frequent market debacles marred their good fortune. It became increasingly urgent that some workable means be found to reduce the price risks inherent in ownership of commodities. Such efforts took place in both the cotton and the grain trades around the beginning of the nineteenth century. Buyers of cotton and grain, particularly those European and English merchants who imported these commodities from the United States, were exposed to price risks of ownership from the time that their agents bought the raw commodities in North America, until the goods were received and ultimately sold on the continent. Typically, this involved a high-risk period of several months' duration. In order to reduce this interval, a number of European and English importers arranged for their purchasing agents to forward details and samples, via fast clipper ships, while the goods themselves were being shipped aboard slower cargo vessels. So aided, these merchants commenced selling their goods on a "to-arrive" basis, while the goods were still afloat. Such contracts were arranged for the to-arrive delivery of specified lots of wheat as early as 1821. Liverpool developed one of the earliest organized to-arrive markets; when the volume of trading expanded sufficiently to attract speculators and full-time brokers in "arrival" contracts, an outdoor trading place was established on an area adjoining the site of the present Liverpool Cotton Exchange Building.

In 1866, the first trans-Atlantic cable came into service. A Liverpool cotton importer, John Rew, conceived of a way to limit price risks, by arranging for his American correspondents to immediately report their purchases for him, by cable. He then sold to-arrive contracts in an equal quantity on the theory that, if prices declined, he could offset his "actuals" losses through a gain on the short to-arrive sale. Within a short time, other importers imitated this practice, and there soon developed a thriving volume of trading in to-arrive contracts. This practice became known as "hedging," a term still commonly used today.[2] Discussing the development of modern futures trading in the cotton industry, Fleming states:

> Originally, the Liverpool "to-arrive" contracts named a specific vessel. As the usefulness developed of trading for deliveries more remote than those of a vessel currently loading or afloat, the original contract was revised to provide for sailing within a specified month. As the use became more general of steam cargo vessels, trading began in contracts for delivery in New York or in Liverpool in a specified month. Then the contracts came to be known as "futures" contracts instead of "to-arrive" contracts.
>
> Use of futures contracts became so extensive that adequate contract forms and rules and provisions for adjudication of differences and enforcement of contracts had to be worked out. In 1868 the New York Board of Cotton Brokers was organized, with a fixed set of rules and regulations for trading for future delivery. In 1870, 106 merchants and brokers organized the New York Cotton Exchange and rented trading rooms.[3]

Coincidental with the introduction of to-arrive trading in Liverpool, grain trading evolved in the United States on a to-arrive Chicago basis.

In his book Edward J. Dies vividly recalls the development of Chicago as the major grain center of the time:

> Like the finger of destiny, the historic pilgrimage of pioneers pointed ever Westward, straggling onward in unending lines. "Caravans of Faith" they were called as they joggled along Illinois and into Iowa. Theirs was a profound faith, the faith of the dreamer striking out for the land of his dreams.
>
> The acreage which the pioneers planted to grain continued widening each year. They shipped their grain to Chicago, then an ugly little town cuddled on the shore of the lake. Part of the money received in return was quickly converted into farm implements. These implements meant larger production. Subsequently, the stream of grain that poured into Chicago bulged the sides of the little town and made necessary almost constant expansion of marketing and storing facilities.[4]

In the early 1850's the volume of grain shipped into Chicago was so heavy that many streets became completely congested with produce-laden wagons. The existing cash markets were inadequate to handle the vast influx. With most merchants overstocked and banks unable to finance

2. Hedging is discussed in detail in Part VI.
3. Lamar Fleming, Jr., Chairman of the Board, Anderson Clayton and Company, in addressing a symposium sponsored by the New York Commodity Exchanges, in New York, November 7, 1961.
4. Edward J. Dies, *The Wheat Pit,* Chicago, Argyle Press, 1925, p. 10.

additional inventory expansion, farmers were forced to sell for whatever prices they could get. Prices of grain plummeted, and many farmers lost not only their grain, but their teams and wagons as well.

To avoid the recurrence of such widespread distress selling, the more enterprising and far-sighted grain producers began to offer contracts to deliver a specified quantity of grain at a designated place within a given number of days. This marked the introduction of to-arrive marketing in the United States, and stimulated the development of the Board of Trade of the City of Chicago. The Chicago Board of Trade, as it is commonly called, was officially established in 1848, but did not function as an organized futures exchange until 1865.

The development of trading in to-arrive contracts in the United States represented a major advance in the field of marketing, providing elements of flexibility not present in earlier cash markets. Forward sales could be made on the basis of samples, or even on description of goods by reputable merchants. Delivery time could be extended over a period of months, although actual title of ownership was transferred at the time that the to-arrive agreement was executed. Thus was introduced the concept of a negotiable title to goods, which could be traded back and forth many times prior to settlement via delivery. For example, in August 1856, during a period of rising prices and speculation occasioned by the Crimean War, it was reported that a single parcel of 15,000 bushels of corn passed through 14 different hands during a 2-day period, ultimately settling time contracts amounting to approximately 200,000 bushels.

The pattern of rising prices and speculation in commodity markets which developed during the Crimean War (1854–1856) was duplicated on a much larger scale during and just after the Civil War. In this period of greatly expanded world commerce, weaknesses of the to-arrive system of marketing became evident. Through the to-arrive contract, the burden of price risk had been successfully shifted from the seller of commodities (the farmer and producer) to the buyer of commodities (the processor, manufacturer, and importer). This latter group was forced to seek higher profit margins as compensation for their additional price risks. However, marketing competition exerted pressure on profit margins as well as on the price spread between producer and consumer. Moreover, after assuming the risks of ownership, trade firms frequently found themselves unable to arrange sufficient bank loans on their unhedged inventory. And this, in turn, inhibited the expansion and development of the commodities industry.

It was obvious that the risk of price fluctuation in ownership of commodities had to be transferred once more. But to whom? There existed, at that time, just a limited number of speculators willing to trade in to-arrive contracts. What the commodity markets needed was a much larger speculative following, to provide the breadth and liquidity that was lacking.

Unfortunately, the sole medium of commodity speculation was the to-arrive contract. This "contract" contained too many variable factors to attract sufficient nontrade speculative capital. First of all, to-arrive shipments varied in grade and quantity. A speculator not closely connected with a particular commodity could rarely determine in advance exactly what goods were involved in any given transaction. Prices were frequently established through secret "deals," with large operators enjoying price advantages over small traders. The nontrade speculator was unable to ascertain the price of his goods at any given time. In addition, terms of payment varied, being subject to individual bargaining.

The lack of an effective mechanism to enforce contract compliance was another serious weakness in to-arrive trading. A speculator had no guarantee that the other party to a transaction would fulfill his contractual obligation, particularly if a substantial settlement was involved. Also, there was no assurance that the goods, upon delivery, would be in good condition and of the prescribed grade and quantity.

These impediments to the expansion of commodity markets were recognized. Specific measures were taken to improve both the exchanges and the contracts, and to encourage large-scale speculative participation. Thus, the modern futures contract and organized futures exchanges were developed, replacing the earlier to-arrive system of marketing.

During the past century, the futures contract and the operations of the commodity futures exchanges have been greatly refined. The basic elements of futures trading have been standardized to meet the requirements of both trade firms and speculators. A futures contract, regardless of the commodity, specifies the quantity, the grades deliverable, and delivery location. A standard contract grade is specified, with a schedule of premiums and discounts established to provide for delivery of other approved grades. In order to be eligible for delivery, the actual commodity must have been inspected to insure that it meets the contract quality standards, and must have been stored in an approved storage facility.

Trading may be conducted only during prescribed hours, on specified licensed exchange and between exchange members only. Prices must be established openly by public outcry through bids and offers, and payment in full must be made at the time of delivery.

Commission firms and commodity solicitors who handle customers' orders and who solicit business are qualified and registered. Each major futures exchange operates in conjunction with a clearing house, which simplifies clearing and settlement of transactions and ensures contract compliance.

Thus, the modern commodity futures market has evolved into a complex mechanism, serving a number of essential functions in our marketing system. The established theory that the primary function of the futures market is to provide facilities for hedging is, according to many authorities, too narrow an approach. According to Professor Cox, "the basic service an exchange performs is to provide an efficient procedure for setting competitive prices quickly in a free and open market."[5]

The futures market provides the most effective mechanism yet developed for setting commodity prices, thereby facilitating the movement of commodities through all stages of production and distribution. It enables commodity tradesmen to reduce their risk of loss from price fluctuations by substituting a "basis" risk for a price risk.[6] Since hedging reduces the capital risk of commodity ownership, industry is enabled to operate on lower profit margins, thereby keeping costs and ultimate market prices at competitive levels.

Another important function of the futures market is to encourage the maximum extension of bank credit to help finance hedged commodity inventory. Even the largest commodity firms finance inventory primarily with borrowed capital. Commercial bankers consider properly hedged commodity inventories an excellent risk, and will lend trade firms substantial capital at prime interest rates.

The futures exchanges, through their respective clearing houses, "clear" their members' futures contracts. Inasmuch as trades are cleared through the clearing house, which is substituted as the "other side" to each trade, the clearing house assumes all the rights and liabilities of the original parties to the contract.

Finally, the commodity exchanges serve as information banks and conduits to both the trade and the speculative community, by collecting and disseminating vital statistics and reports. Futures exchanges are particularly interested in furthering public understanding of the operations of the commodities market and of its role in the overall economy. Spectators are encouraged to visit the commodity futures exchanges and to observe their operations.

5. Reavis Cox, Professor of Marketing, Wharton School of Finance and Commerce, in addressing a symposium sponsored by the New York Commodity Exchanges, in New York, November 6, 1959.
6. This will be discussed in Part VI.

CHAPTER 2   The Commodity Futures Contract

How is it that the futures market can function so well—effectively providing an instant, liquid market for both buyer and seller? The answer lies in the unique nature of the futures contract, and in the operation of the supporting institutions of the commodity exchange and the clearing house.[1]

Essentials of the Futures Contract

A futures contract is a legal instrument which binds both the buyer ("long") and the seller ("short") to the fulfillment of certain obligations. The buyer, barring an offsetting transaction in which the long commitment is closed out (sold), must accept delivery of the cash commodity when tendered, sometime during the delivery month for the respective future. The seller, unless he has previously closed out (bought) his short position, must deliver the cash commodity sometime during the delivery month for the respective future. Delivery is at the option of the short, with respect to the date of delivery (at any time during the delivery period), the particular grade of the cash article, and the place of delivery (subject to limitations and conditions specified by the respective exchange).

A standard grade, conforming generally to the most important grade of each commodity traded in the cash market, is established for each commodity future. This standard grade is deliverable against the futures contract at "delivery price" (the price existing at the time of delivery), with cash settlement of the price difference from the original contract. However, to promote a broad and equitable market, other grades of the cash commodity may be delivered at specified premiums or discounts from delivery price, as illustrated in the following tables:

1. The commodity exchange and the clearing house will be discussed in Chapter 3.

9

Standard Contract Grade(s)
(as of January 1971)

Commodity	Grades(s)
Corn	No. 2 yellow corn
Cotton	Middling 1 inch cotton
Oats	No. 3 extra heavy white oats
	No. 2 heavy white oats
	No. 1 white oats
Soybeans	No. 2 yellow soybeans
Silver (N.Y.)	Refined bar silver assaying not less than 999 fineness

Tenderable Grades of Soybeans (Chicago Board of Trade) (as of January 1971)

Grade	Differential
No. 2 yellow soybeans	Contract price
No. 1 yellow soybeans	3¢ premium
No. 3 yellow soybeans (14% or less moisture)	2¢ discount

Futures contracts have been standardized to ensure equity for both buyer and seller. Standardized items are: contract size; basic contract grade deliverable at contract (delivery) price; other tenderable grades plus their respective premiums and discounts; and approved "spot" depositories and delivery locations. Only the price at which the trade was executed, the delivery month, and the names of the buying and selling clearing firms distinguish the individual futures contracts.

Most Active Futures Trading Months, for Selected Commodities

Live cattle	February, April, June, August, October, December
Cocoa	March, May, July, September, December
Cotton	March, May, July, October, December
Grains (Chicago)	March, May, July, September, December (Except soybeans, which are traded in January, March, May, July, August, September, November)
Pork bellies (Frozen)	February, March, May, July, August
Silver (N.Y.)	January, March, May, July, September, December
Sugar No. 11 (World)	March, May, July, September, October

Commodity futures contracts begin trading with a maximum life varying from 9 to 18 months.

Trading Units: Maximum Daily Price Fluctuations

Each futures exchange establishes a standard contract size, called a unit of trading, for each of its commodities. For example, a contract of cocoa consists of 30,000 pounds, a contract of silver consists of 10,000 troy ounces, and a contract of soybeans consists of 5,000 bushels. At times, an exchange will change the size of one of its contracts if the change would better serve the interests of all parties. For example, in August, 1970, the Commodity Exchange, Inc., New York, reduced its standard copper contract from 50,000 pounds to 25,000 pounds. It was felt that this smaller contract would broaden and materially increase both trade and speculative interest in the copper market.

Futures exchanges also specify maximum daily price limits of trading. No trade may be executed at more than a specified number of cents or points above or below the official close of the previous trading session or, in some markets, not more than a specified number of cents or points above the low or below the high for that day's trading session. Once the limit has been reached, trading may continue only at or within the prescribed limit.

Trading limits were established to lessen the possibility of particularly violent short-term price fluctuations by providing overnight "cooling-off" periods. Concurrently, commission firms are afforded an opportunity to issue overnight margin calls, when necessary. In the event of extreme price changes, the cash markets, operating without any maximum price limits (and, for certain commodities, the London markets), serve as a "safety valve." However, a limit move in a future can be followed by additional limit moves on succeeding days. Some futures exchanges suspend trading limits for an expiring future during all or part of the delivery period,

	Trading Unit (Contract Size)	Maximum Price Fluctuation (Advance or Decline from Previous close)
Cocoa	30,000 pounds	1¢ per pound
Copper	25,000 pounds	2¢ per pound
Corn	5,000 bushels	8¢ per bushel
Pork bellies	36,000 pounds	1½¢ per pound
Silver	10,000 troy ounces	10¢ per ounce
Soybeans	5,000 bushels	10¢ per bushel
Wheat	5,000 bushels	10¢ per bushel
Sugar No. 11 (World)	112,000 pounds	½¢ per pound

allowing the expiring future to more perfectly reflect the precise supply-demand conditions existing in the cash market.

Criteria for Futures Trading

Why is futures trading limited to certain commodities? Why is active trading in these commodities limited to just certain months of the year? During the past century, futures trading has been attempted in many commodities. Why has it proven successful in cocoa, silver, grains, and frozen pork bellies while there are no major organized futures markets for such commodities as tea, coal, tobacco, petroleum, or steel?

A number of commodity and industry conditions are required for a successful futures market. In the first place, the supply and demand factors should not be dominated by just a few concentrated interests. Before futures trading should be considered, a broad, orderly and continuous free cash market must exist. Sulphur, for example, would not be suitable for futures trading because the world's supply is controlled by a few large producers.

A second requirement is the trade's cooperation in establishing and then using a futures exchange for hedging. Studies have indicated that broad trade hedging participation tends to attract speculative capital in volume.[2] A petroleum futures market never developed largely due to the reluctance of the leading producers to participate in futures trading.

A major stimulus to trade hedging is a relatively stable relationship between the cash and the futures markets. This relationship is most consistent when both the cash and the futures commodities are in the same basic form. As a commodity moves from the raw to the finished state, the price relationship between the two tends to deteriorate, rendering hedging progressively less effective. The wool industry provides an excellent example. Raw wool can be readily and effectively hedged. But in the progression from raw to semifinished woolen fibers, and finally to finished goods, the price relationship diverges and the advantages of hedging are progressively diminished.

Hedging is also facilitated when the commodity is generally produced in surplus, with at least a moderate carryover remaining at the conclusion of each production year. If a commodity were in such short supply that producers could be assured of selling their total production at will, the necessity of limiting the speculative ownership risks by hedging would be greatly reduced.

2. Refer to James S. Schonberg, "The Grain Trade: How It Works," Exposition Press, Jericho, N.Y., 1956, Chap. 12 and Part 2 of *Futures Trading Seminar,* Madison, Wisc., Chicago Board of Trade, 1960.

Another important prerequisite for futures trading is that the commodity must be clearly classifiable as to grade and quality, and that this classification be uniform throughout the industry. Thus, any two bushels of No. 2 yellow corn must, at all times, be interchangeable. One of the reasons that futures trading is not conducted in tea, while it does exist in cocoa, coffee, and sugar, is the extreme difficulty of defining and classifying the diverse grades and qualities of tea.

Finally, the commodity should be at least reasonably storable. The more perishable the commodity, the less stable its ownership tends to be and the greater are the risks of dealing. Most fresh fruits and vegetables, for example, are considered too perishable for exchange futures trading. As a matter of fact, when the citrus industry sought a hedging market for domestic orange production, they developed an exchange contract (traded on the Citrus Associates of the New York Cotton Exchange) in frozen orange concentrate. Trading is conducted in certain semiperishable commodities, such as shell eggs and potatoes, and these commodities are frequently more volatile in price than the more stable commodities.

Futures Trading Months

Only certain months are traded in each commodity. Each exchange establishes the trading months for its commodities, choosing generally those months in which trade interests have the greatest need to hedge. Because this varies from one industry to another, there exists no uniformity in the active trading months of different commodities. As an example, futures trading in Chicago wheat is actively conducted in the March, May, July, September, and December futures. July is the first month of the new crop of winter wheat, and the July future provides a hedging medium for purchasers of cash wheat. The new crop of spring wheat comes to market around September, and can be hedged in that delivery month. The December future facilitates hedging against grain stored during the three or four months that navigation is closed due to frozen lakes. The March future represents the mid-point between heavy winter storage and heavy spring consumption and marketing, while the May future can reflect either old or new crop fundamentals, depending upon which is more dominant during that particular year.

And finally, conducting trading in just certain specific months tends to concentrate the entire trading volume in a half-dozen or so futures, resulting in a more broadly traded market interesting to both speculative and commercial interests.

CHAPTER 3 Commodity Exchanges in Action

The Chicago Board of Trade

To maintain a commercial exchange; to promote uniformity in the customs and usages of merchants; to inculcate principles of justice and equity in trade; to facilitate the speedy adjustment of business disputes; to acquire and disseminate valuable commercial and economic information; and generally to secure to its members the benefits of cooperation in the furtherance of their legitimate pursuits.

With this statement of purpose, the preamble to the Rules and Regulations was adopted over 100 years ago by some 80 merchants who founded the Board of Trade of the City of Chicago. In terms of this statement, little has changed since its adoption. It has helped to guide the operations and development of one of the most important commodity exchanges in the world, where trading is conducted daily in corn, oats, wheat, soybeans, soybean oil, soybean meal, silver, plywood, choice steers, and iced broilers. Today, the Chicago Board of Trade constitutes the world's largest cash market for corn, and handles about 90 percent of the United States' trading in grain futures.

ORGANIZATION OF THE CHICAGO BOARD OF TRADE

The Chicago Board of Trade, a contract market licensed by the U.S. Department of Agriculture, is a not-for-profit association consisting of 1,402 members. The Board of Trade does not engage in any buying or selling of commodities or commodity futures. Its primary function is to conduct a public marketing institution, providing facilities where farmers,

14

merchants, manufacturers, and speculators, or their designated agents, can gather in a free, auction-type market to trade in commodities for either immediate or future delivery.

Membership is a personal privilege and carries with it ethical and pecuniary responsibilities. Applicants for membership must be at least 21 years of age and of acceptable moral and financial character. Prospective members must be approved by the Exchange and, once approved, must find a current member who is willing to sell his membership at a mutually agreeable price.

The Board of Trade is self-governing, with a chairman and vice-chairman elected each January. A 21-man Board of Directors, including 3 nonmember directors, sets policy and guides the management of the Exchange. Directors serve for three years, with approximately one-third of them being elected each January. These officials (other than the full-time president, who is also a director) receive no salary for their services. Operational and administrative control of the Exchange is vested in a management team consisting of the president, an executive vice-president/treasurer, an executive vice-president/secretary, and three vice-presidents, each responsible for a particular area of the operation. Some 25 elected and appointed committees are responsible for the many phases of Exchange activity, overseeing the work of more than 200 employees.

The Exchange's main source of income is from dues assessed equally upon all members. Additional income is obtained from real estate rentals (the Exchange owns its own building and leases office space), from weighing fees and a variety of special fees charged for services rendered members and member firms.

Services and facilities of the Board of Trade for the use of members include:

1. Transportation Department, which provides grain shipping rates and services in connection with traffic problems.
2. Weighing Department, which supervises the weighing of grain at elevators in the Chicago switching district.
3. Quotations Department, which records all changes in market prices on futures transactions during daily trading sessions.
4. Office of Investigation and Audits, which investigates all prospective members, conducts periodic audits of member firms' books and investigates all matters referred to it by the Business Conduct and Floor Practices Committees.
5. Statistical Services Department, which collects and disseminates statistics pertaining to all phases of the cash and futures grain business.

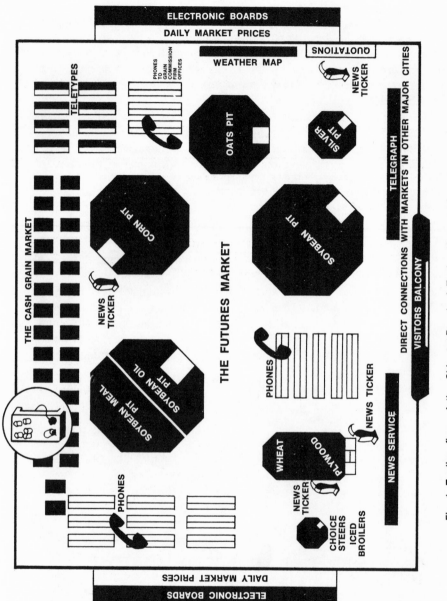

Fig. 1. Trading floor of the Chicago Board of Trade. (Courtesy of the Chicago Board of Trade.)

6. Office of Public Relations, which is responsible for all press relations, advertising and promotion, publications and educational services offered by the Board.
7. Department of Planning and Market Development, which is responsible for the long-term planning and development of new applications for the futures market trading concept.

The heart of the Chicago Board of Trade is the trading floor. This is a vast room; five stories high, a block long, and a quarter-block wide. About two-thirds of the trading floor is devoted to futures trading, with the remaining one-third comprising the cash grain market. These two markets are separate but interdependent.

Futures trading involves contracts for future delivery entered into verbally and confirmed later between two members of the Exchange, either for their own accounts or as agents for others. Grain futures contracts call for delivery, in store of a specified number of bushels of a certain grain of predetermined commercial quality, during a definite month, and at a price agreed upon at the time of the trade. Deliverable grades and other details are established in the Rules and Regulations of the Exchange.

A cash transaction, on the other hand, usually involves a specific lot, a boxcar, truck, or bargeload of a definite grade of grain sold for immediate delivery or to-arrive.

THE FUTURES MARKET

Let us examine the futures market first. Futures trading is conducted in specified areas on the Exchange floor called "pits." Each pit consists of a large, raised octagonal platform, the largest having a diameter of 35 feet, with ascending steps on the outside and descending steps on the inside. There is a pit for each commodity traded. Traders generally position themselves on steps in each pit according to the month in which they are trading. Brokers trading the "flash" month stand in a section beginning on the top step, with a clear view of telephones and price reporters, while those trading in later deliveries stand in other designated areas. Buyers and sellers stand side by side, because each member may buy or sell at any given moment.

Futures trading on the Board of Trade is done directly between members. All "bids" (solicitations to buy) and "offers" (offers to sell) are stated aloud by public outcry so that any trader in the pit can take the opposite side of any trade. The pits are usually extremely active and noisy during trading hours, when as many as several hundred brokers strive feverishly to buy and sell.

In order to effectively communicate with other pit brokers, floor traders simultaneously make use of a system of simple and efficient hand and finger signals, in addition to shouting their bids and offers as required by the Exchange regulations. The dollar-and-full-cents price with the eighth-cent fraction at which each future last traded is kept posted on huge, computer-operated, electronic quotations boards (ComQuote). They line the walls of the trading room, high above eye level. Traders need only indicate with their fingers the fraction of a cent or, with the closed fist, the full cent price at which they want to buy or sell. By holding the fingers of one hand in a horizontal position, they show the various fractions, as illustrated in Figure 2. Just as there is a hand signal for the price, so there

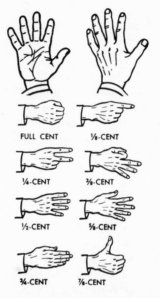

FULL CENT   ⅛-CENT

¼-CENT   ⅜-CENT

½-CENT   ⅝-CENT

¾-CENT   ⅞-CENT

Fig. 2. In futures trading, the hands speak. A trader with his hand up, palm away, is selling; palm toward him, buying. Each finger held vertically indicates 5,000 bushels of grain or one contract of other commodities. Price is shown with fingers held in horizontal positions.

is one to indicate the number of bushels the trader wishes to buy or sell. Each finger held in a vertical position indicates 5,000 bushels (see Figure 2). In addition to utilizing hand signals to indicate price and quantity, traders use their hands to indicate whether they are buying or selling.

Above each pit is a raised platform from which two or more Board of Trade Quotation Reporters constantly observe the changing price picture. As trades are made at prices differing from the preceding trade, a reporter records and time-stamps the new price and transmits it electronically to CBT Quotations Central. In turn, these quotations are disseminated to the ComQuote Boards, to other exchanges, and to thousands of subscriber offices by means of quotation tickers. All these quotations, whether official in the pulpit or on the ticker or the board, are necessarily behind the actual market in the pit. The quotation reporter's record of market prices is timed with a 10-second clock and later appears as an official print-out from the ComQuote System. In a busy market, with trading in five or more delivery months of each commodity, there is a steady flow of quotations emanating from the Exchange for nationwide distribution. The several hundred feet of electronic- and black-boards above the trading floor record Chicago futures prices, current futures in Minneapolis, Kansas City, Winnipeg, and New York, as well as important statistical data collected and disseminated by the U.S. Department of Agriculture.

The Board of Trade method of reporting transactions differs from that of the securities exchanges. While the securities tickers record every trade regardless of price and show the number of shares changing hands, the Board of Trade ticker records only those trades which differ in price from the preceding trade. Volume of trading is not reported by the Exchange until after the close of the market. The Commodity Exchange Authority releases the official volume and open interest totals for all regulated commodities the following day.

A substantial volume of buy and sell orders originates outside of the Exchange and is received on the trading floor by telephone. To accommodate the thousands of calls coming from trade houses and commission firms daily, three batteries of telephone stations are strategically located near each of the pits. As the orders are received by the telephone men, they are written up or taken/received by teletype and rushed by messengers to brokers in the pits. As trades are executed, they are reported back to the originators through these same telephones or teletypes.

The continuous receipt of timely news, statistics and reports is of paramount importance to futures traders. Several broadtape tickers on the Exchange trading floor bring in a constant flow of current news. In addition, another broadtape ticker coming directly from the U.S. Weather Bureau carries overnight weather and the several forecasts issued during the day for the entire country. To augment these weather reports, the eastern end of the Exchange floor contains a very large weather map of the United States, showing the daily national picture of temperature, precipitation, barometric pressure, and wind direction. An automatic printer reproduces weather maps by facsimile as they are developed throughout the day by the Weather Bureau. Private firms also gather weather information from their scattered offices and furnish this information to Exchange floor traders. Additional information is supplied by private firms that gather and circulate commodity news, some of which may be furnished to the broadtape ticker services.

THE CASH GRAIN MARKET

Let us now focus our attention on the cash grain market of the Chicago Board of Trade. On the northern third of the Exchange floor, beneath a series of enormous windows which furnish the most uniform and best light for judging the samples of grain displayed for sale, are some 30 large tables. On these tables are placed small paper bags of grain drawn from cars of grain and graded by the Illinois State Grain Inspection Department.

All cars of grain are sampled and inspected or graded upon arrival in Chicago, and cars are held on the "inspection tracks" until they are ordered to an elevator for unloading. Employees of the Illinois State Grain Inspection Department take an official sample from each railroad car of grain by probing into the grain at five or more different places with a double-tube 11-section trier, 5 feet long. As each probe of grain is drawn, the sectional samples are laid on a canvas and examined for quality, odor, and evenness of loading. The composite samples are reduced and then subjected to a series of laboratory tests to determine their grade, with the basic determining factors consisting of test weight per measured bushel, odor, percentage moisture content, dockage, percentage by weight of damaged grain, and foreign material. Each sample falls into a grade classification according to test results, with the lowest factor determining the grade. The top quality grade of each grain is designated as number "1," and the lowest quality as "sample grade."

The main types of buyers of this cash grain are processors (such as flour millers, corn or soybean processors, and feed manufacturers) and terminal elevators (which store and condition grain with the intention of merchandising it at a later date or shipping it for export). Representatives of the country shippers, or those who have bought grain from the country, move from one table to another seeking out the best buyers. Buyers dip their hands into the samples and carefully examine the grain. They make a quick appraisal of foreign material and damage, squeeze the grain in their hands in a rough attempt to confirm the moisture content notation on the outside of the bag, and may sniff it for objectionable odors. In short, they assure themselves that the sample bears out all of the grade-making determinations noted by the sampling agency.

Like futures, cash grain may be sold before it is owned. A processor or a merchandiser may have a "short" position and cover later on the "spot" or to-arrive market. Similarly, a receiver who contacts country shippers may sell to-arrive short, to an elevator operator, a processor, or a merchandiser. He must cover his short position in the country or in the spot market, necessarily applying a car with a bill of lading date to conform with his to-arrive contract. Any type of grain handler may go long cash grain in the to-arrive market and store or sell it when it arrives in Chicago.

HOW AN ORDER IS ENTERED, EXECUTED, AND REPORTED TO THE CUSTOMER

Many people are quite surprised to learn how rapidly a market order to buy or sell futures can be executed and reported back to the customer. The procedure for receiving, transmitting, executing, and reporting futures orders has been so refined that under normal market conditions the entire operation can be completed within minutes. Let us examine in detail a typical speculative futures transaction on the floor of the Chicago Board of Trade. Except for some minor details, the procedure here could have occurred on any of the major futures exchanges. It should be noted that the actual procedure for handling futures orders varies slightly from one commission firm to another.

Smith, a futures trader in New York, maintains a speculative trading account with Jones and Company, a member of the Chicago Board of Trade. Smith has been closely following the Chicago soybean market. On the basis of his fundamental analysis, consisting of the supply and demand estimates, the normal seasonal pattern of soybean prices, and the current price level, Smith has become "bullish" on soybeans. Although not a pure chartist, Smith considers his commodity charts a valuable tool in the proper timing of futures trading. Anticipating an advance in the price of soybean futures, Smith would like to buy May beans at around $2.25 (per bushel), with an open sell stop order at $2.21½. He is risking about 4¢ per bushel, including commissions, representing $200 per 5,000 bushel contract.

Although quotations on May beans had been running a few cents above Smith's buying ideas, he has noticed that the market has been easing during the past few trading sessions. Upon telephoning his account executive at Jones and Company's New York office and inquiring, "How are May beans?" Smith is informed that May is trading between $2.24⅞ and $2.25⅛ and that the market is relatively quiet. This is the price at which Smith wants to buy beans, and he instructs his account executive to "Buy 10,000 bushels of May soybeans at the market." Since soybeans are usually traded in units of 5,000 bushels per contract, Smith's order represents two contracts.

The account executive handling Smith's account immediately writes up an order to "Buy 10M May soybeans at the market" on a special order blank, noting Smith's account number and name. The account executive then submits the order ticket to his firm's "order room," keeping a carbon copy of the order. Upon receiving the order, the "wire operator" immediately time stamps it and transmits it over the firm's private wire directly to their order room in the Board of Trade building in Chicago.

The Chicago operator will either copy the order onto his own special order form or will paste down the teletype tape copy of the order on a blank form. He will then time stamp the order and pass it on to a telephone clerk who may again time stamp it. The telephone clerk is in direct and continuous telephone contact with Jones' "floor telephone man," stationed at one of the telephone positions on the floor of the Board of Trade. Upon receiving the order, the floor telephone man will write it up and, depending on the type and size of order and the activity of trading, will either hand signal the order visually to Jones' pit broker, or will send the written order via messenger. In the case of Smith's market order, the telephone man would probably whistle or shout to attract the attention of Jones' pit broker, and would signal the order to him. Floor phone men and pit brokers operate together as a well-trained team in quickly and accurately transmitting, executing, and reporting orders, frequently relying upon gestures and hand signals.

Jones' pit broker, upon receiving the order to buy May beans, turns into the bean "crowd." The last trade in May was at $2.25⅛. With a market order in hand, Jones' broker shouts out "⅛ ten May," simultaneously signalling his bid with his hand. A nearby broker with orders to sell May gestures to Jones' broker and shouts "sold." In that brief instant, Jones and Company, acting as Smith's agent, has purchased 10,000 bushels of May soybeans at $2.25⅛ per bushel, for the account and risk of Smith.

The quotation reporter, in the "pulpit" adjacent to and above the soybean pit, notes the transaction, but since it is unchanged from the previous trade, disregards it. Meanwhile, both the buying and the selling brokers note their respective trades on trading cards printed in two colors, one side in blue for "bought" trades and the other side in red for "sold" trades. Any trade that has been "carded" shows the number of bushels involved, the grain and the delivery month, the price, the name of the clearing firm with whom the trade was made, and the initials of the other pit broker. These trading cards constitute the original record of each transaction and become an essential part of clearing records in the offices of the buying and selling firms. Even before the trade is verbally checked between the two brokers who executed the order, Jones' broker endorses the price on the order blank and returns it by messenger to Jones' floor phone man. The executed report is telephoned to Jones' Chicago office where the telephone clerk time stamps it and transmits the report back to the originating office in New York, over the same private leased wire on which the original order had arrived. Finally, the report will be confirmed by telephone to Smith, within minutes after he had placed the order. Before concluding the transaction,

Jones' Chicago office copy of the order is matched against the pit broker's trading card as a double check in the clearing process, and is then used for recording the trade in the customer's ledger account.

Spectators are welcomed at the Chicago Board of Trade, where a special visitors' balcony has been set up, with knowledgeable guides to explain the workings and mechanics of the exchange.

The New York Coffee and Sugar Exchange

Mr. Brown is president of the XYZ Corporation, a large international sugar dealer, headquartered in New York City. The XYZ Corporation is known in the trade as an "operator," a company whose business involves the purchase of raw cane sugar (primarily from Western Hemisphere producers) and the subsequent resale of these sugars to overseas consuming interests.

Let us say that, during the first half of October, XYZ purchases one cargo (10,000 long tons) of raw cane sugar from Brazil. XYZ would like to resell this sugar, on a profitable basis, as quickly as possible. (Notwithstanding the fact that XYZ is located in New York, the sugar is kept in storage in Brazil, and shipped from there directly to the home port of the buyer.) Through its overseas agents, XYZ offers these Brazilian raws to consuming interests in European centers.

Assuming a world sugar price of approximately 3.9¢ per pound (stated as 3.90 in the trade), this 10,000-ton cargo represents an $873,600 commitment. For XYZ, this entails both a considerable cash outlay and the risk of a substantial loss should the prevailing price decline before the sugar is sold. Since XYZ often has several sugar cargos in various stages of purchase and sale, their total investment and risk is considerable. So considerable, in fact, that XYZ, as a prudent business concern, will typically finance (borrow money using its sugar inventory as collateral) a major portion of its inventory, and also hedge or lay off its market risk due to price fluctuations. As a matter of fact, even though XYZ is a well-capitalized, experienced international sugar dealer with an excellent record of sales and earnings, its bankers insist that the bulk of its sugar inventory be hedged or sold ahead as a condition for large-scale inventory financing.

XYZ is unable to immediately resell this sugar to its regular customers. Nevertheless, it is not denied the opportunity to hedge at a profitable price basis. This is accomplished through the machinery of the New York Coffee and Sugar Exchange, Inc.

By hedging its inventory position on the futures market, XYZ will be setting its sales basis on the position and will ultimately have the option of resolving its short futures hedge position in any of the following ways:

1. It may deliver this cargo, or some other cargo of sugar, against its short futures position.

2. It may sell this cargo to one of its regular customers, simultaneously "covering" (buying in) its short futures position.

3. It may, when its short futures position becomes due, "switch" (roll forward) its hedge by covering the existing short futures position and simultaneously selling another, more distant, futures position.

4. It may sell the cargo to another buyer, and the sugar will be priced at the average price that the buyer of the raw sugar purchases an equivalent quantity of futures contracts for the account of the original seller (XYZ, in this case).

5. It may arrange an "A.A." (against actuals) trade wherein the seller and buyer swap futures positions in return for the sale of the actuals.

At the moment, however, XYZ's problem is to get the position hedged. To accomplish this, Mr. Brown, using a direct telephone line from his desk to his broker's booth on the floor of the New York Coffee and Sugar Exchange, Inc., queries the broker's clerk concerning the market. (XYZ Corporation, as an active sugar dealer and hedger, would likely have membership privileges and a direct telephone line right to his floor broker's booth, adjacent to the sugar ring on the Exchange floor.)

The clerk advises Mr. Brown that the market is fairly firm, with some buying, believed to be commission house chart buying, underlying the market. This is just the type of market situation into which Mr. Brown would like to sell (who wants to sell 200 lots of sugar into a weak market?) and Mr. Brown asks for a quote and range on March No. 11 (World) sugar (the contract in which he wants to place his sell hedges). The quote comes back as 3.91 (3.91¢ per pound) bid, offered at 3.93, with the day's high and low for March being, up to that moment, 3.94 and 3.88 respectively.

Mr. Brown gives the phone man a verbal order to sell 200 lots (equal to 10,000 tons) of March sugar No. 11 at 3.89 (it is superfluous to state 3.89 "or better," a floor broker always tries to execute orders at better than his limit).

When the phone man on the Exchange floor receives the verbal sell order, he writes it up on a "sell ticket," indicating the number of contracts, the option (month) to be sold, and the price limit. He then time stamps the order and immediately passes the slip to his floor broker, for execution in the trading ring.

With the order in hand, the broker quickly assesses the market, noting that March is still quoted at 3.91 bid, offered at 3.93. Three brokers are bidding 3.91; one for 5 lots, one for 3 lots, and one for 2 lots.

At this juncture, we shall simulate the broker's ring-trading, presenting both his "trading voice" and his "sotto voice" (representing his thoughts).

(Sotto voice)	This market seems to be developing an easier tone—better hit those bids.
(Trading voice)	SOLD! SOLD! SOLD!
(Sotto voice)	A total of 10 lots sold—no more wanted at this price—and bids at 3.90 are small. This market is thin right here—and, here come other offerings at 3.91. Better fill the demand right away at 3.90.
(Trading voice)	SOLD THOSE 6 AT '90! SOLD THOSE 2!
(Sotto voice)	Only 8 lots at 3.90—no real demand here—better push right through to 3.89 before competitive selling takes the market away from us.
(Trading voice)	SELL MARCH AT '89. SOLD 4 LOTS!

At this point, the broker dictates a brief note to his phone man for transmission to Mr. Brown, noting the slightly weakening tone of the market. Mr. Brown, in the meantime, has been following the market through a sugar ticker tape in his office, and his assessment of the market concurs with that of the floor broker. Desirous of hedging his full 200-lot line, Mr. Brown phones the floor, giving his broker 4 points discretion on the 3.89-limit sell order.

(Trading voice)	SELL MARCH AT 3.90. WHAT?—NO—O.K.—SOLD 2 LOTS AT '89!
(Sotto voice)	Only 6 lots salable at 3.89—we've moved a total of just 24 lots down to this price. Let's see what's wanted here at 3.88. Oh—this is encouraging—this broker across the ring bidding 3.87 for 25 lots—he often represents important foreign interests—this may be what we've been looking for.
(Trading voice)	SOLD YOU 25 AT '87! SELL 20 MORE! RIGHT. 20 MORE! 20 MORE! 20 MORE! RIGHT! SOLD YOU A TOTAL OF 105 LOTS AT 3.87. SELL YOU 20 MORE? NO. O.K.
(Sotto voice)	That's better—let's pull back now—pull all offerings and see if this kind of buying will bring in other demand. What's this? More offerings around the ring at 3.87? Will they offer down? No—looks like they're limited to '87. But where are any bids?—nothing bid, even 2 points down. Better try the 3.86 price with an offer—someone may be waiting to buy on offer only.
(Trading voice)	SELL 1 MARCH AT 3.86.
(Sotto voice)	No buyer—no bid even at 3.85. It's funny there isn't any more demand here now—this is a typical "air pocket" all

right. The only thing to do is to show our entire hand—offer our entire remaining quantity and tell them that's all we have. Some local trader[1] may want to clean up the last of the large sell order—figuring the market could have a good bounce once the offerings have been absorbed.

(Trading voice)   I'LL SELL 71 MARCH'S AT 3.85—ALL I HAVE LEFT!

(From a "ring
trader" across
the pit)   TAKE THEM!

Summarizing this transaction, the XYZ Corporation has just hedged 200 lots (10,000 tons) of raw cane sugar as follows:

10 lots @ 3.91
8 lots @ 3.90
6 lots @ 3.89
105 lots @ 3.87
71 lots @ 3.85

Floor trading, however, represents just one aspect of the total transaction. From the moment that the floor broker reports the trades to Mr. Brown and to the clearing firm which "clears" XYZ's trades (all trades must be cleared by a member of the Exchange, who is as well a member of the New York Coffee and Sugar Exchange Clearing Association, Inc.), the floor broker is responsible for the fulfillment of those contracts. However, the floor broker's responsibility for the trades exists only until after the close of the market, when he or his clerk writes up brokerage slips giving the names of the clearing firm buyers of these contracts, the quantity sold, the month, and the respective prices, to XYZ's clearing firm (the seller).

After the close, the clerks submit their respective purchase/sales slips directly to a member of the Clearing Association who will, later that day, match up the contracts and clear them. In case certain contracts do not match properly, the traders involved will correct the errors on the following day. At this point, the responsibility of the floor brokers to their respective principals ceases. The responsibility, at this juncture, now exists solely between the respective clearing firms. Each clearing firm will then receive from the Clearing Association a copy of its purchase/sales slips, a recapitulation of open positions and other relevant matters, as well as a draft or check for margins required and/or variation margin payable or receivable. In this fashion, the Clearing Association substitutes itself as the buyer to the selling clearing firm, and the seller to the buying clearing firm.

---

1. Professional "ring trader."

PART **II**

THE REGULATION

OF COMMODITY

MARKETS

CHAPTER 4 National Regulation of Commodity Trade

The impact of government regulation on the commodity markets has taken diverse forms and has covered a smorgasbord of commodities—animal, vegetable, and mineral. The most impressive array of controls has evolved in agriculture, in response to pressure from farm interests. But the call for aid has also been heard—and answered—in other sectors of the commodity industry. Thus, silver-purchase programs have been enacted to help mining interests; the acquisition and sale of metals for government stockpile has sometimes been adapted to producer demands as well as to military considerations.

The wisdom or folly of government intervention has been a subject of lively and incessant debate; it is obviously difficult for anyone to comment dispassionately on a matter of such controversiality. To Ayn Rand and the American Farm Bureau, virtually all controls would seem to interfere with the healthy adjustment of supply and demand, via the great balance wheel of free price change. To other farm groups, or to the professionals of UNCTAD[1] and FAO,[2] it seems plain that some commodity markets, left entirely to their own caprice, could play fast and loose with the earnings of producing nations, and might exercise a destabilizing influence on domestic and world trade.

Insofar as is possible, we shall sidestep these political issues. Our concern is not the question of wisdom or virtue of government action in this sphere but the market consequences of such action. In Chapter 5 we shall consider the worldwide scope of selected commodity arrangements and agreements. In this chapter, our attention centers on the origin and development of domestic (United States) controls, with particular reference to agricultural support programs.

1. United Nations Conference on Trade and Development.
2. Food and Agricultural Organization of the United Nations.

Evolution of Farm Supports in the United States

The strong impetus to government intervention in farmers' markets arises from both the politics and the economics of agriculture. On the political side, it is clear that farmers command great congressional influence, and it is exceedingly difficult for any government to neglect "hard times" in the country. Because of the economics of agricultural production and marketing, farmers are often exposed to greater instability and more prolonged periods of depressed selling prices than industrial producers.

In the world of industry, a relative handful of large companies often dominates each major product line. In periods when sales decline, it is common for the automobile or aircraft, aluminum or steel industries to operate below capacity and for output to be cutback in lieu of price reductions. In the vastly more decentralized sphere of agriculture, reduced prices do not readily evoke output cuts. On the contrary, individual farmers may tend to expand production in an effort to maintain income, leading to still greater pressure on prices.

Further contributing to such market declines is the typical inelasticity of demand for farm products. That is, price cuts do not stimulate proportionate increases in offtake. As a general rule, it takes a substantial reduction in farm prices to get consumers to use even slightly greater supplies of eggs or potatoes, corn or wheat, beef or pork, than they would otherwise absorb. Because supply and demand for farm products respond modestly to price changes, relatively small shifts towards surplus or deficit tend to evoke very wide swings in farm prices and incomes. These fluctuations may occur year to year and also over much longer periods or cycles. A prolonged period of favorable demand may stimulate expansion of cultivated areas and improvement in yields. If and when demand diminishes, a lengthy period of chronic overproduction may follow. The most acute swings in agricultural demand and price have been associated with the great destabilizers—the cycle of war and peace, and the partially related cycle of prosperity and depression.

Impact of World War I

In the relatively calm years prior to World War I, the United States government's role in the farm economy was largely confined to unobtrusive services (aid to agricultural research, extension work, crop reporting, and provision for long-term credit via Federal Land Banks). The government posture changed drastically, however, as a direct result of the agricultural boom engendered by World War I, and of the bust which followed soon afterwards.

During World War I, demand for farm products swelled, and to meet this demand, U.S. farmers rapidly acquired more land and machines, built more buildings and facilities and, as a result, assumed bigger loans and heavier taxes and expenses. For farmers, a twin legacy of World War I was expanded acreage and an increased burden of cost and indebtedness. In the immediate aftermath of the war, demand from Europe and other foreign markets swallowed up large quantities of U.S. agricultural production and kept U.S. farmers in fine fettle. By May of 1920, the index of farm prices in the United States rose to 236 percent of its 1910–1914 base. In the ensuing period, however, demand lagged and prices began a decline which accelerated as the 1920's wore on. For agriculture, the decade of the 1920's provided a bitter foretaste of the Great Depression of the 1930's.

By 1921, the farm bubble had clearly burst. Wheat was down to a dollar a bushel from a peak of $2.75 only two years earlier. Other leading farm products dropped even more sharply in percentage terms. Corn sagged to 42¢ per bushel in 1921, down from about $1.85 in 1919. Wool was clipped from about 60¢ to 20¢ per pound over a similar period. In response to increasingly urgent appeals from farmers, Congress passed support bills in 1927 and again in 1928. Both were vetoed by President Coolidge. The farm crisis—deepening in the 1920's—turned to disaster in the 1930's when the Great Depression engulfed industry and commerce, and further dragged down foreign and domestic demand for farm products.

Just before the crash, when the nation's economic woes were still looked upon as transient, the Hoover Administration decided that extension of loans to farmers on favorable terms might enable them to hold back excess production until market conditions improved. In this spirit, Congress passed and the President signed the Agricultural Marketing Act of 1929, establishing a Federal Farm Board with $500 million in lending power. This loan program—begat in hopeful times—proved incapable of withstanding ever-mounting surpluses. For a very limited period, extensive Farm Board financing helped to sustain wheat and cotton prices. But as supply pressures swelled here and abroad, prices of these commodities tumbled with the rest, and the Farm Board sustained large losses on loans which could not be repaid. As a result of this experience it became increasingly *de rigeur* to couple production controls to loan programs to help avoid a repeat of the Farm Board's major fiasco.

Agriculture and the New Deal

The New Deal farm program formed the basis for most of the support legislation in effect in subsequent decades. Included in this program were such elements as:

1. Commodity Credit Corporation loans to farmers at a designated percentage of a "parity" price.
2. Subsidy payments to make up all or part of the difference between the going price and the targeted parity price.
3. Production control by participating farmers in exchange for loans and benefit payments.
4. Marketing quotas in some commodities (subject to two-thirds vote by affected producers).
5. Soil conservation payments as a device to take land out of production as well as to reduce soil depletion.
6. Government purchase of surplus farm products for use in free school lunch programs or for distribution to the needy.
7. Expanded farm credit facilities to help protect farmers from foreclosure, aid tenants in buying farms, and generally improve the availability of short- and long-term loans.

These various agricultural policies were embodied mainly in the Agricultural Adjustment Acts (AAA) of 1933 and 1938, supplemented by the Farm Credit Act of 1933 and the Soil Conservation and Domestic Allotment Act of 1936. This Conservation Act came into being partly because the production controls (instituted under the AAA of 1933) were weakened by Supreme Court rulings; alternatively, the Administration attempted to check production by shifting land from principal soil-depleting crops to grasses and other conservation-oriented uses. However, the conservation program proved ineffectual in this respect, and improved weather and technology led to higher yields, so that agricultural production mounted again in the late 1930's. Despite the partial failure of government efforts, there is little doubt that they helped to alleviate the dire plight of many farmers, tenants, and "dust bowl refugees." The experience of the 1930's also tended to prove that without effective production controls, support programs are often gravely compromised.

The Great Depression ended with the onset of World War II. Associated with this war (and later, in more limited fashion, with the Korean War) was a renewed stimulus to agricultural expansion reminiscent of the World War I boom. Government policy shifted to encouraging output growth in order to meet heavy wartime and postwar needs. After 1949, however, foreign demand dropped sharply while domestic production remained at high levels. Surpluses accumulated and the government once again turned to the defense of farm prices and income by methods similar to those tested in the 1930's.

United States Agricultural Policy Following World War II

Out of the Great Depression and the New Deal experiments which it evoked, came the farm programs of the post–World War II decades. The principal control implements in the government panoply have been price supports, acreage allotments or diversions, and marketing quotas.

PRICE SUPPORTS

Price support programs are financed by the Commodity Credit Corporation (CCC) and administered by the Agricultural Stabilization and Conservation Service (ASC). Direct dealings with individual farmers are handled by the state and county ASC committees. For a designated group of commodities (i.e., corn, wheat, cotton, rice, tobacco, and peanuts) price support is mandatory by law. Support is also mandatory for certain non-basic commodities (tung nuts, honey, milk, and butterfat). For other commodities, support is optional; in recent years, this category has included barley, rye, flaxseed, and soybeans. For all price-supported commodities, the level of price support is fixed by the CCC, taking into account the current parity price for the commodity in question.

Parity Concept. This pairs the current price of a commodity with the purchasing power of that commodity in a selected base period. Under United States farm legislation, the base period chosen initially was the relatively favorable interval, 1910–1914. It should be noted that changes have been made over the years in the precise parity concept used as a basis for support operations. The Agricultural Adjustment Acts of 1948 and 1949 set as an additional criterion the price relationships prevailing between farm commodities in the most recent 10-year period. The formula used to compute parity price for any given commodity started with an "adjusted base price" for that commodity (i.e., its price relative to other farm prices in the last 10 years). It then raised or lowered this base price according to the change in the "parity index" of all prices paid by farmers now, versus 1910–1914. In the wake of the AAA's of 1948 and 1949, the formula for calculating a parity price (say, for wheat) was as follows.

Parity Price Formula

Parity price
for wheat   =   Adjusted base price of wheat   ×   Parity index

OR

$$\frac{\text{Average wheat price received by farmers in last 10 years}}{\text{Average index of all farm prices received in last 10 years (1910–1914 base)}} \times \begin{array}{l}\text{Ratio of prices} \\ \text{paid by farmers} \\ \text{now to prices} \\ \text{paid in 1910–1914.}\end{array}$$

Purely for illustrative purposes, assume that the average price received by farmers for wheat in the last 10 years was $2.00 per bushel, and that the index of all farm prices received in the last 10 years was 2.00 (or two times what they received in 1910–1914). In that case, the adjusted base price for wheat would be $2.00 ÷ 2.00 = $1.00. Now, further assume that farmers are presently paying two-and-a-half times as much for all they buy compared to what they paid in 1910–1914. The parity index is therefore 2.50. Multiplying the adjusted base price for wheat ($1.00) by the parity index (2.50) gives the current parity price for wheat, i.e., $2.50 per bushel.

To determine the actual support level for a particular commodity, the CCC uses an additional formula which sets the percentage of parity according to the so-called "supply percentage" for each crop. This is simply the ratio (in percentage terms) of estimated total supply to estimated consumer demand for the year.

Once these figures have been computed, tables are consulted which give the support level as a certain percentage of parity, depending upon the supply percentage for basic commodities. Ordinarily, these tables list support levels between 75 percent and 90 percent of parity. For nonbasic commodities with mandatory support, the level of support is at the discretion of the Secretary of Agriculture. In extraordinary cases, the Secretary may authorize levels above 90 percent of parity.

Once the support level has been determined, various techniques have been used to achieve this level. The major ones are as follows:

LOANS AND PURCHASE AGREEMENTS

The Commodity Credit Corporation extends "nonrecourse" loans to farmers on storable commodities. The farmer can choose to market his crop or retain it under loan, whichever course is more advantageous for him. He has the additional privilege of turning his crop over to CCC if the market price is below the loan level when the loan matures; or, in the reverse situation, he may pay off the loan and market his crop. In effect, the Loan Program provides farmers with credit at low interest rates, a floor price, and the option to sell at a higher level if the market attains it. At the same time, the Loan Program supports prices by financing withdrawal of supplies.

Ordinarily, loans are obtained by farmers in the 6- to 8-month interval following the harvest, and mature 1 to 3 months after this period of loan availability. At this point, it would be usual for the government to purchase whatever quantity remains under loan. However, sometimes farmers have the option of extending their loan arrangement. This *"reseal"* (or loan-extension privilege) applies to certain grains stored in government-approved facilities.

As an alternative to a loan arrangement, the farmer, for a modest service charge, may enter a purchase agreement with the Commodity Credit Corporation. This purchase agreement is essentially a limited-time option which the CCC extends to the farmer to sell up to a specified quantity at a designated price. For example, a farmer may sign a purchase agreement for 3,000 bushels of wheat. Later, he may decide to sell no wheat at all to the CCC, or to sell any amount up to and including the stipulated 3,000 bushels. His decision must be made during a specified 30-day period. (When loans are also available, the declaration period is usually the 30 days prior to maturity of the loan.)

Both loans and purchase agreements provide price support at around the same level. But each has its own advantages. The loan offers the lure of immediate cash to eligible farmers. On the other hand, a purchase agreement provides price insurance to the farmer who has no pressing need for cash, is unwilling to pay for commercial storage on the crop placed under loan, and/or does not have CCC-approved storage structures on his farm. Loans and purchase agreements may be supplemented by direct subsidy payments and also by outright purchases of selected commodities for price-support purposes.

For the entire support program, a crucial element is the extent to which stocks build up in CCC hands. If prices do not rise above loan or purchase-agreement levels, the farmer will not redeem loan entries and he will fully execute options to sell to the government under his purchase agreement. Accordingly, support programs of the kind described above typically require government willingness to store large quantities of the commodities involved and in time call for procedures to dispose of accumulated surpluses.

An ancient underlying concept is that of the ever-normal granary. Essentially, this involves the Joseph-in-Egypt idea of building up stocks in periods of abundance and releasing them for use in lean years when supplies are low relative to requirements.

SURPLUS-DISPOSAL METHODS

Under prescribed conditions and procedures, stocks accumulated by the government are released to domestic or foreign markets. We may consider briefly what each of the specific programs entails, starting with the outlets which handle the largest volume.

Regular Commodity Credit Corporation Sales or Barter Arrangements: Commodity Credit Corporation offices throughout the country hold regular, publicly announced sales of commodities through competitive bidding on specified quantities and qualities of a commodity. In addition, CCC sells a substantial volume in the world market at prevailing world prices. To help stimulate sales, long-term credits may be extended to foreign countries. Barter operations, under CCC auspices, are carried out through commercial trade channels by United States firms. Under these programs, surplus commodities are exchanged for foreign-product materials.

Public Law 480, Title I. The Commodity Credit Corporation is empowered to sell substantial quantities of surpluses abroad for foreign currencies. As is the case with barter operations, actual sales under Public Law 480 are carried out by private United States exporters. Disposal operations under Public Law 480 have promoted United States export trade in farm products by authorizing sales for foreign currency to importing nations who might otherwise be barred from purchases by lack of requisite dollar exchange. At times, Public Law 480 exports play a key role in determining whether a particular commodity market will be strong or weak. In soybean oil, Public Law 480 sales have often accounted for the bulk of United States exports in any one season.

Public Law 320, Section 32. This law provides for Commodity Credit Corporation purchases from producers, outright subsidies to exporters, and donations to eligible groups. In general, the subsidy to exporters is geared to the difference between the prevailing world price of the commodity in question and the domestic support price. In contrast to the mandatory price-support provisions of the Agricultural Adjustment Act of 1949, Section 32 does not specify which commodities require action, nor how much the Department of Agriculture must pay per unit bought from producers. Section 32 prescribes that commodities are often stored for varying periods; and on the disposal side, the possibility of sales are fully explored before any thought is given to donations. On the other hand, if the commodities bought by the United States Department of Agriculture are not sold, they are donated to groups eligible to receive them. Welfare agencies, nonprofit public institutions, school lunch programs, Bureau of Indian Affairs, and the Red Cross are among the many recipients of these donations.

LIMITING PRODUCTION

Closely related to the price-support program are programs designed to limit crop acreage in order to promote a more favorable balance of supply and demand. This supply restraint takes the form of acreage allotments with or without marketing quotas. Acreage allotments without quotas have been used only rarely and have recently been in effect only on corn. Under this arrangement, the Department of Agriculture determines the appropriate national acreage allotment for each commodity. This allotment is generally fixed at a level sufficient to cover domestic, export, and reserve needs. The national acreage allotment is then apportioned among individual farms on the basis of past history of production of the crop in question.

Acreage allotments with marketing quotas have been established for a variety of crops. For each, a formula specified by law has been used to determine what quantities represent an adequate supply. Here again, a national acreage allotment is determined and is then apportioned among individual farms. The program of acreage allotments with quotas cannot be instituted unless at least two-thirds of the farmers, voting in a referendum, approve the program. The marketing quota for a farm is, in general, the quantity produced on the acreage allotment for that farm. Penalties are specified for producers who exceed quotas.

Restraint in production is also achieved through the soil bank. The soil bank entails two separate programs: (1) the acreage reserve, and (2) the conservation reserve. The acreage reserve seeks to restrict crop production by reducing acreage below established allotments. The farmer receives payments to compensate for loss of income on set-aside land. Similarly, under the conservation reserve, farmers receive payments for taking general cropland out of use for soil-saving purposes. Under either reserve arrangement, the farmer is subject to strict penalties if he harvests a crop on the set-aside acreage.

New Farm Legislation for the 1970's

As we have seen, farm policy in the United States (and elsewhere) is not static; it slowly adapts to new circumstances and to changing legislative attitudes.

In November 1970, Congress gave final approval to new basic farm legislation to replace the Food and Agriculture Act of 1965. This new legislation, effective in 1971–1973, represents a compromise between those forces pressing for gradual abolition of supports and those who desired maintenance of farm income along traditional lines. The 1970 bill moved towards acceptance of concepts enunciated earlier by Agriculture Secretary Hardin in keeping with the Administration's position. These Administration ideas included the following:

1. The continuation of certain support payments and production controls.
2. A greater leeway to farmers in deciding what they would plant.
3. Increased latitude for the United States Department of Agriculture in determining applicable support prices.
4. In general, more scope to free market action.

As finally approved by Congress and the President, the principal feature of the 1970 farm bill was its inclusion of the set-aside concept for wheat and feed grains. Under previous legislation, participating farmers were given an acreage allotment for the commodity in question and had to restrict plantings accordingly. Under the set-aside system, they are told how much land they must withdraw from crop use and devote to conservation purposes; they are then free to allocate plantings on the remainder of their land as they see fit.

By and large, set-aside of cropland is the basic condition for eligibility for benefits under the new wheat, feedgrain, or cotton programs. Critical elements in these programs continue to be loans and payments to participating farmers. In general, payments are still based on a formula comparing the prevailing market price with the parity price for the commodity in question.

In reply to criticism that farm supports mainly benefit the wealthier farmers, the new legislation establishes an annual ceiling of $55,000 per crop on payments to any one producer.

The United States Farm Program and Its Relevance to Price Analysis

We have completed our brief survey of the United States farm program, its changing character and its chief features in recent times. In concluding, it may be useful to comment on some aspects of this survey and, especially, to point up its relevance to price analysis.

First, glancing back at the history of United States agricultural policy, we find it interesting to recall that controls came into being not at the behest of the foes of private enterprise, but rather at the urgent demand of the proprietors of America's soil—independent farmers. It is equally noteworthy that much criticism of farm-support programs today comes not only from tenacious defenders of laissez faire, but also from liberals who believe that the principal benefits of farm supports go to the very few, while the cost is borne by the many. Perhaps the future direction of government agricultural involvement will depend on an alliance between conservative noninterventionists and liberals who want to reorient government welfare spending. This may gradually reduce the influence of agricultural supports and restrictions on commodity markets.

Until the remote day (if ever) when such controls are dismantled, it is obvious that anyone interested in analyzing the fundamental market outlook for a particular agricultural crop must be exceedingly well informed about the currently applicable government programs. How much "free supply" will be available to meet demand this season? To what extent might changes in the loan level or in acreage set-asides affect the outlook for the new crop? If there is any near-term tightness, does the Commodity Credit Corporation have stocks large enough to cover it, and at what prices will the CCC make its holdings available? Based on the loan level and the CCC selling price, it is often possible to delineate a likely range of price fluctuation, and also to consider the chance based on legislative considerations, for prices to move either above or below this expected price zone. At times, a trader can rely substantially on the strength of support just below the loan level, and still have a chance of "scoring" well if circumstances take the stronger turn. However, the futures market is usually adept at "equalizing odds." Thus, early in a season, futures may trade at a premium over tenable support levels; in the usual case, longs may eventually be penalized by loss of this premium, while profits will be attained only under more extraordinary circumstances.

In each case, one key to successful analysis and trading is a careful evaluation of possible developments within the framework of thorough knowledge of the limits (if any) set by the existing support program. Regrettably, there is no general formula we can give, but we shall attempt some further guidelines in our later chapter on fundamental analysis.

The Commodity Exchange Authority

The United States Government's role in commodity markets is of two principal types: (1) basic intervention, which seeks to influence a commodity's supply, demand, or price, in keeping with prescribed policy goals (the farm program is an excellent case in point); and (2) policing action, which is designed to set and enforce rules of fair play in commodity trading. The regulations established under the Commodity Exchange Act are clearly of this second type.

Pressure for regulation of commodity trading developed concurrently with commodity trading itself. As noted in Chapter 1, trading activity in futures surged with the great expansion of agriculture and trade in the late nineteenth century. As futures markets grew, occasional market "corners" and other forms of price manipulation brought vehement protests from farm groups and legislators. At other times, public ire was aroused needlessly, by sharp price moves of innocent origin. Free markets are often volatile creatures and, in exuberant moments, their action may lead farmers or users to suspect skulduggery where none exists. In this context, one function which the government may usefully serve is that of a watchdog, helping to prevent illicit or manipulative action, as well as to clear unfounded suspicion.

Public reaction against real or imagined unfair trading practices ushered in passage of the Grain Futures Act of 1922, the pioneer United States legislation in this field. The 1922 Act established the basic guidelines and procedures which still define the government's role in the regulation of commodity trading. Under this Act, futures trading in regulated commodities could only be conducted on federally licensed exchanges designated "contract markets," with supervision of trading being shared between each respective exchange and the government.[3] The two facets of this supervision included: *self-regulation:* the assumption of responsibility for proper conduct by the exchanges themselves, and *government regulation:* under the purview of the U.S. Department of Agriculture.

This principle of cooperative supervision was renewed in the Commodity Exchange Act of 1936, the successor to the 1922 Grain Futures Act. The new legislation modified and strengthened the provisions of the earlier Act, and extended the number of commodities under regulatory coverage. Further changes and additions were made by Congress in later legislative revisions of the 1936 Act.

The Commodity Exchange Authority (CEA) is the agency of the United States Department of Agriculture which administers the Commodity Exchange Act. As provided in the law which it administers, the basic functions of the CEA are policing contract markets and futures trading to prevent market manipulation and unfair trading practices; collecting and disseminating information and statistics concerning futures trading; and providing registration and other requirements for floor brokers and commodity firms (futures commission merchants).

More specifically, the CEA's responsibilities include:

1. Preventing price manipulation, corners, and dissemination of false or misleading crop and market information; observing floor trading; and investigating alleged and apparent statutory violations.

3. Regulated commodities are primarily domestically produced agricultural and livestock commodities, and are regulated by the U.S. Department of Agriculture.

Speculative Limits on Position and Daily Trading Under the Commodity Exchange Act (as of June 26, 1971)

Commodity	NET POSITION LIMITS Long or Short in One Market		DAILY TRADING LIMITS on Purchases or on Sales in One Market	
	One Future	All Futures Combined	One Future	All Futures Combined
Wheat, Oats, Barley, Flaxseed	2,000,000 bushels	2,000,000 bushels*	2,000,000 bushels	2,000,000 bushels*
Rye	500,000 bushels	500,000 bushels	500,000 bushels	500,000 bushels
Corn, Soybeans	3,000,000 bushels	3,000,000 bushels	3,000,000 bushels	3,000,000 bushels
Cotton	30,000 bales**	30,000 bales**	30,000 bales**	None
Shell eggs	150 carlots	150 carlots	150 carlots	150 carlots
Potatoes: Maine Round White	Mar. future, 150 carlots Apr. future, 150 carlots May future, 150 carlots Other futures, 300 carlots	350 carlots	Mar. future, 150 carlots Apr. future, 150 carlots May future, 150 carlots Other futures, 300 carlots	350 carlots
Potatoes: Idaho Russet Burbank	Mar. future, 150 carlots Apr. future, 150 carlots May future, 150 carlots Other futures, 300 carlots	350 carlots	Mar. future, 150 carlots Apr. future, 150 carlots May future, 150 carlots Other futures, 300 carlots	350 carlots

* 3,000,000 bushels if 1,000,000 bushels or more of total represent spreading or the closing of spreads in the same grain between markets.
** Does not apply, except during delivery month, to trades or positions which represent straddling or the closing of straddles between futures or markets.

Limits do not apply to *bona fide hedging transactions or positions.* For complete information see specific orders of the Commodity Exchange Commission.

Source: United States Department of Agriculture, Commodity Exchange Authority, June 26, 1971.

Guide to Reporting Levels Under the Commodity Exchange Act
(as of January 20, 1969)

Each trader is required to file reports with the Commodity Exchange Authority when he holds or controls open contracts in any one future of any commodity on any one contract market equal to or exceeding the amounts shown below. A report is to be filed for the first day a trader acquires such a position, for each subsequent day on which he makes a trade, and for the first day his position falls below the reporting level. A trader having a reportable position must report all of his trades and positions, regardless of size, in each future of the commodity on all contract markets. For complete information on reporting requirements, see Parts 15, 18, and 19 of the CEA regulations.

Commodity	Reporting Level	Reporting Form Number
Wheat, Corn, Oats, Rye, Soybeans, Barley, Flaxseed	200,000 bushels	203, 204*
Grain sorghums	11,200,000 pounds (200,000 bu.)	
Cotton	5,000 bales	303, 304*
Butter	25 carlots	403
Shell eggs**	25 carlots	
Frozen whole eggs**	25 contracts	503, 504*
Potatoes	25 carlots	603, 604*
Wool**		
Wool tops**	25 contracts	803
Soybean oil		
Cottonseed oil	25 contracts	1003
Soybean meal		
Cottonseed meal	25 contracts	1103
Live cattle**	25 contracts	1203
Cattle products	25 contracts	1303
Live hogs		
Frozen pork bellies	25 contracts	1403
Frozen skinned hams		
Hides	25 contracts	1503
Frozen concentrated orange juice	25 contracts	1603

* Series 04 reports are filed weekly by reporting merchandisers, processors, and dealers, showing positions in the cash (spot) commodity when the futures position is reportable.

** A trader with a reportable position in any one future of any one type of contract in this commodity is required to report his trades and positions in all types of contracts in the commodity on all markets. For detailed instructions, see Section 18.00, paragraphs (e) wool and wool tops, (f) shell eggs and frozen eggs, and (g) live cattle.

SOURCE: United States Department of Agriculture, Commodity Exchange Authority, January 20, 1969.

2. Licensing commodity exchanges as contract markets, and reviewing rules of contract markets to determine conformity with statutory requirements.

3. Registering futures commission merchants and floor brokers; establishing minimum financial requirements for futures commission merchants; auditing books and records of futures commission merchants; and maintaining an extensive reporting system designed to keep the actions of futures commission merchants, floor brokers, and traders under surveillance.

4. Insuring trust-fund treatment of customers' regulated margin moneys and equities by requiring futures commission merchants to segregate and protect such funds. A futures commission merchant must segregate funds deposited to margin regulated commodities from those used to margin nonregulated commodities, and is specifically prohibited from comingling customers' regulated funds with its own funds.

5. Establishing statutory limitations on speculative positions and trading activity. If and when a speculative position reaches a specified reporting level, the speculator must file reports with the CEA detailing all his transactions. In addition, no speculator may assume a total number of contracts in excess of a CEA stipulated position limit, nor may he exceed the daily trading limit on purchases or sales of a commodity in a single market. (See the tables on pp. 309–307 for the position and trading limits and reporting levels for each commodity as currently specified by the CEA).

6. Compiling and publishing reports and other informational material relating to activity and operations on contract markets.

7. Issuing warning letters, or compliance notices to individuals or firms deemed to be in violation of the Act; or in more serious cases, issuing a complaint calling for administrative hearings. Such hearings could lead to a cease and desist order, to suspension, or revocation of a commission house or broker's registration, or to criminal proceedings.

In the fiscal year ending June 30, 1970, the CEA's regulatory powers embraced 22 commodities, including grains, soybeans and their products, livestock and livestock products, and eggs and potatoes. Futures trading in these regulated commodities was conducted at 11 licensed exchanges located in New York, Chicago, Kansas City, and Minneapolis.

In short, the CEA functions both as a watchdog to assure equitable rules of futures trading for those engaged in trading regulated commodities, and as a source of information and statistics concerning market operations in regulated commodities.

CHAPTER 5 International Commodity Controls

Since World War II, governments the world over have accepted wider responsibility for economic stability and growth—both domestically and, as a necessary corollary, in the sphere of international trade and development. One facet of this new economics has been increased attention to the primary products (raw materials) which play a predominant part in the export earnings of the so-called developing countries.

For the wealthier industrialized nations, an interest in commodity problems does not necessarily reflect a benevolent concern for the welfare of poorer lands. Many developed nations are themselves major exporters of primary goods. Apart from any direct economic involvement, they are often motivated by political considerations, noble or otherwise. Above such political considerations stands the plain fact of the economic interdependence of nations. The developing countries are major markets for the more industrialized lands, and any severe contraction in the former's purchasing power must affect the latter's trade and well-being. Today, it is a generally accepted notion that commodity problems have broad ramifications affecting the health of the international economy and the aspirations of poorer lands. Commodity problems are part and parcel of the broader problem of economic development.

Increasingly, the postwar literature about commodities has crystallized several other related concepts. First, it is self-evident that measures designed to heal or relieve distress in a particular commodity market are often means of supporting or raising export earnings of producers of raw materials. This leads to explicit recognition that "commodity arrangements" often constitute an important form of aid to developing nations.[1]

---

1. The term "commodity arrangements" is used here to encompass the entire spectrum of policy initiatives described later in this chapter.

Such aid is obvious when importing countries agree to measures which will make them pay more for the primary products they buy. A transfer of purchasing power also occurs when prices are maintained at higher levels than they would be otherwise.

But if commodity arrangements are to be viewed, at least in part, as aid instruments, then it is only reasonable to consider the efficiency of such arrangements compared to other forms of aid. Much of the criticism of commodity agreements in recent years has focused on their alleged inferiority compared to direct aid measures.

The critics of commodity arrangements contend it is better to provide loans or grants to build highways, or exchange guarantees to spur private investment, or technical assistance on a project basis. The supporters of such commodity action-plans argue that these specific aid forms are wanted too, but commodity arrangements are valued complements.

Aside from these differences, all parties now agree that commodity arrangements constitute only one possible set of prescriptions for dealing with the trade and economic needs of developing countries. At times, other aid techniques may offer similar benefits without posing obstacles to market adjustment, and without involving the magnitude of operating costs required of some commodity controls.

Finally, specialists in this area recognize that commodity arrangements are not all of the high-voltage variety, entailing quota restrictions or other mandatory controls. Rather, there exists a full spectrum of possible measures ranging from mild and nondirective techniques to controls of a strictly compelling nature.

Before we survey this spectrum of alternative measures, it is perhaps useful to recall some of the classic problems which gave rise to commodity arrangements, and also to highlight recent milestones in the evolution of commodity policies.

Impetus to Commodity Arrangements

Symptoms of malaise in world trade, involving primary commodities, have been evident to varying degrees throughout this century. But (as in the case of the United States) the most powerful impetus to national and international government agricultural involvement was the Great Depression of the 1930's. During this period, a host of international commodity agreements came into being (e.g., in wheat, sugar, tin, etc.), paralleling the domestic agricultural supports instituted in the United States and Western Europe.

Depression-born anxieties lingered until well after World War II. A major source of concern was the extreme reaction of commodity markets to cyclical fluctuations in the developed countries. The comparative vulnerability of primary commodity markets was starkly revealed in the 1930's. By and large, prices for primary commodities sank far more than prices of more highly processed goods.

Technically, the economist saw the explanation for this greater weakness in the inelastic supply and demand characteristics of most primary commodities. As we observed earlier, demand and supply are said to be "inelastic" when a given percentage price change does not evoke a corresponding change in supply, or a proportionate and opposite change in consumption. Because demand and supply are inelastic, a relatively modest surplus is difficult to deplete; prices must drop to extremely low levels before usage rises enough or output falls enough to close the gap. For agricultural commodities, the problem is sometimes compounded by a tendency on the part of some producers to increase output when prices decline, in a self-defeating effort to maintain income.

The spread of depression influences from developed to developing countries proceeds not only via direct changes in demand for primary products, but also through a tendency for protectionist forces to grow stronger, leading to restrictions on competing imports from developing countries.

Through mechanisms of this sort, cyclical contractions or expansions in demand in developed countries are transmitted in magnified form to the primary trade and balance-of-payments of developing countries. Thus, according to a United Nations' estimate, the 1957–1958 recession in the United States and other Western countries, coupled with slight increases in the cost of goods purchased in industrialized lands, led to a loss in import capacity. This loss was equal to six years of lending to the developing countries by the International Bank for Reconstruction and Development (at 1956–1957 rates).[2]

Instability in the earnings of primary exporters originates in cyclical and year-to-year variations in supply—as well as in fluctuations in demand and changes in import policy of developed countries. If, for example, one year sees a bumper crop 25 percent above that of the preceding season, prices may drop 50 percent or more, with the paradoxical result that producers earn less for growing and selling more. From a longer-term standpoint, the problem of supply instability takes a different form. Periods of high prices lead to general expansion in capacity; by the time output reaches a peak, prices weaken, setting the stage for the next cycle phase.

The problem of achieving greater output and price stability remained the core concern of international commodity thinking from the early 1930's to well after World War II. This concern was reflected in the Havana Charter drawn up at the 1947–1948 meeting of 50 countries participating in the

2. *United Nations World Economic Survey 1958,* pp. 6–7.

United Nations Economic and Social Council. The Havana Charter projected one aim of international commodity agreements: to moderate cyclical fluctuations in price without interfering with long-term trends. However, the Charter went further. It also foresaw the need for facilitating an increase in consumption or for transferring resources from overexpanded to new industries. Forward-looking in another way, the Charter set the principle—honored in virtually all subsequent commodity actions—of cooperation on equal terms between producers and consumers.

Through the 1950's, commodity discussions still focused their attention largely on the question of stabilizing producer returns. However, by degrees (though never completely), attention shifted perceptibly to the problem of raising the level and growth rate of export earnings. Two factors contributed to this elevation of goals. On the positive side, some reduction occurred in the need for stabilization as such, largely because of reduced cyclical variations in industrialized lands. For this reason, fluctuations in the exchange earnings of developing countries have been less acute in the last decade or two than they were in earlier years.

The second reason for thinking more about the level and trend of earnings, and less about stability alone, originated in one of the more disturbing trends of the 1950's—the marked tendency for the "terms of trade" of primary producers to deteriorate. In other words, prices of primary goods which developing countries export declined relative to the cost of the more sophisticated goods they buy. Hence the "real value" (or purchasing power) of primary commodity exports shrank. Accordingly, commodity producing countries found themselves in the unenviable position of having to offer larger quantities of primary commodities to obtain a given "bundle" of manufactured goods. Factors contributing to this adverse trend were: (1) production efficiencies permitting greatly expanded output of many primary products; (2) technological innovations leading to synthetic development of substitutes for some primary products, or permitting processors to obtain more usable extract from each unit of raw material; and (3) the broad tendency of demand for primary products to grow slowly (or more nearly in line with population), while demand for other finished goods rises at a faster rate.

In the late 1950's and early 1960's, it came to be widely appreciated that, unless something was done to accelerate the earnings growth of the less industrialized lands or to otherwise provide them with purchasing power, any hopes for accelerated development would quite likely be shattered.

The beginning of the 1960's "development decade" saw leading nations —East and West—commit themselves more or less explicitly to programs for supporting and raising income of poorer countries and not just to stabilization. Prominent in its support for commodity agreements, France envisioned measures which would boost commodity prices above 1962 levels and thus raise income of primary producers. Without accepting such a blanket commitment, the United States moved towards sympathetic consideration of commodity agreements as one possible trade-and-aid package for developing countries.

A significant landmark in the evolution of United States policy was the August 1961 meeting of the Alliance for Progress at Punta del Este, Uruguay. Here, the United States and other American Republics agreed not only on the desirability of commodity price stabilization, but also on a need to overcome "secular deterioration" in the terms of trade of hemisphere producers, and the need to promote growth in foreign exchange income received from exports. One outgrowth of Punta del Este was greater consideration of "compensatory finance" schemes designed to help make up declines in export earnings of developing countries. Also, after Punta del Este, the United States gave its decisive support to successful negotiation of an international coffee agreement, a particularly significant pact in commodity history. While selectively accepting commodity agreements or other international commodity controls, the United States has remained flexible in its approach. It has evolved a policy of case-by-case study of commodity problems in full awareness of the range of difficulties and the wide spectrum of prescriptive alternatives.

Types of Commodity Arrangements

Underlying the case-by-case approach is a recognition that the character of the problem differs for each commodity, and that the therapeutic approach should vary accordingly. Thus, confronted by chronic price weakness and mounting supply pressures in coffee, the United States decided it could accept an international commodity agreement because there existed adequate political support at home. This was a clear economic rationale, and there was no practical possibility of providing aid funds large enough to offset the consequences of any sharp price weakness. The root of the problem in coffee was an overexpansion in production, and curbs on output seemed the only ultimate solution. In other cases (e.g., rubber and jute), a key source of difficulty was competition from synthetic products. In such cases, different policies might be suitable; an agreement might seek to regularize supplies of the material product, and assure stable and inviting prices.

In short, the appropriateness of different commodity policies will depend on economic, political, and technical characteristics of the particular commodity, on the willingness of leading producers and consumers to tolerate a decline in foreign exchange earnings of primary producers, and on the availability of compensatory finance.

Depending on factors of this kind, different levels of action will seem suitable for different situations. These different "action-levels" may be classified as follows.

I. Consultative Arrangements
   A. A special conference (or series of conferences).
   B. A continuing study group.

II. Other Nonregulatory Arrangements
   A. A formal or informal agreement to remove trade barriers or otherwise expand free markets.
   B. An agreement or other arrangement designed to promote consumption, or encourage transfer of resources to new uses.
   C. Indicative (or target) planning.

III. Regulatory Arrangements (incorporating one or more of the following techniques):
   A. Multilateral contracts.
   B. Buffer stocks.
   C. Import or export quotas.
   D. Other (e.g., production control).[3]

CONSULTATIVE ARRANGEMENTS

When a commodity problem first begins to appear pressing, the first logical step is for the parties involved to begin discussing the nature of the problem and to gather information that might be relevant to its solution. This "consultative approach" may take the form of a conference or series of conferences, or a more permanently established study group. Quite often, a study group will be the first step to more directive action. Or it may simply provide a center for multinational discussion, statistical compilation, and a regular review of market prospects. Typically, research, education, and publicity are used to help spur individual countries to adopt policies which will contribute to market stabilization.

Study groups have existed for rice and grains, citrus and cotton, bananas, cocoa, jute and hard fibers, oilseeds and their products, rubber, and lead and zinc. International conferences have established other continuing information entities, such as the International Cotton Advisory Committee (ICAC). Like a study group, the ICAC has collected and disseminated cotton data, kept track of all developments affecting cotton,

3. Adapted from Irwin Shishko's, "The Coffee Outlook Under a Model International Agreement," *Commodity Yearbook 1964*, pp. 19–28; republished in *Guide to Commodity Price Forecasting*, New York, Commodity Research Bureau, Inc.

and recommended measures it deemed appropriate for maintaining and developing a sound world cotton economy.

Consultative arrangements are often the springboard for multinational action calling for varying degrees of member discipline and control. Broadly speaking, the milder, less directive commodity arrangements are classified here as nonregulatory (noncontrol) plans.

NONREGULATORY ARRANGEMENTS

Characterized by a wide variety, these forms are distinguished by the largely voluntary nature of cooperation and by the tendency to focus on goals which do not call for an elaborate organizational or control edifice. Thus, the Olive Oil Agreement (operative since 1959) focused mainly on encouraging consumption to help check increasing competition from low-cost substitute oils. Without formal agreement or explicit export quotas, members of the Lead and Zinc Study Group have, at times, voluntarily curtailed offerings in order to prevent acute price weakness.

These noncontrol arrangements discussed so far usually concentrate on one or two specific problem areas. A more comprehensive approach entails an effort to simultaneously influence supply and demand forces so as to encourage long-term equilibrium at reasonable prices. The terms "indicative" or "target" planning may be applied to this second, more embracing type of nonregulatory commodity arrangement.

More specifically, indicative planning is a noncompulsive approach to economic planning pioneered in Western Europe. It is a technique by which government and industry draft a set of comprehensive guidelines for balanced growth; individual firms are encouraged to follow these guidelines out of an enhanced appreciation of the economic possibilities and self-interested awareness of their role in the overall plan.

As applied to commodity problems, the main idea of indicative or target planning is that producers and consumers jointly set goals for themselves to help establish and maintain long-run statistical equilibrium. No doubt, these goals have to be reviewed regularly in the light of revised supply and demand conditions, and other new factors in the relevant commodity situations. This type of planning is nonregulatory in that it imposes no mandatory controls. Instead, it invites producers and consumers to find their own means of fulfilling commitments which they themselves deem appropriate to accept.

One of the first published attempts to apply indicative planning techniques to a particular commodity problem, was a 1962 article.[4] About the

4. Irwin Shishko, "Target Planning in Cocoa," *Candy Industry and Confectioners Journal,* August 28, 1962, p. 5.

same time, similar concepts were entertained by FAO and UNCTAD economists.

In subsequent years, increasing attention has been devoted to the possible usefulness of a broader type of indicative planning—one which encompasses many commodities. The logic of a multicommodity plan goes back to the basic problem of allocating land and labor. For example, if one wishes to consider the need for limiting acreage in coffee, one must simultaneously explore the possibilities for alternative livestock or crop production. The FAO has worked on an Indicative Plan for World Agriculture, one which takes into account the need for a more comprehensive and interconnected approach to international commodity problems.

REGULATORY (OR CONTROL) ARRANGEMENTS

As previously suggested, consultation on commodity problems may, in turn, lead to the development of some kind of "indicative plan." To the extent that the countries concerned see fit to translate this plan into a set of formal commitments including enforcement machinery and sanctions for noncompliance, the arrangement then evolves into a "regulatory" or "control" agreement.

Such an agreement may be regional in character (e.g., the export quota agreement in coffee set up between Latin American producers in 1957–1958); or it may go beyond a regional basis (e.g., the Cocoa Producers Alliance of 1964–1965, including Brazil and the leading West African producers). It should be noted that both of these arrangements failed, as did most other pacts in which producers acting on their own sought to control the market.

Commodity agreements, whether regional or international, are usually classified according to the type of control instrument on which they depend most heavily. The three main types are: (1) the quota agreement, entailing restrictions on shipments, on sales and, perhaps, on imports; (2) the buffer stock arrangement, under which a central authority buys at the bottom of a central price range and sells at the top; and (3) the multilateral contract agreement binding importers to purchase set quantities if prices fall to specified floor levels, and committing exporters to offer stipulated amounts if prices rise to preassigned levels. These types of agreements do not exhaust the possibilities, since agreements could also be based on other measures such as production controls, commitments to expand consumption, or price guarantees by importing countries.

Quotas, buffer stocks, and multilateral contract arrangements all have one principal common element. They seek, in one way or another, to confine prices to a prescribed range. In short, they are stabilization-oriented. On the other hand, certain alternate techniques mentioned above —production controls and consumption controls—are directed towards overcoming long-term disequilibrium.

Nowadays, international commodity agreements utilize several of these control techniques rather than concentrate on any one single type of arrangement. However, it is convenient here to illustrate the different kinds of agreements by describing relatively pure types operative in recent years.

International Wheat Agreement (Multilateral Contracts)

The International Wheat Agreement (IWA), initiated in 1949 and renewed successively thereafter, has two distinctions. First, it is the sole instance of an agreement based on multilateral contracts. Second, it is the only such agreement covering a commodity grown mainly in the temperate zone and of predominant concern to developed countries.

The experience under the Wheat Agreement points up the difficulty of establishing a price range that is both attuned to market conditions, and satisfactory to buyers and sellers. In the first four years of the International Wheat Agreement, market prices ruled above the then-established Agreement price zone ($1.20/.50–$1.80). Under the provisions of the Agreement, importing member nations were assured of being able to buy up to 95 percent of the agreed quantities at the stipulated maximum zone price, regardless of the then-existing free market price. Thus, the agreement operated entirely in favor of importers. In the next few years, the price zone was raised to $1.55–$2.05 at the exporters' behest; but correctly anticipating a price decline, many importers including the United Kingdom withdrew. As a result, the percentage of world wheat trade covered by the second IWA dropped from 60 percent initially to 25 percent. Later, when the agreement was renegotiated for the third time, participation was increased by cancelling the commitment of importers to buy guaranteed quantities at the floor prices and instead requiring them only to buy a percentage of their requirements from exporter members within the specified price range. The concept of "guaranteed quantities" was also abandoned, and instead exporters undertook to supply average commercial requirements of member importers within the assigned price range. The 1959 agreement also excluded the increasingly important trading of wheat under special arrangements, especially concessional sales from developed to underdeveloped countries.

It is interesting to note that the stronger mandatory provisions of the IWA's were gradually weakened or eliminated. In some ways, the more indicative provisions proved most valuable. That is, the IWA's provided a forum encouraging countries to readjust their national support policies and to utilize surpluses to assist needy countries.

International Tin Agreement (Buffer Stocks)

The International Tin Agreement (ITA) is the unique example of a pact founded on buffer stocks, but salvaged under duress by the imposition of export quotas and negotiation with outside suppliers.

The postwar ITA, established in 1956, ran parallel in form to the tin arrangements operative prior to World War II. Initially, producing members contributed nearly two months' world coverage to the buffer stock. The manager of the stock was obliged to buy and sell at the floor and ceiling prices respectively, but could also exercise discretion in buying or selling in the vicinity of these same price limits.

From the beginning, the ITA found funds inadequate to permit exclusive reliance on buffer stock operations, even when these were reinforced by production controls. In 1957 and 1958, prices declined in the face of buffer stock purchases and sharp output curtailment by members, with weakness influenced by heavy sales from the USSR (predominantly re-export from China). Price weakness was ultimately overcome by an informal understanding with the USSR limiting exports from that origin, and also by the imposition of export quotas. Tin prices have also been unsettled by uncertainties regarding United States stockpile release, and it has become regular practice for this country to consult with the International Tin Council regarding possible changes in stockpile acquisition or disposal policy.

The principle of producer-consumer cooperation enunciated in the Havana Charter is reflected in the ITA as in all major postwar agreements. In the Tin Council (the ruling body of the ITA), producers and consumers each have equal aggregate votes.

International Sugar Agreement (Export Quotas)

Sugar has recently returned to active membership in the family of international commodity agreements, after a dormant period which largely reflected the United States-Cuban impasse. The export quotas established under the old sugar agreement have been inoperative since 1961.

A new five-year International Sugar Agreement (ISA) was concluded in October 1968 and came into effect in 1969. It is essentially an export quota arrangement. Quota adjustments are geared to prescribed trigger prices, with an outside price range of 3.25–5.25¢, for Caribbean port (stowed basis). Exempt from quota control are exports of sugar under "special arrangement," which includes exports under the Commonwealth Sugar Agreement, Cuban exports to socialist countries, exports under the African and Malagasy Sugar Agreement, and shipments to the United States for domestic consumption.

The ISA thus deals with the remaining "free market," a market which because of its residual nature may be extrasensitive to rather small changes in aggregate supply and demand. In 1970, free market trade came to around 8.5 million tons, or little more than ⅛ of world production and use. One problem the agreement faces is nonparticipation by the United States, and the EEC. The United States has contended that it objects to lack of progress on two "hard core" issues: (1) the problem of controlling re-exports of Cuban sugar by the communist countries; (2) the desire of European Common Market countries for an export quota of 1.2 million tons (four times that offered by UNCTAD Secretary General Raul Prebusch, the Agreement's chief protagonist and organizer).

In the opening years of the new Agreement, the world statistical position grew stronger, and with the help of quota restrictions, prices advanced. In this situation, neither of the problems suggested by the United States posed overtaxing problems. In future years, however, difficulties may arise from these sources; and still more, perhaps, from the continuing efforts by tradi-tional importing countries to achieve self-sufficiency (or export status) as the EEC has done.

The Sugar Agreement's export quotas are backed up with a commitment by importing countries to limit imports from nonmember exporters to 1966–1968 levels, and to prohibit such imports when the prevailing price is below 3.25¢.

International Coffee Agreement (Quotas and Diversification Goals)

In the 1960's, the case for an international commodity agreement was perhaps strongest of all for coffee. Here was a commodity of particular significance to developing nations. Moreover, this commodity faced a clear and present danger of declining to price levels which would seriously impair producer earnings and adversely affect world trade.

Thus the new International Coffee Agreement came into being in 1963 with "tremendous and unprecedented political backing."[5] It was supported by the trade (e.g., the National Coffee Association of the United States) as well as by the overwhelming majority of producing and consuming coun-tries. As opposed to earlier stop-gap efforts, the Coffee Agreement is long-

5. Irwin Shishko, "The Coffee Outlook under a Model International Agreement," *Commodity Yearbook 1964*, p. 23.

term in the sense that it seeks to gradually restore statistical equilibrium, as well as to provide an immediate defense against price weakness.

For short-term stabilization purposes, the main control instrument in the new Agreement is export quotas, supplemented in a very significant way by consumer aid in policing quota compliance. As a tool in enforcing quotas, the Agreement provides that all shipments of coffee from member countries must be accompanied by "certificates of origin." Importing countries agree not to admit coffees which lack the appropriate certificate, and also to limit imports from nonmembers whenever the International Coffee Council decides this is necessary.

Exempt from quota limits are exports to a stipulated list of new markets. The intention of this clause is to encourage growth of consumption in new areas. However, for most of the life of the Agreement to date, the clause has also encouraged very large shipments of so-called "tourist coffees," exports seeking to escape quota restrictions by claiming a new market destination, while being routed sooner or later to conventional markets.

Despite an impressive panoply of control measures, the Agreement found it necessary for several years to adopt a tolerant view towards over-shipments and "tourist coffees." Later, however, controls over such violations became more formidable and escape hatches were gradually closed. As long as surpluses exist, one question will always be: Will effective export restraint build pressure for some countries to break away from the Agreement? The answer depends, in good part, on the evolution of production in different areas. The Agreement contains important clauses aimed at production control and diversification.

In 1963 and after, the Agreement was strengthened by a succession of frost-damaged crops in Brazil. Largely because of this setback to output in the foremost producing country, recent years have seen a working-off of world stocks (mainly in Brazil). The possibility now exists that the period of chronic overproduction has ended and tomorrow's problem may (for a time at least) be one of limited supply. If so, the "long-term" Coffee Agreement is at least a "short-term" triumph, in that it has helped to promote stability and preclude a disastrous market downturn in a difficult transitional period.

Some observers, however, still feel that as long as world prices remain at present levels, the incentive to production expansion in coffee remains large; at some future date, world coffee may again encounter the kind of problems which gave rise to the Agreement.

An interesting feature of the pact is its response to consumer interests, and to pressure from different groups of producers for larger shares of the coffee market. Modifying the original quota arrangement, a system of "selective quota adjustment" was introduced which permitted separate adjustment of export entitlement for four different groups of coffees. This system was initially helpful in permitting African producers to expand exports of Robusta coffees in response to increasing roaster demand for less expensive coffees. Later, Brazil successfully sought to boost demand for its coffee by launching an aggressive marketing campaign featuring concessional prices to roasters who agree to buy more than usual quantities. These changes in producer selling efforts and export allowances highlight the fact that, in the long run, *agreements adapt to changes in the balance of forces between different producers and groups of producers.*

Concluding Comments

The survey of commodity arrangements presented in this chapter suggests some of the problems and pitfalls which impede international control efforts, and indicates areas where such efforts might be useful and effective.

A strong case for a control agreement exists when (as was the case for coffee) an immediate threat is posed to the exchange earnings of developing countries, when alternative aid of compensating magnitude is not available, and when widespread support exists among both producing and consuming countries. Even so, regulations designed to stabilize prices should probably be complemented by long-term measures which seek to restore fundamental equilibrium.

In many cases, it seems wise to consider whether a healthy long-term statistical position can be best attained via consultative or indicative arrangements rather than by regulatory techniques. That is because "fundamental disequilibria" call for efforts to guide the long-term development of production and consumption. On the other hand, control agreements (of the buffer stocks, multilateral contract, or quota varieties) are essentially directed towards short-run stabilization rather than long-run adjustment.

Each type of control agreement has its particular susceptibility or weakness. Buffer stocks entail high financing and storage costs. (Of course, it is the relatively low cost of storage for tin and some other metals which makes them more likely candidates for buffer stock arrangements.) Financial resources of the buffer stock may be exhausted in times of stress and export quotas may be useful to support the operation. The choice of an appropriate price range is difficult for all types of control agreements; given altered conditions, multilateral contracts may tend to operate in favor of exporters or importers.

Export quota agreements are difficult to enforce, and it appears that consumer participation is needed to help police them. In a sense, all agreements are relatively frail vessels which break down in the face of acute economic or political disturbance. This, however, does not preclude their usefulness in the long stretches of living history which are neither severe nor disastrous.

The two most basic criticisms of commodity agreements concern: (1) their negative effect on the automatic adjustment mechanisms of a free market, and (2) their alleged inferiority as a form of aid to developing countries.

The first criticism calls attention to the fact that price support deters a shift of resources out of areas of overproduction. It thus tends to preserve fundamental disequilibria, and also by supporting inefficient producers, discourages the rationalization of production that is one key to economic development. There are several possible answers to this criticism. One is that it is possible for individual countries (e.g., Brazil) to set domestic prices which discourage overproduction even while reaping the benefit of a higher world price. The second answer is that production controls under an agreement may encourage the transfer of resources which would otherwise be prompted by the market's painful whiplash. Neither of these answers is satisfactory to those who see the market mechanism as the most efficient lever for change.

As two possible cases in point, one might ask oneself: (1) What would have happened if an effective coffee agreement had not come into being in 1963? (2) How might the world cocoa picture have differed if a cocoa agreement had been reached when it was initially considered in 1953?

Looking at coffee first, the authors presume that, in the absence of an agreement, many more producers would have been "driven to the wall" and Brazil's surplus stocks might now be totally depleted. However, it is exceedingly difficult to imagine what the cost would have been in human, economic, and political terms; in our opinion, the result probably would have been exceedingly disturbing for a period of years at least.

Now, let us suppose that a cocoa agreement had been established in 1953 and not deferred for consideration until more recently. Doubtless, the absence of a cocoa agreement helped to bring about a very speedy downward adjustment in both price and production. In the presence of an effective agreement, prices might well have been sustained at higher levels. In that event, by the late 1960's cocoa producers might have found themselves carrying burdensome stocks, and perhaps exploring schemes for elimination (or destruction) of surpluses. By the same token, however, chocolate manufacturers might not have had reason to be gravely concerned about a cocoa shortage and runaway prices in 1968–1969. It is not so easy to say precisely how a balance can best be struck between excessive interference in free markets, and action to moderate those extreme price fluctuations which are considered objectionable by both producing and consuming nations.

The second major criticism of commodity agreements concerns their efficiency as aid instruments. It has been observed that:

1. Economic aid directed towards specific priority-projects may be a much more effective way of promoting development.
2. Commodity agreements dispense aid without regard to the relative need of recipient countries, and also without being able to assure that the benefits go to those who will use them for development purposes.
3. In some commodities, a portion of the gain from commodity agreements goes to developed countries.[6]

In short, it is argued that "commodity agreements, in contrast with economic aid and private foreign investment are least likely to place added resources in the hands of those who will use them most effectively for development purposes."[7]

The point is also made that "if fifteen underdeveloped nations were benefiting from a commodity agreement, it might be extremely difficult to withdraw or modify the agreement because of political changes in one of the countries."[8] At this point, some representatives of the underdeveloped countries would surely reply that (as they see it) one reason for agreements is to avoid the ability of developed nations to attach political strings to aid. FAO and UNCTAD representatives would certainly agree that other forms of aid may be as desirable or even more so. But they would regard the two (agreements and aid) as complementary, not mutually exclusive. As a practical matter, they would doubt that sufficient economic aid would be forthcoming from developed nations to preclude the need for some kinds of constructive action in the commodity field.

In the eyes of the UNCTAD and FAO experts, no single approach will suffice. Investment guarantees, compensatory finance, greater freedom of access for the exports of developing countries—all these and more should go hand in hand with commodity arrangements tailored to the particular characteristics of the market in question.[9] Few can contest the need for simultaneous consideration of trade and aid, commodity arrangements, and

6. For details, see "Commodity Agreements, Their Role in the World Economy," Washington, D.C., United States Chamber of Commerce, 1963.

7. *Ibid.*, p. 33.

8. *Ibid.*, p. 33.

9. This point is effectively summarized by FAO economist Gerda Blau's "International Commodity Arrangements and Policies," CCP 65/3, Rome, Food and Agricultural Organization of the United Nations, 1964.

development planning. Division arises over the character of the policy mix and the degree to which the more regulatory measures should be utilized. In judging the issues, let us simply recall that the ultimate concern is with the well-being of peoples and nations, and that a grave development gap is a grave threat to all.

PART III

FUTURES

AS A PRICING

MEDIUM

CHAPTER 6

Seasonal Factors and Crop Years

The Seasonal Nature of Producing and Marketing Commodities

The production and marketing of commodities is, on the whole, a seasonal business. Unlike manufacturers, who may be able to regulate their production to conform to variations in seasonal or cyclical demand, the farmer can exercise little discretion concerning when to plant his crops. Planting time is determined for him by the type of crop, the geographical location of his farm, and by the weather. Nor can the farmer significantly advance or defer harvest to take advantage of market conditions. As an example, the bulk of the U.S. corn crop, amounting annually to some 5 billion bushels, must be harvested between October 1st and November 15th despite the fact that the corn will be consumed during the entire year. Harvesting of U.S. agricultural commodities occurs, in most years, as follows:

Wheat	May through August
Oats, barley, and cotton	July through September
Soybeans	October through November
Corn	October or November through December

Therefore, from the time that the Texas winter wheat crop begins moving to market in volume late in May, harvest of agricultural commodities expands as the combines work northward. Around September, when the harvesting of wheat, oats, cotton, and barley has been pretty much completed, the soybean crop is about ready to move in commercial quantities, to be followed in about a month by the corn crop. Weather sometimes delays harvest past these dates, while early portions of crops are sometimes ready for market sooner. Corn in Texas is very much ahead of corn in the Corn Belt and soybeans on sandy soil in central Illinois are harvested before soybeans in other areas.

A portion of the harvest is marketed directly to mills, processors, exporters, and terminal elevators; but the bulk of the grain not actually consumed on farms is trucked directly to the thousands of country elevators that dot our farmlands. Generally, these country elevators do not have the facilities to store this vast quantity of grain. Their primary function is to serve as the initial factor in the distribution of agricultural commodities, and they can operate profitably only by expeditiously handling and marketing the grain. During the height of the harvest movement, long lines of trucks can be seen waiting to unload in front of country elevators. This grain must either be sold and delivered or shipped on consignment in order to make room for newly arriving supplies. Even the large terminal elevators located adjacent to the principal grain marketing centers of Chicago, Duluth, Kansas City, Minneapolis, and Buffalo frequently become congested as thousands of grain-laden railroad cars continue to arrive from country locations.

It follows, therefore, that cash prices of agricultural commodities tend to be under pressure during the period of harvest and its accompanying heavy marketing. Gradually, thereafter, the pressure of harvest abates and farmers begin concentrating on harvesting a later crop, and on preparing to plant the next season's crop. Concurrently, commodity cash prices tend to experience a seasonal recovery as the current production begins to move out through the regular channels of distribution into the hands of exporters, processors, millers, terminal storage centers, and consumers.

From time to time, the government loan program has been a major depository for surplus agricultural production. Low commodity prices not only encourage heavier utilization but also attract an expanded volume of grains into the government loan program and, eventually, into the government's hands. This, plus the policy that government grain holdings may not be resold in the domestic market except at prices generally above the level of support prices, tends to create a condition of artificial scarcity in commercial channels, giving additional impetus to the postharvest price recovery.

Even nongrain commodities (with the exception of metals and other industrial commodities, where production can be more or less controlled) exhibit similar seasonal price tendencies. Cash values tend toward weakness during periods of heavy marketing, with higher prices likely later in the season.

The following table presents the normal seasonal cash price patterns for a number of commodities. It should be emphasized that this data represents an average of cash commodity price movements over a long period of years and that deviations from this long-term seasonal pattern may occur during any given year.

Normal Seasonal Pattern of Cash Commodity Prices

Commodity	High	Low
Cocoa	January–March	June and December
Corn	August	November–December
Cotton	July	October–December
Eggs	November	March–April
Potatoes	June–July	October
Soybeans	May	October–November
Wheat	May	July–August
Wool	December	June

Crop Years: Old and New Crops

Agricultural commodities are harvested annually and, in each commodity, one day is designated as the beginning of its crop year. For example, July 1st is the beginning of the crop year for wheat, oats and rye in the United States, even though their harvests may have been in progress before July 1st. The reason for this statistical designation is that during the month of July there is a sufficient flow of newly harvested grain to terminals to fully affect prices based on new crop conditions. Statistics of carryover from the preceding crop represent only old crop grain.

The distinction between old and new crop futures follows logically. An old crop future is one whose delivery period expires prior to the full-scale harvesting of the new crop, whereas a new crop future trades during the period when new crop supplies are substantially available for delivery. Trading is conducted simultaneously in both old and new crop futures. For example, in November, trading in wheat on the Chicago Board of Trade is conducted in the December, March, May, July, and September futures. December, March, and May wheat are old crop futures, because any wheat delivered against them will represent old crop grain harvested the previous summer. On the other hand, the July and September futures represent new crop months, inasmuch as the harvest should be sufficiently advanced by that time to permit the delivery of newly harvested wheat.

Although domestic consumption of agricultural commodities will not usually vary appreciably from year to year, even a small variation (particularly towards the end of the marketing year) can be a most important influence on the size of the old crop carryover. This will exert a direct effect on the price of the expiring old crop future in relation to the price of new crop futures. On the other hand, the size of successive crops (representing the supply) can show marked variations. Old crop futures will normally sell at premiums to new crop when there is a relative tightness, or the expectation of a relative tightness, in old crop supply. As an example, on September 25, 1970, May 1971 wheat at Chicago, the last old crop future, closed at $1.69. On the same date, July 1971 wheat, the first new crop future, closed at $1.58. This 11¢ premium for May wheat over July was due primarily to the expectation that old crop supplies would be small relative to the demand.

The distinction between old and new crop futures is not quite as simple in the case of soybeans and corn. Although October 1st is technically considered the beginning of their crop year, the corn and soybean harvests frequently commence early enough to render new crop supplies available for delivery against the September future, and hence to influence the price of the September future. Although more applicable to the soybean crop (since soybeans are normally harvested several weeks earlier than corn), the September future of these two commodities can represent either new crop or old crop futures. This distinction is important to the pricing of the September future. In the case of soybeans, when the free carryover is small, old crop futures (July and August) will likely trade at premiums over new crop futures (November and January). This type of situation encourages farmers to harvest as early as possible in order to benefit from the premium prices on old crop futures, so that the September future could be considered new crop. On the other hand, when free carryover is expected to be ample, resulting in old crop futures being priced below new crop (assuming no change in the government support price for soybeans), there is little incentive for new crop soybeans to be rushed to Chicago for delivery against the September future. The result is that the bulk of deliveries would be made against the November and January futures. In this case, the September future would be considered old crop.

CHAPTER 7 The Relationship Between the Cash and Futures Markets

The cash and the futures markets are two separate but closely related commodity markets. The cash market refers to the regular commercial channels for buying, selling, storing, and distributing actual (cash) commodities. The futures market refers to the organized exchange trading of standardized contracts for the future delivery of commodities.

An important distinction between the cash and futures markets is that only about 1 percent of the total volume of futures transactions is settled by delivery of the actual commodity, whereas virtually all cash transactions result in physical delivery. Another difference is that, in cash transactions, the precise grade and quality of the commodity are specified; while in a futures transaction, the seller has the option of delivering any one of several tenderable grades. Commodity exchanges establish a "basis grade" for each commodity, which is deliverable at contract price. Other grades of the commodity may be delivered, but at specified premiums or discounts to contract price.

Trading is conducted differently in the cash and the futures markets. Cash transactions may take place anywhere in the world, at any time and between any individuals. Furthermore, cash transactions are privately negotiated between the buyer and the seller, so that the trade terms are likely to vary with each transaction. Futures transactions, on the other hand, may be executed only by exchange members in the designated exchange ring or pit, during established trading hours. All trades must be publicly announced by open outcry and a record of transactions is immediately noted and disseminated to interested parties. Finally, most of the important terms of the futures contract are standardized, so that the only details which vary for each trade are the names of the buyer and seller, the delivery month, and the contract price.

The most important relationship between the cash and the futures markets—and certainly the one commanding the greatest attention on the part of both hedgers and speculators—concerns price. The difference in price between a particular grade of the actual (cash) commodity and a designated future (in the same commodity) is called the "basis." At any given time there exist various "bases" for each commodity, reflecting the following variable factors: the cash price for the particular grade and quality of the actual commodity; the price of the particular commodity future; the time of shipment or delivery; and the commodity destination.

The "basis" is quoted as the number of points or cents which the actual commodity is trading above or below the price of the corresponding future. When the price of the cash commodity is higher than the future, the basis is "on"; when the price of the cash commodity is lower than the future, the basis is "off." The basis of each commodity can fluctuate, and during the life of any given future, may change from "on" to "off," or vice versa, in response to changing fundamental or technical factors.

Bases in the New York Cocoa Market on December 14, 1970

Grade	Basis		
Ghanian	425	over	March*
Nigerian	400	over	March
Superior Bahia	325/350	over	March
Ariba (Ecuadorian)	175	over	March
Sanchez	10	under	March

* The range of March cocoa for the day was:

Open	27.70
High	27.78
Low	27.65
Close	27.74

The "basis" and its fluctuations are major factors which directly influence the many operating decisions of commodity trade firms. It is through changes in the "basis" that trade firms either profit or lose on their hedging operations. Trade firms attach such importance to it that the price of the actual commodity is frequently quoted in terms of the "basis" rather than in dollars and cents. For example, the price of a particular grade of cash corn may be quoted "2¢ off December." So long as this quotation is maintained, the price of that particular cash corn will fluctuate directly with the price of the December future, always 2¢ lower.

Although the price of the cash commodity may be higher or lower than the price of a distant future, the spread between cash and futures prices must narrow as each future approaches expiration.[1] Ultimately, the cash and expiring futures prices must coincide on contract terms (except for technical variations due to transportation and handling) because of the possibility of traders accepting or making delivery of the cash commodity against the expiring future. If the cash commodity were priced below the expiring future, a trader would have a guaranteed profit by buying the cash commodity, selling the expiring future (short), and delivering the lower priced cash commodity against his short futures commitment. This spreading would continue until the discount of cash to futures was eliminated. On the other hand, if the cash commodity were priced higher than the expiring future, a trader could buy the expiring future and sell the cash to arrive. He could accept delivery of the actual commodity against his long futures position, and deliver it against his short to-arrive commitment. This spreading would continue until cash lost its premium to the expiring future. Cash versus futures spreading is an intricate operation and is usually the exclusive province of experienced, well-financed professionals.

There exist three basic types of futures markets (classified by price structure): (1) a *"carrying charge"* (*"premium"*[2]) market refers to a market where each future sells at a premium over the previous future; (2) an *"inverse"* (*"discount"*) market refers to a market where each future sells at a discount from the previous future; and (3) a *"flat"* market refers to a market where all futures trade at approximately the same price. In a "carrying charge" grain market, the first future of the new crop may be priced below the last old crop future, but succeeding new crop futures will sell at successive premiums (see the table below).

Future Quotations (as of December 30, 1970)

"Premium" Market		"Discount" Market		"Flat" Market	
Silver (New York)		Soybean Oil (Chicago)		Sugar No. 11 (New York)	
Jan. 1971	162.50	Jan. 1971	11.63	Mar. 1971	4.38
Mar.	165.00	Mar.	11.55	May	4.38
May	167.50	May	11.40	Jul.	4.40
Jul.	170.00	Jul.	11.28	Sept.	4.39
Sept.	172.50	Aug.	11.04	Oct.	4.39
Dec.	176.30	Sept.	10.58	Mar. 1972	4.36
Jan. 1972	177.60	Oct.	10.18		
Mar.	180.10	Dec.	9.85		
		Jan. 1972	9.75		

1. Subsequent references to the cash commodity will refer to the deliverable grade, which is deliverable at contract price and is usually the most important grade of each commodity in the cash market.
2. Also called "contango" in European markets.

Carrying Charge (Premium) Market. This is the most common type of market structure, existing when the current supplies of a commodity are in excess of requirements. In such a buyers' market, the excessive stocks tend to depress the cash price and hence the price of the nearest future, and buyers have no incentive to aggressively bid for supplies. Under these conditions, where each future is priced higher than the preceding one, the price spread between successive futures should theoretically reflect the costs of owning and storing the cash commodity, namely: interest on capital, storage charges, commissions, insurance, transportation, and handling charges. In practice, carrying charges vary, depending on the commodity and its location, on the competitive position of buyers and sellers, and on whether the cash commodity owner has his own storage facilities. Premiums in a carrying charge market cannot exceed full carrying charges (except as noted in the next paragraph), and they rarely even equal the full charges. If they did exceed the costs of carrying the commodity, trade houses would buy the near future and sell the distant. They would accept delivery of the cash commodity against their long position, store the cash commodity, and deliver it against their short commitment in the distant future. Their profit would be the price spread between the two futures minus the costs of owning, storing, and delivering the cash commodity. This type of spreading would continue until the premium of the distant future over the nearby future narrowed to less than full carrying charges.

Only in the case of perishable commodities can the premium on a future exceed full carrying charges, and even this is a rare situation. Where there exists a threat of the cash commodity spoiling or being reduced in grade, traders may be reluctant to risk taking delivery of the cash commodity for storage and eventual redelivery against a short futures position. Under such circumstances, traders might not initiate this spread until the premiums exceeded the normal carrying charges by a sufficient margin to justify the additional risks.

Inverse Market. Such a market is likely to develop: when current commodity stocks are below anticipated requirements; when there exists a tightness of deliverable supplies relative to the open interest in the expiring future; or when the forthcoming new crop is expected to be very large or will be supported at a lower price than the old crop (applicable to commodities under government price support programs). In such a sellers' market, cash buyers are forced to bid up prices in order to secure their current requirements, while "shorts" in the nearby futures, especially in the expiring future, must aggressively cover their positions to avoid the anticipated difficulty of obtaining deliverable supplies in the cash market. This tightness of actuals, and the ensuing demand for nearby futures, inverts the normal price relationships, causing each later future to sell at a discount from the preceding one.

Unlike a premium market, where the maximum premiums on the distant futures tend to be limited by the carrying charges, in an inverse market there exists no such limit to the potential premium of the near futures over the distants. The extent of inverse premiums is largely determined by the degree of scarcity of the cash commodity. If deliverable stocks of a commodity are small relative to existing demand, as expressed by the open interest in the expiring future, "shorts" will be forced to cover by buying the expiring future whatever the price. From time to time we witness a "short squeeze," where the price of the expiring future vigorously advances to substantial premiums over distant futures. The "short squeeze" is one of the risks in being short an expiring future especially in a flat or an inverse market.

Flat Market. A relatively rare situation, this exists when supplies of the cash commodity are adequate to meet the existing demand, and the commodity is produced throughout the entire year. In such a market, carrying charges are usually of minor importance, because production can often be geared to match the near-term demand, so that minimum supplies need be stored. Certain metals sometimes exhibit this flat market tendency.

Before closing this discussion of commodity price relationships, it should be emphasized that commodity prices are constantly fluctuating in response to the free market forces of supply and demand. The commodity pricing mechanism tends to efficiently regulate production and allocate consumption by means of the changing price relationships between the cash and the futures markets, as well as between the various futures. These changing price relationships guide commodities through trade channels from producers to ultimate consumers by inducing smaller production and greater consumption when prices are low, and greater production and lesser consumption when prices are high. In practice, a carrying charge market encourages commodity firms to buy and store the cash commodity and to hedge in a distant future. In such a situation, the futures market pays at least part of the carrying costs (trade firms will normally carry actuals only if they are "paid" to do so). On the other hand, an inverse market, with premiums for the cash commodity and the nearby futures, encourages commodity firms to sell their excess commodity stocks and to secure their required supplies through buying hedges in the distant futures. This is especially applicable in the grain business, where many grain merchants will sell their cash supplies if they cannot profitably hedge in the futures market. As inverse spreads widen, additional cash supplies attracted by the higher prices tend to be marketed or to be delivered against short futures positions, while cash buyers will either reduce their consumption or seek lower priced substitutes.

CHAPTER 8 How Futures Prices Are Established

Prices of commodity futures, like the weather, are always subject to change. At any given moment the price of a commodity future represents the collective estimates of all buyers and sellers as to the future supply and demand for the commodity, and price fluctuations reflect the continuous revision of these supply and demand estimates. This premise, however, calls for some qualification. It cannot account for an error in prevailing collective thinking; those who are wrong may represent the dominant force. It also neglects the influence of hedges, which at times may be placed in the market with no thought whatsoever of whether prices are likely to advance or decline. Forceful trading, too, can distort prices. At times speculators may be responsible for temporarily running a market out of proportion to its basic economic value.

Pricing of an agricultural commodity for future delivery usually begins even before the commodity is planted. This can be of great assistance to producers, who are able to use price as a guide to planting. It also enables feeders to plan feeding requirements, and foreign buyers to determine where and when to buy needed supplies.

In a free market, the supply of a commodity consists of the carryover from the previous crop, production from the current crop, and imports. On the other side of the balance sheet is the demand, consisting of domestic usage, exports, seed requirements, and the reserve required for the year-end carryover. (This basic equation ignores, for the time being, the role of the U.S. Department of Agriculture, or agencies of other governments, in buying, storing, and marketing vast quantities of commodities.)

Prior to harvest, these various factors which comprise the supply of a commodity are recorded by frequent government reports. The most important of these, in the case of U.S. agricultural crops, are the *Farmers'*

Intentions to Plant and the monthly *Crops Reports,* which put crop plantings and development into sharper focus. As each report is issued, futures prices adjust to the newly estimated supply-demand relationship, and to its comparison with previous estimates. Once the crop has been planted, weather and plant disease are two principal factors influencing the final size of the crop, whether it be corn in Illinois, cocoa in Nigeria, or potatoes in Maine. Many substantial corn and soybean rallies have been sparked by unexpected droughts and heat spells during the crucial growing period prior to harvest. However, once the harvest actually commences, traders keep a close watch on its progress in the important producing areas.

Actual yields at harvest may reveal a higher or lower production than was anticipated. Plant damage during the growing period may not show until harvest time; for example, small corn kernels will require a larger quantity to make up one bushel, therefore such corn will yield a smaller corn supply. After harvest, when the final production has been established, the attention of traders shifts more to the question of demand. Export sales, weekly reports of exports, crush (in the case of soybeans), consumption, stocks on hand, and movements into and out of terminal storage are carefully scrutinized and analyzed. Other important reports include weekly purchase figures for cocoa and storage and slicing reports for pork bellies.

In discussing the adjustment of prices to changes in supply and demand, Schonberg states:

> In markets, and more so in futures markets, prices constantly change and act to keep production and consumption in balance. The only "fair price" as stated by Professor James A. Boyle many years ago is the "equilibrium price" which coordinates production and consumption. This is the price which moves the whole crop into consumption without a shortage and without a carryover. . . . It has been the free cash markets and the futures markets, even though handicapped by the price support laws, that have guided the grain through the trade channels from farmers to consumers.[1]

Freely fluctuating commodity prices tend to coordinate production and consumption because low prices of an oversupply commodity tend to induce a greater rate of consumption, frequently at the expense of higher-priced substitutes. High prices, on the other hand, tend to price a scarce commodity out of the market by reducing consumption and encouraging the use of lower-priced substitutes. Corn and other feed grains, and cottonseed oil and soybean oil are two sets of commodities which, for many purposes, are interchangeable depending on relative prices. High prices, moreover, tend to allocate supplies of a scarce commodity over a longer

1. James A. Schonberg, in addressing the Futures Trading Seminar sponsored by the Chicago Board of Trade, Chicago, 1960.

period of time, pending the arrival of a new crop or of additional supplies of the same crop, which may have been attracted to the market because of the higher prices.

Besides being influenced by supply and demand for the actual commodity, prices are influenced in a more direct sense by the buying and selling of futures contracts. A major factor in this respect is the prevailing psychology of the trade and the public. Notwithstanding economic supply and demand factors, changing prices can directly induce additional buying or selling. Price fluctuations caused solely by previous price changes are considered "technical" in nature. They are usually of temporary duration and can be precipitated by large-scale speculative liquidation or short covering, heavy spot month deliveries or the "touching off" of large stop orders. This type of "technical" price fluctuation tends to be short-term in nature and will not change the basic longer-term price trend. Nevertheless, it can cause considerable discomfort to those traders who, although having a position in accordance with the major market trend, may be too thinly margined or too nervous to withstand the adverse "technical" price move.

Regardless of their cause, price fluctuations and the active effort to profitably anticipate them comprise the principal interest of both trade firms and the public, and will receive the major emphasis throughout much of this book.

PART **IV**

COMMODITY PRICE

ANALYSIS

CHAPTER **9** **On Seeking Profits in Commodities**

> It's easy to make money on Wall Street. All you
> have to do is—buy when the price is low. Then, as
> soon as the market goes up, sell and take your
> profit.
>
> —MARK TWAIN

Part IV focuses upon one central theme: How to make money in commodities? It can be done. In fact, there are individuals who have won the commodity game consistently, converting modest margin accounts into substantial fortunes. However, such success does not come easily, except in the imagination. For a great many nonprofessional traders, the pursuit of profits in commodities is at best frustrating and elusive. Many are called by the lure of high-leverage in commodity markets. Few are chosen to reap the glittering rewards.

The Problem of Prediction

The average trader's chance of success will be much greater if he has a thorough and realistic understanding of sound trading technique, and of the pitfalls he is likely to encounter along the not-so-primrose trading path.

One fundamental difficulty concerns the problem of prediction. To make money in commodity futures, it is not sufficient to estimate prices with fair accuracy in the light of available information. Your estimate must be different from, and better than the forecast already registered in today's futures market quotation. To be a successful commodity trader, you must outguess the market.

This point merits reiteration and reflection. A futures market is usually a fairly accurate price barometer of all the facts and opinions which are known, surmised, or guessed about a particular commodity. Today's futures price reflects the consensus of all the people who are trading that commodity; it mirrors their evaluation of a commodity's present and future price outlook. If we think that the price of a particular commodity future is going to rise or fall, it is either because we believe our judgment is better than the market's, or because we think we know something which most people in the market do not know.

There is still another reason why a trader may believe that a market will either rise or fall. That (disastrous) "method" of price analysis can be called the "wishful thinking" approach, based primarily on the trader's existing market position. Thus, a trader may believe that prices will rise— or fall—simply because he is already long or short. This market approach is very prevalent, particularly among small, public speculators. Although it will be discussed in detail in subsequent chapters, let us say, at this point, that *a trader should be long the market because he is bullish—and not be bullish because he happens to be long.* Of course, the same logic applies, concerning a short position and a bearish market viewpoint.

Tomorrow's price changes are likely to depend on tomorrow's news—or anticipated news—the next change in the weather, the soon-to-be-released crop estimate, or the unforeseen strike or revolution. From the standpoint of most traders, it is a matter of pure chance whether tomorrow's news will be bullish or bearish. Since futures respond to such news, price changes in futures have an important random element.

Ordinarily, the commodity news which is published in the daily press is of little trading value. Much earlier, it had come over the ticker of brokerage and trade houses, had been acted upon by traders and, so, had been "discounted" in the futures market. The more swiftly and perfectly the market reacts pricewise to news, the less will be its remaining bullish or bearish significance.

We will see later that even when a market seems to be following a clear trend, there may be a lack of momentum in the indicated direction; more than that, there may not even be a directive force underlying the apparent "trend." Chance, the careless artist, may simply have drawn an intriguing but meaningless line on the chart of time.

Fortunately, difficulties of this kind do not preclude successful trading. But they do complicate the game, and make it a hard one to beat without uniquely good methods or privileged access to important market information.

Insiders and Outsiders

What sort of players are best suited to win the frequently irrational Monte Carlo of the commodity markets? One would think, quite naturally, that the odds would favor the "insiders," the professionals.

In each commodity, trading in actuals and in futures is the constant preoccupation of men trained "on the firing line" to buy or sell on behalf of large specialized trade houses or industrial users. Each of these firms invests a great deal of time and money in an effort to stay in touch with every factor which might influence its commodities. The object, wherever possible, is to stay "one jump ahead of the market" in order to maintain that competitive "edge" which will enable the firm to profit in its dealings.

For example, a large cocoa importer or chocolate manufacturer may have a private representative in the cocoa growing areas whose duty it is to keep close tabs on crop conditions and developments. The same firm may also have a European branch or agent who provides a firsthand account of demand conditions in important consuming areas, while the firm's trading department is in constant touch, by wire or phone, with buyers or sellers throughout the world.

Even such "insider" firms do not consistently make money. From time to time, their trading departments suffer losses, occasionally quite serious ones. Some of these losses perhaps flow from correctible errors. Perhaps better statistical analysis could have made crop observations more meaningful; or in other ways, the firm could have made better use of the information available to it. It would seem, however, that even with optimum methods, and even with an inside edge on market news, anyone who trades regularly must often lose. The difficulties are enough to prevent most people in the commodity business from regularly relying on outright speculation as the main source of their profits.

By contrast with a professional, the speculator is usually an outsider. He must, as a rule, work with second- or third-hand information, received after it has already been scrutinized and acted upon by large dealers and other professionals. He has no special representatives in critical areas, no string of correspondents, and rarely is he trained as an economist or trader.

Can this trader approach the not very consistent speculative success of the professional, whose everyday business involves commodity dealings? If so, by what legerdemain? One possible solution for the amateur trader is to place reliance on the counsel of commodity brokers or advisors.

Brokers and Advisors

A list of commodity dealers, brokers, and advisory services can be obtained from any of the commodity exchanges, commercial banks, or the classified directory.

Indeed, we think, there are notable weaknesses in the way most commodity brokers carry out market research and dispense opinions to the public. Many firms (including some of the largest) have not measured the value of the trading recommendations which they continue to offer confidently to all comers. They have not critically reviewed the success or failure of their past suggestions. Nor have they attempted to seriously use systematic methods, based on modern economics and statistics.

The fact that so many commission firms have failed to build a thoroughly professional research staff is partly a matter of historical precedent. Years ago, the commodity business was small, and most diversified commission houses did not find it worthwhile to spend much money on it. The tradition of thrift in spending on commodity research is still generally prevalent. Commodity research has remained the stepchild of Wall Street.

It is time for a change. And the best way, we think, for such a change to come about, is for the public to begin demanding more quality research and more careful release and review of commodity opinions by those who issue them.

Sources of Trading Guidance

How should the average trader go about selecting a broker or advisory service? In making a choice, it seems advisable to follow certain basic dictates.

1. Inquire around financial circles to find out which firms have good reputations, especially in the commodity (or commodities) in which you are interested.

2. Among those eligible, concentrate on those firms who will give you a complete and precise record of their trading recommendations, especially those with successful trading records.

3. Also give preference to firms whose methods seem professional.

4. Test before you trade. For at least a month or two, follow every recommendation the firm makes by "paper trading." For each buy or sell recommendation, enter the opening price the next day. In the same way liquidate on paper when advised to do so, and tally up your profits and losses.

In the case of an advisory service, you can sometimes get back copies of that service's opinions by requesting them, or you may find them at your broker's office. Take the time to go over these thoroughly before you start trading on the service's advice.

In checking the results of past trading recommendations, be sure the broker, the service, or your own reckoning has taken into account commission charges, and has allowed for the "execution gap" that often exists between the price at which a buy or sell is first favored, and the price at which you can actually execute your order.

Let us assume you have found an advisory service which a careful tabulation indicates has been making profits consistently. Even this is no guarantee of success, because the particular service may have been enjoying a "hot" period. But if the service has a good reputation, and also seems to be using professional methods (as later chapters of this book may help you to judge), then you may be willing to start trading.

If you want to give your advisory service a fair try, you are probably well advised to follow all the recommendations they give. If you pick and choose between them, you have changed the odds of success from what you thought they were on the basis of the service's opinions only. That may be all right, but your method is no longer what we are presently discussing. Instead of guiding yourself solely by expert (and partly tested) advice, you are being directed by a composite opinion, which now includes your own expert or inexpert judgment.

One way to eliminate your own subjective involvement is to open a "managed account" where that is feasible, with a service selected in the manner indicated above. Such an account authorizes another party to trade on your behalf, and for your risk or profit.

Another worthwhile possibility is that you might trade through a dealer in actuals who is also a member of the exchange in question, and can execute your orders in the same way as any Wall Street brokerage firm. In some cases, this will give you the benefit of an "insider's" knowledge of a given commodity market. However, if you are a small trader, a dealer of stature may not want to take the trouble to handle your account. He is simply too busy tending his actuals business to spend much time talking to speculators, especially in those times when opinions turn out badly, and questioning calls multiply.

If you are a large trader, you may wish to talk to several dealer-exchange members about the possibility of placing your orders through them in return for their guidance and information or, in effect, their partial or complete management of your account. As was suggested above, an advantage of this arrangement lies in the dealer's large fund of experience and knowledge. The main weakness is that the dealer may be too close to the market; he may rely too heavily on personal judgment and too little, perhaps, on objective, systematic methods.

The speculator who is interested in a managed account has another alternative: to place his money in a commodity fund.[1] As its name implies, this is a commodity analogue of a mutual fund in securities. Experience of commodity funds to date has not been encouraging, however. Despite guidance by experienced commodity people, a number of such funds have performed badly. Clearly, one would wish to investigate new funds carefully before investing.

Whether you trade with a dealer or broker, or seek the guidance of an

1. The fund may be in either a corporate or (limited) partnership form.

advisor, you may find that decision-making is often based on rather vague and subjective standards—a "feel of the market," a broad reading of the chart, and statistics. This is changing. As time passes, more and more attention is being paid to systematic methods of analysis. But so far, commodity research and opinion owe more to the folklore of Wall Street than to scientific approach.

The Folklore of Wall Street

As the phrase is used here, the "folklore of Wall Street" is the Street's heritage of commodity trading ideas, written and unwritten. It is a blend of common-sense economics, trading maxims, and helpful hints garnered over long years of market experience. It is a "folklore" rather than a science because it is subjectively formulated in a way which appeals to the intuition, but is not easily tested.

These Wall Street commodity ideas are part insight and part myth. For the commodity economist, there is a great deal of work to be done separating the useful insight from the mythical chaff. This means, to an increasing extent, formulating commodity concepts and trading ideas in ways that can be *tested,* a real challenge to commodity brokers and advisors.

Earlier, we suggested how one might select a broker or advisor to help guide your commodity trading decisions. But what if you intended to "do it yourself"? In that case, your quest must be for rational and workable methods which might help you to trade with some justifiable confidence and hope of success. You will also need a broker who will execute your orders and maintain your account efficiently and reliably.

It is useful to start with a critical but not unfriendly view of the maxims commonly accepted on Wall Street. Of these, the following are perhaps the most popular:

Go with the market; do not buck the trend.
> It is usually unwise to try to pick the top or bottom of a major bull or bear market. It is often better to buy on signs of an uptrend market, and to sell on indications of a downtrend.

Stop your losses; let your profits run.
> Bad trades are inevitable. The important thing is to terminate them before they grow costly. Be prepared to admit you are wrong. When you are right, be patient. Do not permit a good profit to turn into a loss.

Watch out for a turn when market opinion seems one-sided.
> Inevitably, bullishness is overdone at the top of a market, and bearishness at the bottom. This truism encourages the "contrary opinion" philosophy which holds that a very high index of opinion in one direction, particu-

larly when accompanied by a record-high open interest, is often a prelude to a market reversal.

Confine your trading to situations of unusual appeal.
There is wisdom in patience. Wait for situations in which profit potential seems unusually high. Trade infrequently, unless your particular trading plan reasonably requires you to take positions often.

If anything is wrong with these maxims, it is that they are obvious in implication, but not so obvious in application.

Certainly, we would all like to let our profits run, and severely limit our losses. However, as soon as we begin trading, we find that if we limit losses too closely, we incur a great many losses; and if we let profits run too freely, we lose many of them by overstaying the market. The problem is to design specific trading tactics which, in practice, will keep the magnitude of losses low in relation to the magnitude of profits.

Other Wall Street maxims appeal to the intuition but, once again, do not suffice to objectively guide trading decisions. For example, the adage "trade with the trend" seems almost another way of saying "get on the winning side." Without specific rules it is not so easy to identify trends that are not, in actuality, "false starts" or temporary reversals in an existing trend. We would all like to pick trends that will continue; the question again is: How? (A question we shall tackle in detail in ensuing chapters.)

These criticisms of Wall Street's maxims should not be overdone. There is something to be said for this conventional wisdom, even if it is often somewhat vague. It offers an informed viewpoint, an attitude which is probably conducive to a healthy trading psychology.

One should be prepared to accept losses, and not permit them to grow beyond a predetermined limit. As a general rule, it is probably unwise to buy in the absence of a sign that a downtrend has run out of steam, or to sell in the face of an apparently unchecked bull market. If, as an exception to this rule, you have a specific scale-down buying program, then it is wise to decide in advance whether you are prepared to carry the resulting position indefinitely and pay the cost. If you consider selling scale-up, remember there is no limit to the extent to which the market can go against you. It is probably wisest to decide firmly at what point you will admit being wrong, and exit resolutely if not happily.

As we said before, most of the popular trading "rules" originated in the rough battleground of Wall Street experience. These findings were not developed or tested in any systematic way. It would be exceedingly helpful to examine the actual trading experience of great numbers of commodity speculators. A careful study of their experience might cast further light on the factors which influence success or failure.

Fortunately, one such study, *An Analysis of Speculative Trading in Grain Futures,* has been conducted by the Commodity Exchange Authority. Although based on a pre–World War II period, and subject to some special influence due to market characteristics of that period, the CEA study, nevertheless, retains its relevance and interest.

CEA Study of Grain Trading

The CEA study, published in 1949, was based on an examination of the actual trading records of nearly 9,000 traders over a nine-year period, 1924–1932.[2] It covered over 400,000 transactions in grain futures, all on the Chicago Board of Trade.

The first and most striking observation of this study is that, among speculators in the group, losers outnumbered winners by 3-to-1, and in the aggregate, speculative net losses were nearly six times net profits. These highly negative results were undoubtedly influenced by the fact that the period under study was, on balance, one of major decline in grain prices. Even allowing for this factor, the study is both a telling commentary on the difficulty of successful commodity speculation, and a revealing hint as to some of the behavioral patterns which contribute to triumph or defeat.

Most speculators, the study found, tend to trade on the long side. The ratio of long to short positions was approximately 2-to-1. This preference is not as overwhelming as is sometimes thought, but it is enough to create a serious loss bias in a period of predominantly weak prices, or even during a generally two-way market.

It should be noted, however, that many of those speculators who were consistently short (during this period of generally declining prices) actually finished with net losses rather than profits. These net losses occurred even though the consistent "bears" were right more often than they were wrong; the "bears" actually made a greater number of profitable transactions than losing ones. In the aggregate, however, they lost money because their average loss per transaction on the wrong side of the market materially exceeded their average gain per transaction when they were right.[3]

As the CEA observes, the main factor responsible for the predominance

2. By Blair Stewart, *An Analysis of Speculative Trading in Grain Futures,* Technical Bulletin No. 1001, Washington, D.C., U.S. Department of Agriculture, Commodity Exchange Authority, October 1949.

3. In simple mathematical form, we can say that the condition for profit is: $(N_L \times L) < (N_p \times P)$, where N_L is the number of completed loss transactions, L is the average loss for each such transaction, N_p is the number of profit transactions and P is average profit for each such transaction. The short traders in the CEA survey were able to make N_L (number of losses) less than N_p (number of profits) but they also managed to score an average profit P more than proportionately lower than average loss L.

of losses was "the small traders' characteristic hesitation in closing out loss positions."[4] Evidently, the small trader acted against Wall Street's first maxim: Instead of cutting losses, and letting profits run, he tended to cut profits and, if not actually letting losses run, at any rate, showing greater reluctance to cut losses.[5]

As the CEA points out, it is not reasonable to imply all one has to do to trade successfully is to follow a simple maxim about liquidating profits and losses. "If success could be achieved so easily, there would be few unsuccessful traders on futures markets."[6]

As we interpret it, however, a most significant conclusion to be drawn from the CEA study is that *most traders become more reluctant to liquidate when the market goes against them. This may well be the single most important cause of unsuccessful futures trading.* The evidence suggests that traders tend to defer action not only when they are losing, but also when they are beginning to see their profits fade.

[In general the] liquidation pattern [seems to be one] in which traders tended to cut profits and losses when they were increasing, but refrained from closing out either profitable or unprofitable trades when price movements were tending to eliminate them.[7]

Most traders were inclined to initiate their buy transactions during downmarkets and their sell transactions during uptrends. Thus, their first impulse was to "shop for good value," rather than go with the trend of the market. The one trader in the CEA sample who made the largest profits also followed this pattern. However, he displayed more frequent willingness to trade on "movement," buying as prices rose, and selling as prices weakened.

Another CEA finding is instructive to those who want to know what makes some people win and others lose in the game of futures trading. The heaviest loser in the group of speculators surveyed "traded through a large number of complex cycles with much in-and-out trading."[8] The speculator who made the largest profits operated in trading cycles which were "predominantly simple, and in-and-out trading was quite rare."[9]

4. Blair, *op. cit.,* p. 129.
5. Most traders covered in the CEA study operated on a small scale and stopped trading before profits or losses were very large.
6. Blair, *op. cit.,* p. 7.
7. *Ibid.,* p. 124.
8. A "cycle" is the combination of trades by which a trader assumes long and short positions and subsequently liquidates them. In a "simple cycle" a trader builds up a position—long or short—and then liquidates it. In a "complex cycle," he may buy or sell various positions during the cycle, thus making him simultaneously long and short; or expressed differently, he "straddles" all or part of his initial position.
9. Blair, *op. cit.,* p. 30.

It would seem that the more complex trading pattern of the "losers" reflected a tendency, once again, to defer liquidating a loss position (or a dwindling profit), this time by "straddling" (that is, taking an opposite position in another delivery month). Thus, a complex trading pattern is probably more the result of losing methods than the cause of losses. However, it may well contribute to losses by encouraging an evasion of correct strategies, as well as by adding materially to commission charges.

What other characteristics separate the most successful traders from their less fortunate and much more numerous brethren? Does one's professional status, occupation, or training make any difference? Rather surprisingly, the CEA study shows comparatively little difference in trading results for those of different occupational backgrounds. In fact, the CEA report suggests that special knowledge of the commodity traded did not help greatly. In all groups, regardless of background, speculative losses greatly exceeded profits. However, we attach some significance to the fact that the group with knowledge of the grain business lost somewhat less than others, and materially less than the lowest groups. Specifically, the percentage of traders who made profits was 29 percent for the group of managers in the grain business, and 21 to 22 percent for farmers, clerical, and manual workers.

Thus, a broad knowledge of a specific commodity is somewhat helpful, but in most cases is not sufficient to guarantee profitable commodity trading.

Even if no one factor is decisive, it may be constructive to start our "how-to" discussion with an appreciation of some of the behavioral principles which influence success or failure.

Who Wins and Who Loses in Commodity Speculation?

Below, we have combined some of the Wall Street trading maxims discussed earlier with the lessons learned from the CEA study, to draw a profile of the "Winners" and "Losers" in commodity trading.

Winners tend to:	Losers tend to:
Consider purchases on strength as well as on reactions. Consider sales on signs of weakness.	Buy on weakness. Sell on strength.
After a major upswing, wait for evidence of top formation before selling. After a major decline, wait for evidence of bottom formation before buying.	Buy when price seems low enough. Sell when price seems too high.
"Let profits run" but when they begin to fade markedly, liquidate.	Take profits quickly. If they begin to fade, hold tight.

Regard any pronounced loss as proof that liquidation may be in order. Protect positions with "stops," or liquidation.	Once a loss develops, wait for market to come back to permit liquidation on more favorable terms.
Straddle only when straddle itself has merit.	Straddle a loss position to defer taking the loss.
Consider short and long positions equally meritorious, and act on both sides.	Trade primarily on the long side.
Know as much as possible about the commodity traded and the method used.	Rely on tips and intuitive reaction to particular market situation.
Wherever possible, test a method before putting money on it; test advisory service or broker before following recommendations.	Follow advice of the most convincing broker or advisory report; if that proves wrong, try someone else.
Prevent a good profit from turning into a loss.	"Watch" as profits erode.

So far, the trading precepts we have discussed have only broadly indicative value. They tell you to "let your profits run" but offer no precise advice as to when to take them. They advise limiting losses, but without saying how much. In short, they remain maxims rather than specific trading guides.

Let us see how we go about devising rules of market behavior which are clear-cut, objective, and more realistic.

"Decision Rules" for Commodity Trading

Formally speaking, one solution to the problem—how to trade profitably —entails formulating "decision rules," preferably rules which are rational and unambiguous, and which can be tested. We'll see that some of the rules in popular use are more subjective and more difficult to test than others.

Following established precedent, we can classify decision rules into two main types: fundamental and technical. To this we might add a third class, which attempts to combine both fundamental and technical considerations.

THE FUNDAMENTAL APPROACH

This approach is based on an analysis of the economic factors and the environment in which they operate. It seeks to determine the underlying causes of price change, as rooted primarily in supply-demand relationships.

It addresses itself to one main problem: that of gauging value. It asks the primary question: *What should the price be under the indicated economic conditions?*

THE TECHNICAL APPROACH

On the other hand, this approach is concerned with the behavior of the market itself. It seeks to predict tomorrow's price in today's and yesterday's observed price pattern, and in an analysis of the relative strength of buyers and sellers (the technical condition of the market). It focuses its attention on both the problem of gauging the actual price trend, and that of evaluating its momentum. The basic question it raises is: *Where is the market heading?*

We shall devote our attention first to the technical approach, because it is broader and more straightforward than fundamental analysis, and because it links readily with the general trading principles and precepts which we have discussed in this chapter. We shall see that the decision rules of the technical analyst are, to a large extent, efforts to implement in an objective, highly-organized manner, the popular trading maxims discussed above.

CHAPTER 10 Introduction to Technical Analysis

What Is Technical Analysis?

Technical analysis of futures price movements embraces a study of the actual price fluctuations (as opposed to the basic economic factors which may have caused those price fluctuations). The technician relies on the daily action of the market as expressed on the ticker tape and in chart form by price, volume of trading, and open interest changes (number of contracts outstanding), to help him determine when to buy, to sell or to stand aside. Concerning the philosophy of technical analysis, Commodity Research Bureau states:

> The purpose of chart reading is to measure the relative strength of buying and selling pressures. If it can be demonstrated that buying pressure at the prevailing price level is more powerful than selling pressure, it is logical to assume that prices will rise. On the other hand, if selling pressure overpowers buying pressure, the assumption is that prices will fall.
>
> If we substitute the word "supply" for selling pressure and "demand" for buying pressure, we can reduce the measurement to that of supply and demand. Accordingly, chart analysis seeks to determine at what point supply exceeds demand and vice versa; also, when they are in approximate balance.[1]

As suggested in Chapter 9, a central goal of commodity analysis is the development of decision rules for profitable trading. What distinguishes technical analysis from other methods is the kind of rules it evolves, namely those which are based solely on the behavior and condition of the market.

The one variable which is crucial to the technician's interpretation is, of

1. "How Charts Are Used in Commodity Price Forecasting," New York, Commodity Research Bureau, Inc., 1955, p. 1.

course, price. Price movement is the chief barometer of all forces—natural, economic, or political—which affect a commodity market. Hurricane or drought, strike or revolution, business upswing or recession—all these, and more, find expression in market action. To the astute technician, the price pattern is prophetic as well as historic. The market is our best predictor.

Admittedly, some of the patterns may be misleading. And so the technician often turns to other market indicators to help him gauge the meaning or significance of price moves. Quite likely, he will take into account (in ways which we shall explore later) changes in the volume of trading, and in the open interest. He may also examine the relative strength of buyers and sellers. Is the market overloaded with speculative longs? How soon is first notice day (the first day on which shorts may issue notices of intention to deliver against a maturing contract)? Are deliverable supplies ample, and tenders likely to be large?

In its broadest application, then, technical analysis embraces subjective areas in which the market psychology of traders interacts with their actual commodity positions. For the most part, however, the focus of technical analysis is on exact numerical measures, specifically price, volume, and open interest. We shall also develop the thought that, because of its objective numerical character, technical analysis lends itself to computerization.

Approaches to Technical Analysis

The technician's handbook includes a variety of tools and methods, ranging from the informed and subjective, to the more disciplined, objective and mathematical.

In outline form, we catalogue the following technical approaches:

    I. Tape or board reading.
   II. Price chart analysis.
      A. Price trends.
      B. Support and resistance.
      C. Consolidation (reversal and continuation).
      D. Price formations and patterns.
      E. Measurement rules.
      F. Wave theory.
  III. Volume and open interest analysis.
  IV. Other technical indicators.
      A. Measures of relative performance.
      B. Study of periodic price performance.
      C. Opinion survey and contrary opinion theory.
   V. Computer-oriented methods.
      A. Mathematical trend analysis.
      B. Moving average and other trading systems.

C. The computer as chart reader.

D. Formulating and testing decision rules.

Let us emphasize at the outset that these listed approaches are not all-inclusive nor are they mutually exclusive. In particular, computer-oriented methods are sometimes only an automated way of applying technical concepts included under other headings. However, quite apart from the stylishness or handiness of computer use, we shall see that the computer makes possible real innovations in technique of analysis. Furthermore, the application of computer methods encourages explicit statement of one's theories in ways that can be tested.

In this chapter, we shall examine the principal technical methods in detail, especially today's most popular approach—chart analysis, as well as technical analysis using computer methods. But first, a few introductory words about several of these methods, starting at the more subjective end of the scale.

TAPE READING

Among technicians, a select few are "tape watchers" or "board readers," who follow each new price tick and compare it with their mental record of the market's recent performance. Above all, they are searching for a signal that a significant change is imminent or underway. Like other technical analysts, tape watchers are sentries on the lookout for any unusual movement in the market underbrush. Often an abrupt price change on large volume is their cue to action. Typically, the tape watchers seek to profit from small moves, sometimes scalping only a few points at a time as day traders. Tape watchers are essentially mental chartists, with a short-term trading viewpoint.

Nearly every broker's boardroom has its contingent of "regulars," a generally congenial assortment of old-timers, whose days are spent in trading from the tape. It is most interesting to observe these traders—many of whom are extremely apt and successful speculators—as they operate. If you sit with them long enough, the conversation will eventually turn to the subject of charts and chart trading. On that subject, most tape traders are unanimous in their disapproval. After all, these boardroom buffs, veterans of countless bull and bear cycles, have observed hosts of fellow speculators come and go and they still trade from the tape, not from charts. Or do they?

Although you may never convince him of it, the tape trader who buys when the market crosses above a previously impregnable level on heavy volume operates in almost exactly the same way as does the experienced chartist who buys an upside breakout on a stop order. The similarity does not end there. Both the tape trader and the chartist employ many similar basic techniques, designed to get them into a position as a move is beginning, and to ride with the position so long as the trend remains favorable. The reader should bear in mind this relationship between tape trading and chart trading.

Is it really possible to consistently interpret market action as a valid forecast and guide to profitable trading? Many floor traders will testify from experience that it is. However, an interesting possibility (to which we shall give further attention later) is that the immediate trend of the market may have diminishing predictive significance; forecasting accuracy may shrink as the time horizon is extended.

Although the distant view may be blurry, the fact is that most traders are interested in more than a one-hour or one-day projection. Their aim is to catch larger, more lasting price moves. And this requires them to decide when the profit potential—medium or long range—more than outweighs the risk of loss. As an aid to their decision-making, the most widely used implement is, of course, the price chart.

CHART ANALYSIS

Whatever its limitations, the price chart understandably has won the loyalty of many commodity traders. The chart is picture history, a kind of succinct commodity profile. At the very least, it is a handy, easily understood reference to a commodity's past range and volatility and a ready indicator of projected price turns and trends.

Charting, the principal tool of the technical analyst, has attracted an increasing following among commodity traders. What accounts for this? In the first place, charting has been thoroughly and enthusiastically publicized in much of the current financial literature. It is considered relatively simple to absorb the basic principles of charting so that with little more than a brief indoctrination and supplied with a pencil, a straightedge, and chart paper, any trader can join the expanding ranks of "market technicians." Furthermore, maintaining price charts is simple work; the chartist need not concern himself with the seemingly complicated mass of commodity reports and statistics which are regularly issued.

Unfortunately, there is temptation on the part of many commodity traders to regard charting as a simple, automatic trading system and to blindly rely on "playing the charts" to provide trading ideas. Successful trading requires much more than a brief period spent daily with charts. It is not sufficient to compare current chart formations with certain standard historical chart patterns and then to react to them in some prescribed manner. To trade profitably, the technician must become expert at his trade. This can only be gained through study, hard work, and experience.

Those who think of technical analysis as a science, find it an inexact science at best. In fact, many experienced operators consider it an art because the skill, finesse, and experience of the technician are without doubt the essential ingredients for profitable trading.

To succeed, the chartist must remain independent and objective. This is more easily said than done. Self-discipline is required to maintain a market position when one is constantly confronted with confusing and even contradictory news and advices. Even experienced traders will sometimes abandon a good position for no better reason than that they got bored with it, or that they heard that an important trade firm was rumored to be taking on a position contrary to theirs.

The technician must constantly check and recheck his conclusions, taking nothing for granted. Any position must be abandoned, whether at a profit or a loss, whenever an objective analysis indicates that it is unsound.

The outstanding weakness of charting, then, lies in its complete dependence on the interpretive skill of the technician. It has often been observed that there are really no bad charts, only bad chartists. Many neophytes, after a series of discouraging losses, have abandoned their technical studies because "they just don't work." This fairly common phenomenon is further proof that there are no shortcuts to trading success and no substitutes for experience, knowledge, and hard work.

Another weakness of charting stems from the belief that, although the true fundamentals of a commodity situation are unknown to the speculator, these facts may be known and acted upon by large trade houses and other professional traders, whose buying or selling causes price changes which can be studied and analyzed on charts. In reality, however, certain events such as drastic weather changes, military action, and political developments most often occur unexpectedly. Prices may not have completely discounted these occurrences, in which case the chartist may be caught off-guard. There is very little that can be done to protect a position in such a situation except to be alert to recognize the sudden change in market trend, to be quick to assess its probable significance, and to abandon or reverse an existing position if it appears warranted.

THE ROLE OF THE COMPUTER IN TECHNICAL ANALYSIS

The information contained in a chart and, as we remarked earlier, the main technical indicators, are numerical. There is, therefore, no reason why all of a chart's story cannot be told in tables. It appears, however, that most traders prefer the graphic to the tabular. To them, "a picture is worth a thousand numbers" and, in fact, often contains that many figures.

While the public may balk at numbers, the specialist welcomes them, especially in this computer era when complex numerical operations can be executed in an instant. Numbers are grist for the computer mill. And since the key technical factors are numerical, it is especially appropriate for technical analysis and the computer to join forces.

Like the human chartist, the computer can project a trend or trend channel, interpret a formation, determine when a turn has occurred, and (if we so instruct) factor in volume and open interest changes to help gauge the significance of a price move. But unlike its human counterpart, the computer has no latitude for vagueness, emotion, or indecision. The computer must be "talked to" in a language that is definite and unambiguous, and it will respond in the same way.

This is not to say that computer methods are invariably superior. It may be true (as some chartists will contend) that there are subtleties in price behavior which are quite unlikely to be recognized in a computer program. Certainly, there are nonquantifiable factors—both technical and fundamental—which may be recognized by an alert mind yet might escape a sophisticated numerical calculus.

Nevertheless, the development of computer methods is a challenge to conventional commodity research. It is a reminder that theories about commodity analysis should be expressed as explicitly as possible, and until they are tested in some systematic way, should be regarded simply as interesting hypotheses.

On Testing Commodity Theories

The fact is that, in large part, the trading concepts now current on Wall Street have never been precisely formulated or tested. We suspect that many favorite ideas (including some which are held by the authors) may prove to be scientifically unsupportable. One of the goals of this book is to initiate a more critical attitude towards existing analytic concepts and a more scientific approach to their formulation.

The first step in this approach is to state our hypotheses in a manner which is operationally significant, that is, one which is clear, unambiguous, and subject to either proof or refutation. We might illustrate this with reference to one of the cardinal beliefs on Wall Street, the faith in the persistence of established trends. Generally speaking, the first technical tenet in commodity analysis is the "law of momentum." Stated loosely in the "old fashioned way," this law says that once a trend has commenced, it tends to endure (at least until a significant countervailing force intervenes).

Intuitively, those with trading experience feel there is truth in this "law." But as stated above, its impact is neither clear nor precise. We are left to decide subjectively what constitutes an "established trend"; moreover, we have been given no specific guidelines to help determine whether or not a significant counter-trend has developed.

Is an erratic price increase an uptrend if it involves an advance of 1¢ or 5¢ over a period of one day or one week? Do we say the trend has persisted (thus fulfilling the law of momentum) if, after we identify an uptrend, the market goes up ½¢ and then turns down; or goes down 2¢ and then up 3¢? Unless we state our hypothesis more explicitly, we can neither verify nor refute it.

How can the "law of momentum" be expressed in a way that is operationally significant? We might start by defining "uptrend" or "downtrend" in one specific way, and then by framing testable hypotheses about a trend's predictive significance.

Let us say, for example, that we instruct our computer to fit a linear trend to 20-day intervals of price action starting on every fifth day for a period of 1 year. We now define the trend of the market according to what the computer tells us about the slope of the fitted trendline. We say the trend is up if the 20-day slope is positive, and down if the 20-day slope is negative. Of course, we could also estimate each 20-day trend without a computer, but with significantly more man-hours of work.

Let us state a specific trend hypothesis:

Hypothesis. If the trend (as defined above) is up, then more often than not, the price one week later will be up. Conversely, if the trend is down, then more often than not, the price one week later will be down.

This hypothesis is one which we can very easily verify. As an illustrative test, we asked our computer to perform this trend analysis, looking at 50 20-day segments of cocoa data in an arbitrarily selected year (1964). The result of this analysis: No consistent difference existed in the direction of the market's move in the week following an uptrend as opposed to the week following a downtrend. In other words, prices went up about as often as they went down in this 5-day period after a 20-day uptrend; and the same indifferent performance followed a 20-day downtrend.

Does this mean that trends have no predictive significance? Have we disproved the "law of momentum"?

No, our trial run simply indicates that a 20-day linear trend is of little or no use in predicting the direction of a price move one week later. It does not prove that a 15 or 30-day trend would be equally worthless as the basis for a 1-week price projection. Nor does it disprove the usefulness of a 20-day trend in projecting 1 day ahead or 2 weeks ahead.

There is, however, one critical inference which we might reasonably draw from this single experiment. A trend is not as self-evident as it appears from charts or records of price moves after the moves have occurred. That which seems obvious about trends (and their persistence) becomes much less obvious when we try to say exactly what we mean and to open the door to a test of our accuracy.

As we suggested earlier, there are a great many popular ideas in the commodity world which need to be translated into specific, testable hypotheses. In our judgment, this is a vast, largely untapped area of research, and one to which students of economics and statistics (econometrics) might well address their attention. It is also an area in which commission houses and advisory organizations with a claim to professionality must conduct more disciplined study.

In this chapter, we shall frequently express popular technical trading concepts as hypotheses in need of testing. Our first major assault—friendly but critical—will be on the interpretation of price charts. Before we consider the chartist's aims and assumptions, it seems best to outline briefly the methods of constructing the most basic and widely used types of chart.

Chart Types and Their Construction

The two most widely used types of price charts are the vertical line chart and the point and figure chart. Both are easy to construct and maintain. As a simple "how-to-do-it" guide we shall work out these charts using price data covering trading during February, 1971, in September 1971 New York silver.

Sample (A) of this data is a reproduction of the price information which is published in those leading newspapers which include commodity coverage. For every future of all commodities traded, a daily newspaper commodity table reports the opening price (or bid), the highest and the lowest prices at which trades actually occurred, and the final closing price. There usually follows a column indicating the net change (plus or minus) from the previous trading session. Typically, the newspaper will also recap the number of contracts traded and the open interest (total number of contracts outstanding) for each future.

Sample (B) provides detailed price information which does not appear in the daily press. It presents an intraday chronological record of price changes. This detailed summary of daily price changes is generally available at a modest cost from each respective exchange, or may be obtained by subscription from a private statistical service.

Sample Commodity Price Data (A)
September 1971 New York Silver

Date	Open	High	Low	Last	Volume	Open Interest
Feb. 1, 1971	166.10	168.00	165.50	167.60	1,878	39,185
2	168.00	169.60	166.90	168.50	2,344	38,829
3	169.50	169.80	168.50	169.00	1,599	38,922
4	168.30	168.30	166.70	167.10	1,418	38,914
5	166.50	167.80	166.40	167.60	1,168	38,865
8	167.80	168.40	164.60	166.00	1,811	38,820
9	164.60	166.00	163.30	163.80	2,501	38,726
10	164.10	165.80	163.70	165.50	1,579	38,565
11	165.90	166.80	164.50	165.70	1,931	38,491
16	165.50	166.30	165.10	165.30	1,682	38,316
17	165.90	166.70	165.50	165.60	1,149	38,267
18	166.00	166.50	165.50	166.00	1,260	38,262
19	166.40	167.50	166.40	167.50	1,937	38,067
22	167.20	167.50	166.00	166.20	1,843	38,265
23	166.20	166.50	163.80	164.40	2,810	37,671
24	164.30	165.50	163.80	164.00	3,956	37,734
25	164.00	165.20	163.70	165.10	2,577	36,109
26	166.00	167.00	165.60	166.70	1,717	36,020

SOURCE: *The Wall Street Journal,*

Sample Commodity Price Data (B)
September 1971 New York Silver

Date	Daily 50-Point Price Changes				
Feb. 1, 1971	166.50	165.50	167.50	167.00	167.50
2	169.50	167.00	168.00		
3	169.50	168.50			
4	167.00	167.50	167.00	167.50	167.00
5	166.50	167.50	167.00	167.50	
8	168.00	165.00	166.00		
9	164.50	165.50	163.50	164.00	
10	164.50	164.00	165.50		
11	166.50	164.50	166.00	164.50	166.00
16	165.50	166.00	165.50		
17	166.50	165.50			
18	166.00				
19	167.50	167.00	167.50		
22	166.00	166.50			
23	164.00	164.50			
24	164.00	165.00	164.00		
25	164.50	164.00	165.00		
26	167.00				

SOURCE: Courtesy of Morgan, Rogers and Roberts, Inc., New York.

THE LINE CHART

The most universally popular chart is the vertical line (bar) chart. Figure 3 is based on the price data presented in sample (A) and, as noted above, is readily plotted from the daily statistics published in many newspapers.

A line chart records the high, low, and closing prices for a commodity future, and may also include the total volume of trading and open interest. The chart is set up with the vertical axis representing the price scale and the horizontal axis the time scale. Since this is a daily line chart, the horizontal axis will be divided into units of five squares each, representing the five trading sessions of each week. (The chartist may also choose to maintain supplementary weekly or monthly line charts, as an aid in long-term price analysis and projection.) The vertical axis will be subdivided into tenths for commodities quoted in $\frac{1}{10}$'s or $\frac{1}{100}$'s of a cent, and into eighths for grains, which are quoted in $\frac{1}{8}$'s of a cent.

We shall begin by setting up the price scale along the left vertical axis, placing the current price near the center of the page. After setting up the horizontal (time) scale, we are ready to plot the chart. Referring to the daily price summary (sample A), draw a vertical line down the appropriate date column to connect the day's high and low prices. Then, enter a small horizontal "tick" corresponding to the day's closing price or, if the close is given as either a split price or a bid-and-asked price (e.g., $1.38\frac{1}{4}$ – $\frac{1}{2}$), use the midpoint. The opening price is generally not recorded on the chart. Remember to skip a space in the event of a holiday, so that each Monday's trading will be recorded in the first space of each week's subdivision.

We can see from Figure 3 how the high-low-close data from sample (A) (see p. 97) is translated into line chart "language." At the bottom we record daily volume and open interest figures (total combined volume and open interest for all months, rather than the figures relating to the specific future which we are charting). The product of our efforts is a composite graph of price, volume, and open interest which presents a comprehensive profile of both the price action and technical condition of the commodity under study.

THE POINT AND FIGURE CHART

A point and figure chart records the chronological succession of price changes based on a scale which the chartist selects. Figure 4 is a 50-point chart of September 1971 silver, obtained from price-change data in sample (B) (see p. 97).

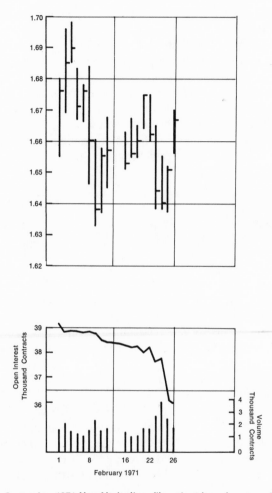

Fig. 3. September 1971 New York silver (line chart based on sample [A]).

The chart is set up with the vertical axis representing the price scale. There is no time scale on a point and figure chart, as trades are recorded chronologically, without regard to date. We can therefore consider the horizontal axis as merely a series of columns in which successive price changes are recorded. A single day's trading activity may be contained within a single column, or several columns, depending on the extent and succession of price changes.

Prices are recorded in the appropriate squares, using X's to mark advancing prices, and O's to mark declining prices. Continue marking in the same vertical column until the price reverses by one square; then advance to the next column and continue charting. Each vertical column of X's represents advancing prices; each vertical column of O's represents declining prices. Each column must have at least two squares filled. In the event of a price gap from one day to the next, you may record the gap by marking a "dot" in the center of each "gapped" square.

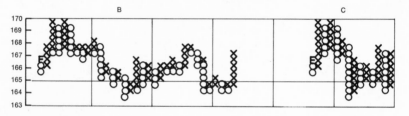

Fig. 4. September 1971 New York silver (50 point chart based on sample [B]).

Although there is no formal recognition of any time parameter, it is customary to mark the first square of each month with the first letter of that month, instead of the standard X or O. In addition, some chartists blacken the final square of each day's entry in order to be able to refer to prices from any particular trading session.

Referring to sample (B) (see p. 97), the first trade was 166.50, and this is noted (record an "F" in the 166.50 square to denote the first trade in the month of February). Prices thereafter declined to 165.50, necessitating the next two squares down to be O'd. From 165.50 the market firmed, with prices moving up to 167.50. Therefore, the chartist would advance one column to the right, and record X's in squares representing 166.00, 166.50, 167.00 and 167.50. From there, he would again have to advance into the next vertical column to record the next price of 167.00. Charting is continued in this manner.

In our point and figure chart example, a 50-point interval was selected as the scale for price fluctuations. We could have constructed a 10-point chart, recording every 10-point fluctuation. This would afford us the most intensive, finely detailed view of price action possible in silver trading, since the minimum price fluctuation is 10 points. Such fine detail might be desirable for a scalper or day trader, but would not be necessary (or even desirable) for someone with a longer-term trading viewpoint. On the other hand, we could have used a 100-point chart in order to study broader, more substantial price movements.

Some traders prefer to maintain several charts; a 10- or 20-point, finely detailed chart for short-term swing observation, and a 50- or 100-point chart for an overall view of longer-term formations. A large-unit chart can generally be constructed from a detailed chart (e.g., one can construct a 50-point chart from a 10-point chart), when required.

POINT AND FIGURE REVERSAL CHART

An important variation of the point and figure chart is the point and figure reversal chart. In a reversal chart, we do not advance into the next chart column until the market reverses direction by a preordained increment. Using Figure 4 (p. 100) as an example, let us assume that we decided to convert this to a 3-block reversal chart. Therefore, we would not advance a column of either X's or O's into the next column unless the market had reversed by at least 3 boxes (150 points). The effect of this charting method is to eliminate the short-term "jiggles" which tend to confuse and distort analysis of market trends. The choice of reversal parameters is virtually limitless, since two distinct variables are involved: box size and reversal increment. It is the technicians' objective to select a reversal combination which will minimize losses due to whipsaw (by eliminating premature breakout signals on random minor fluctuations), and maximize profits (by encouraging the trader to maintain his winning position until the market trend actually reverses).

In their study, Dunn and Hargitt's Financial Services reviews and analyzes 10 years of trading data for 16 commodities.[2] A total of 263 futures contracts were studied, using 28 different reversal combinations with each. The conclusion of this comprehensive study: There exists no universally satisfactory reversal combination; a different reversal combination was found to work best with each of the 16 individual commodities. This study is an excellent example of the advanced commodity research currently being undertaken. We reprint below the summation of the soybean analysis from this study.

On the following pages trade statistics are given for each January contract from 1961 through 1970 and each July contract from 1960 through

2. *Point and Figure Commodity Trading: A Computer Evaluation,* Dunn and Hargitt's Financial Services, Inc., 124 West State St., West Lafayette, Indiana, 1970.

1969. A total of 20 contracts have been traded. Soybeans since the early 1950's have been one of the best performing commodities available to the trader. As the summary table indicates, many chart parameter combinations yield excellent reliability and profits. The 4 x 1 and 1 x 7 charts each are quite acceptable for January Soybeans. The 4 x 1, 1 x 4, 1 x 5 and 1½ x 4 charts are appropriate for July Soybeans. Clearly July Soybeans trade better than January, however, the profits obtainable from January are well worth going after. Of all these good methods the 4 x 1 and 1½ x 4 charts appear best. The 4 x 1 chart yields total profits of 335.254¢ with 30 of 52 trades successful (58%) for an average per trade return of 6.447¢. The 1½ x 4 chart yields a total profit of 208.748¢ with 30 of 59 trades successful (51%) for an average return of 3.538¢ per trade. Either of these charts is good, but the 4 x 1 appears to be somewhat superior to the 1½ x 4 chart. These charts perform so well that it is recommended that both be traded simultaneously; that is, one contract via each chart. Together they yield 544.002¢ profit with 60 of 111 trades successful (54%) and an average return of 4.900¢ per trade.

It is interesting to note the results of the chart recommended by a popular and well-advertised PF chart service. They used a 1 x 3 chart which over this period yielded a net profit of 27.758¢. It pays to do your homework![3]

THE MOVING AVERAGE CHART

A trading system based on moving average charts represents the closest approximation of a "do-it-yourself" automatic trading system available to the public speculator. The major virtue of this trading approach lies in its complete objectivity; human judgment and decision are limited to the selection of the particular system. From that point, trading decisions are based entirely on the mechanical, arithmetic signals provided by the moving average system.

The moving average chart is self-descriptive and, in its basic form, simple to start and maintain. After determining what period moving average to keep, the technician must compute, following each day's close, the average closing price for the period under review. For example, in the case of a 10-day simple moving average, the technician would add the closing prices for the past 10 days and divide the sum by 10. Let us illustrate this with reference to the price data, presented earlier, for September 1971 silver (sample A, p. 97).

It is not necessary to retotal all the closing prices every evening. For simplicity of calculation, the technician merely adds the latest closing price to his total, subtracting therefrom the oldest closing price on the list. Referring to the above figures for the 10-day moving average, on day #11 the technician would add that day's closing price to the sum of the past 10

3. *Ibid,* p. 46. By permission.

Calculation of 10-Day Moving Average
September 1971 Silver

Date	Closing Price	Total Last 10 Closings	10-Day Moving Average
Feb. 1	167.60		
2	168.50		
3	169.00		
4	167.10		
5	167.60		
8	166.00		
9	163.80		
10	165.50		
11	165.70		
16	165.30	166,610	166.60
17	165.60	166,410	166.40
18	166.00	166,160	166.20
19	167.50	166,010	166.00
22	166.20	165,920	165.90
23	164.40	165,600	165.60
24	164.00	165,400	165.40
25	165.10	165,530	165.50
26	166.70	165,650	165.70

days' closings, subtracting day #1. This process is repeated every evening.

Moving averages are most commonly used in conjunction with the line chart for the particular commodity, being interposed as a curve over the line chart (as in Figure 5).

In addition to the basic type of moving average, as presented here, it is possible to devise various types of complex moving average systems. These will be discussed in a subsequent chapter.

What Do Charts Show?

As implied above, there are two kinds of information one may hope to derive from charts:

1. *A record of past behavior:* charts may be seen as a visual index of price change in the commodity under review.
2. *Projection of future behavior:* charts may be viewed as a forecasting device; an analytic tool for projecting the likely direction and extent of future price movements.

There is little reason to question the contribution of charts in their first role, as a convenient record of market action. The difference of opinion arises over the alleged predictive value of this widely used technical device.

Can charts really tell us anything about tomorrow's price? Or is the next market move dependent on new events which are, from the point of view of most traders, purely chance occurrences?

To examine this question in a concrete way, the following specific chart pattern is presented for commodity X. This pattern could represent oranges or cocoa as easily as the price of tea in Formosa.

How do we interpret Figure 6? First, it may seem reasonable to infer that commodity X was in a downtrend from 100 to 50. Reversing, it then moved from 50 to 115; in the final stretch, X appears to have turned down again. In retrospect, it may seem that profits could have been made by going with the trend. For example, one might have sold (short) at point A

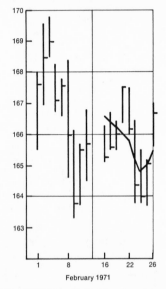

Fig. 5. September 1971 New York silver (moving average chart).

$= 85$, when the formation penetrated the uptrend line T_1. The short position would have been covered and a long position initiated at point $B =$ 75, when X moved over the downtrend line T_2. This would have been sold at point $C = 100$, when X dropped below uptrend line T_3.

This might make it appear that Figure 6 has developed trend patterns with predictive significance. This appearance, we shall soon see, is quite deceptive. For, in this case, the movement of prices shown has no relation at all to the next turn in the "market."

The chart pattern for X, our mystery commodity, is in this case merely a "random walk" based on the toss of a coin. We have drawn our chart by moving up one box each time our coin toss was "heads" and down on each "tails" reading. In this way, after many tosses, we arrived at the pattern shown in Figure 6. If we wish, we can generate still more interesting and elaborate chart patterns by using more elaborate randomizing methods. In all cases, the *ersatz* charts we get will resemble the ones which portray real price movements.

We may conclude from this illustration that an interesting pattern does not necessarily indicate predictive significance.

Even if we clearly understand why a trend has developed, the next price change may still be capriciously unrelated to the existing trend. Assume, for example, that the market for commodity Y depends largely on a government price support which is currently $2.00. Suddenly, rumor has it that the support level may be raised to $4.00. However, the government decision to raise or not to raise the support price is uncertain (let us say it is a 50:50 proposition). Under these circumstances, the market may rise to

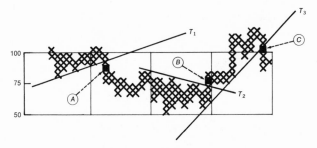

Fig. 6. Commodity X (point and figure chart).

$3.00. The trend, as shown on a chart, may be up unmistakably. But whether the market's next move will be up to $4.00 or back down to $2.00 remains a matter totally dependent upon chance, much like the heads-or-tails game by which we generated the random chart pattern.

In this last example, the market has merely "discounted" available news about a possible increase in the support price. That is, the market has priced itself in such a way as to take into account the estimated likelihood of a support price increase. Let's consider another hypothetical case in which the likelihood of a support price increase from $2.00 to $4.00 is 75:25. In such circumstances, the market might rise to $3.50. This time, the chart uptrend would have predictive significance for we have assumed that the chances are 3-to-1 that the market will rise further to $4.00. It should be noted, however, that the amount gained if the price did rise to $4.00 would be $0.50, or only one-third of the risk inherent in a sudden price drop back to the $2.00 level. If one could "play" a situation like this four times, one might anticipate three profits of $.50 each and one loss of $1.50; we say the expected gain (or loss) is zero.

In other words, the market—operating with customary elusiveness—has priced itself in such a way as to balance the two sets of odds with which each trader is concerned: (1) the likelihood of success, and (2) the profit-loss ratio. When these two sets of odds offset one another, we say the market has "discounted" the available information.

There is one important qualification to this discussion. We have assumed above that the market would react instantly to the anticipated change in the government price support level. However, in many real market situations, the factors influencing change only become known by degrees. In such circumstances, the trader may be able to alter the second set of odds (the profit-loss ratio) by limiting his losses. For example, in the case described above, he might buy at $3.50, instructing his broker to sell out if the price dropped to $3.25 or less. In this case his profit potential might be $.50, with his loss potential something nearer to $.25. It is difficult to state these odds exactly because the market might drop to $3.25, causing our trader to liquidate at a loss, and then rise to $4.00.

In summary, we have seen that impressive-looking chart patterns may be generated by merely random forces; for this reason, trends are sometimes of limited predictive value. Even where a trend does have predictive value, the odds may not be inviting from a trading standpoint. A small profit may not be worth pursuing if the risk is inordinately high. Often, the market seems to price itself in such a way as to establish a risk high enough to offset an apparent profit potential.

To trade successfully, a correct analysis and projection of chart formations and other technical indicators must be combined with sound trading techniques. These subjects will be explored, in depth, in subsequent chapters.

CHAPTER 11 Chart Analysis

The Trend of the Market

In analyzing a futures price chart, the technician should first determine the trend of the market (basic direction in which prices are moving). Trend analysis is one of the most important facets of charting, and success or failure in technical analysis is largely dependent on the timely and accurate recognition of price trends. Stated very simply, a market can move only in three possible directions: up, down, or sideways. Although this statement sounds obvious, the fact remains that it is actually difficult, at times, to determine the trend direction of a given market.

An "uptrend" is characterized by prices fluctuating in a succession of higher highs and higher lows; a "downtrend" by a succession of lower highs and lower lows. A market which moves indecisively in a broad sideways direction is called a "sideways" "trend," or a "congestion area."

Within any major trend, lasting for as little as a few months to as long as several years (world sugar was in a major downtrend for three years, from 1964 through 1966), there frequently occur minor counter-trend moves which may last from just a few days to several weeks. A study of past markets clearly indicates that all bull markets are periodically interrupted by minor (downward) reactions, and that minor rallies are a standard element of bear markets. The extent of the minor counter-trend depends upon the magnitude and steepness of the existing major trend, the price level and the current technical condition of the market. The chartist must be aware of both the major and the minor trends and must, at all times, be able to distinguish between the two. It is primarily the major market trend, providing the basis for the extended price moves, that should concern the serious market student and which will be stressed in this book.

An important characteristic of major price trends is that, once established, they tend to persist for long periods of time; in fact, for much longer than most traders anticipate. Although, based on either sharp analysis or just plain luck, many speculators do establish good market positions near the beginning of a major price move, nearly all take their profits long before the move has run its course.

The Trendline

The trendline can be a very useful tool in making an objective determination of price trends. A trendline is a penciled line on a chart, tangent to the trading bottoms of an uptrend, or to the trading tops of a downtrend. As soon as a chart pattern develops into two successive highs or lows, a lightly penciled trendline can be drawn. This should be considered as a provisional trend. Then, as the chart pattern develops, the technician should be alert for either a confirmation or a rejection of the original trend projection. Figure 7 illustrates this principle.

In Figure 7, we see that prices traded in a sideways trend, between 3.60 and 4.03 for some six months, from May through October. During the end of October 1970, an upside breakout occurred, with prices rising quickly to 4.45. This was followed by a decline to the 4.14 level and then a return rally right back to 4.45. At this point, the chartist, wielding his mighty marker, drew a provisional trendline (T). The first critical testing point had now been reached. Clearly, if prices continued their retreat, back to the original 4.03 breakout level, the trendline T would no longer be intact, and the market's direction would again be open to question. On the other hand, if the market advanced above the recent 4.45 rally high, the chartist would rest firmly on his hypothesis that the market's momentum was up, along a path best defined by the trendline T.

It should be noted that, even if prices had returned to the 4.03 breakout level, the market would not necessarily have struck out. Chartists recognize that after an upside breakout (such as occurred at the 4.03 level), prices sometimes revert to the original breakout level, before a sturdy consolidation occurs for any extensive move.

In the case of our sugar market, the bullish trend was fully justified, with prices ultimately advancing to the 5.00–5.20 level, before encountering unyielding resistance.

Trendlines are not necessarily straight lines. They may curve or they may begin as a straight line and then curve. Chartists who recognize only straight trendlines are apt to miss many valid nonlinear trendlines.

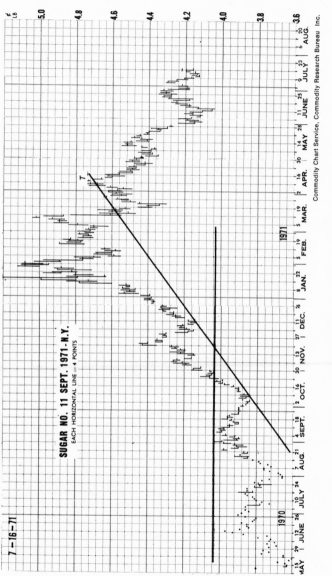

Fig. 7. September 1971 New York sugar No. 11 (trendline).

The Trend Channel

Some price trends are sufficiently orderly to enable the chartist to draw a line parallel, or nearly parallel, to the trendline and tangent to the rally tops in an uptrend or to the reaction bottoms in a downtrend. These two parallel trendlines constitute a "trend channel," with trading activity largely confined within the two lines. Short-term traders may be inclined to trade against the trend channel by liquidating long positions at the upper line with the idea of rebuying on a reaction, or covering short positions at the lower line and then reselling on a rally. Trend channels tend to indicate short-term price objectives, based on the assumption that prices will continue to find support at the lower line (points A, C, and E on Figure 8) and resistance at the upper line (points B, D, and F). In Figure 8 line T is the major downtrend line, line T_1 is the opposite boundary, and channel T $-T_1$ is the downtrend channel.

Like other formations, trendlines are hardly invincible. It therefore may happen that prices will descend below the bottom line of a downtrend channel, or above the top line of an uptrend channel. Clearly, this indicates that the existing trend (whether up or down) is accelerating, and it therefore may be appropriate to redraw the trend channel to conform to the steepened price formation.

Experience suggests that when an existing price trend gains sudden momentum in this manner, the accelerated market action may be the "blow-off" which precedes a trend reversal. We cannot be certain of this. We can only watch our newly drawn trendlines with particularly zealous attention for a possible change in price direction.

Wave Theory of Trend Analysis

Chartists have always eagerly sought to discover any regularities which might help them to anticipate the formation or termination of a price trend. One belief which enjoys fairly popular support is the idea that a trend typically evolves in three succeeding waves.

This three-phase thesis lacks any sophisticated theoretical basis, or so far at least, any objective proof. Yet it enjoys wide enough credibility to lead us to think that, like some folk medicines or prescriptions, it may well have some true value. Its proponents rationalize it rather vaguely. Some suggest that the first upswing in a major bull market represents a stage of youthful discovery; the next one of mature recognition and adaptation; and the last one that mixes belated zeal of the late-comers with the flagging strength of old age.

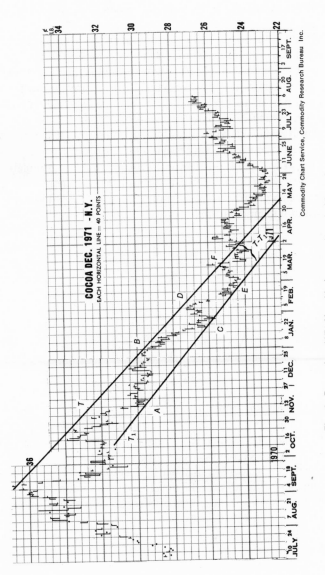

Fig. 8. December 1971 New York cocoa (trend channel).

One evident difficulty is that it is easy to argue intuitively for almost any number of stages; say for example: infancy, youth, middle age, maturity, and old age. Also, from observation of price movements, one realizes that swings are not always so easy to count. Is Figure 9 a two-, four-, or six-phase uptrend?

As implied above, the three-wave theory has survived such criticism and has, in fact, fathered a more elaborate variation. The Elliott Wave Theory was originated by the late R. N. Elliott, who argued that complete price movements tend to occur in five waves: three in the direction of the major trend, and two as part of a corrective reaction in the opposite direction.

In Elliott's view, each of the larger waves (one, two, and three in Figure 10) can themselves be analyzed into submovements of five small waves each. That is, there occur three successive minor upswings up to point 1 in Figure 10, then two small downswings from 1 to 1a, completing the miniature five-wave movement. Insofar as one is able to identify an Elliott Wave count, one presumably has significant insight as to the market's current phase and impending move.

Fig. 9.

In connection with the Wave Theory, many traders believe that during the course of a major price move, there is a frequent tendency for market corrections to retrace 40–50 percent of the preceding advance or decline. The possibility of a correction behaving true to form and halting at about the halfway mark is considered particularly likely if the 50 percent correction level coincides with a recently developed congestion area. That is, merely to reaffirm the existence of support (or resistance) at a certain point, helps to make it a likely target.

An excellent example of the practical application of the Elliott Wave Theory to commodity price forecasting is Figure 11.

Mathematical Trend Analysis

Our description of a trend and the interpretation of its characteristics can be made more precise with the help of some simple mathematical tools.

For example, after a trend has manifested itself as previously suggested (i.e., let us say the pattern already shows three successive lows, or three successive highs), we can "fit" a trendline to the price data using the least squares method (described in any introductory statistics text). Unlike the trendlines drawn earlier by inspection, the mathematically fitted line will not pass through either the highs or the lows of the observed price movement, but will move up or down the middle lane. For example, given a series of closing prices as shown in Figure 12, the mathematically fitted least squares straight lines would approximate T_1 and T_2 respectively.

Notice that in each part of Figure 12, we have drawn two lines paralleling the fitted trendline, and enclosing the price movement. These two lines constitute a trend channel, but in this case, one which can be delineated precisely by mathematical means. For example, the lines L_1 and L_2 can be located at a computed distance from the trendline T in such a way as to enclose 95 percent of all the observed closing prices. In exact statistical language we might say, draw L_1 and L_2 two "standard error" units away from T. This is basically a statistical statement that the two channel lines

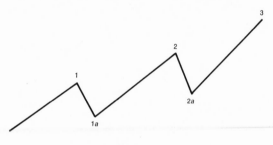

Fig. 10.

have been mathematically placed in such a way as to enclose 95 percent of the price activity; and, if we wished, we could vary this percentage level.

The first conclusion we can reach here is simply that a trendline and parallel channel lines can be drawn using certain mathematical rules, thus giving us a method that can be repeated objectively in the same way at any time. In fact, a computer can be programmed to carry out this operation every day, or every week, or whenever we deem it appropriate. (We will discuss computer methods in a later chapter.)

Our second observation has to do with measuring the kind of price formation which has evolved. This formation is completely described by two characteristics of the mathematically fitted trendline and its parallel channel lines: (1) the slope of the line (s); and (2) the scatter around the trendline, as measured by the vertical distance (d) of L_1 (and equally of L_2) from T.

In general, a trend is more likely to endure if its slope is high, and its

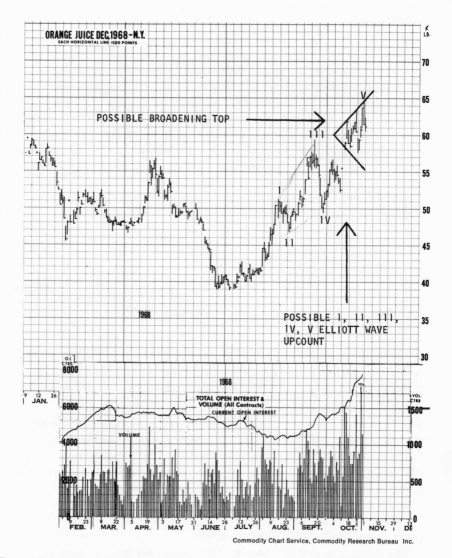

ORANGE JUICE DEC.1968-N.Y.
EACH HORIZONTAL LINE =100 POINTS

POSSIBLE BROADENING TOP

POSSIBLE I, II, III,
IV, V ELLIOTT WAVE
UPCOUNT

TOTAL OPEN INTEREST &
VOLUME (All Contracts)
CURRENT OPEN INTEREST

VOLUME

Commodity Chart Service, Commodity Research Bureau Inc.

Fig. 11. December frozen orange juice. A major top may be forming. At this writing, it could take the shape either of a broadening or a diamond top. The third wave into new season's highs only to fall sharply is bearish action on Elliott analysis. We would liquidate all longs and stand aside for now. (Courtesy Commodity Research Bureau, Inc.)

scatter is low. In other words, when a trend is lean and steep, as pictured in (B) of Figure 12, it has more momentum or thrust than when it is broad and shallow, as shown in (A). As a corollary, it is reasoned that a rather loose A-type trend is easier to reverse than a tight trend of type B. From this, we can arrive at two hypotheses about trend reversals as indicated by our own mathematical calculation or by computer.

Trend-Reversal Hypothesis 1. When a breakout occurs from a mathematically defined trend channel, this breakout is more likely to augur a complete turnabout and a new trend when s is low and d is high. (The breakout from a loosely formed trend lends itself more easily to the dominance of new forces, since the old ones are weak.)

Trend-Reversal Hypothesis 2. When a breakout occurs from a mathematically defined trend channel, this breakout is likely to augur a decelera-

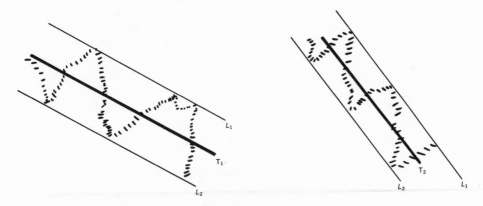

Fig. 12. Mathematically fitted trendlines. A. Low slope (s), high scatter (d). B. High slope (s), low scatter (d).

tion of the existing trend or a sideways movement (rather than a complete trend reversal) if s is high and d is low. (The breakout from a tight and steep trend may simply indicate a loss of momentum, without necessarily implying that the powerful existing forces have been reversed.)

Fundamental Factors as an Aid in Trend Analysis

In attempting to gauge the likely timing and duration of commodity price trends, we shall no doubt wish to investigate fundamental factors, since these often suggest bounds to any period of unalleviated bullishness or bearishness.

It is clear, for example, that if one is dealing with an annual agricultural crop, the biggest economic motive force to price change may be year-to-year variations in production. For this reason, as a new season approaches, any established trend becomes more suspect; for another crop year often brings at least the possibility of a reversal in supply conditions.

On the other hand, industrial commodities (for example, a leading metal like silver) are frequently more subject to longer-term cyclical variations in demand than to annual output changes. Thus, price trends may be of longer duration. These influences must be considered in subtle detail for each commodity, rather than generalized by commodity group. For example, industrial copper may have severe short-term swings reflecting strikes or weather impediments in mine areas, while agricultural crops like cocoa may have several years of declining price due to a partly cyclical supply expansion.

The pure technician may reason that one can learn a great deal about the past habits of a particular commodity, including any consistent tendency towards specific trading cycles, simply by studying the past record of price action. Certainly, this is one useful way to hunt for timing regularities; but in the opinion of the authors, it should be complemented by a detailed current analysis of supply/demand characteristics of the commodity under review.

Although no broad generalization can be made concerning the extent of commodity price trends, some consistency has been noted in the performance of individual groups of commodities. For the sake of this discussion, let us divide commodities into three basic groups: *industrial* (e.g., copper, lumber, and silver); *agricultural* (e.g., frozen pork bellies, soybeans, and wheat); and *perishable* (e.g., eggs and potatoes). The unavoidable overlapping of some commodities (e.g., potatoes, which can be both agricultural and perishable) need not invalidate this point. Industrial commodities tend to produce the longest-term trend cycles, due to their relative stability of supply and demand. They are more subject to the longer-term business and economic cycles than to the shorter-term vicissitudes of rain, drought, and spoilage. Next, with respect to the length of trend cycles, are the agricultural commodities. As pointed out in Chapter 6, prices of agricultural commodities tend to make seasonal lows around harvest time which, of course, occurs around the same time each year. Although government marketing activities (e.g., the government's role as both a buyer and seller of cotton) may distort this historical pattern, it still is generally valid. And finally, perishable commodities tend to fluctuate in the shortest-term cycles. This is because perishables have all the uncertainties of production and consumption common to all other commodities; additionally, ownership of perishable commodities involves risk factors due to the hazards of spoilage, deterioration, and reduction in grade.

Hypotheses on Trend Validity

Assume that a trend has begun. The problem confronting the technician is: What is the likelihood that this trend will endure? In what we have referred to earlier as the "folklore of Wall Street," we can perhaps identify several hypotheses regarding trend validity. We state these as follows:

Hypothesis.1. Each time a market finds unyielding support at an uptrend line, or resistance along a downtrend line, the trend is gaining strength. That is partly because additional traders are coming to recognize the power of the trend, and to identify its line of operation. At the same time, counter-trend positions are likely to be closed out or even reversed at these points, adding further momentum to the existing trend. The longer a trend persists, the greater the chance it will continue until some new force intervenes to precipitate a reversal. (Here again, the fact that a trend attracts its own following is basic.)

Hypothesis 2. A trend has greater validity if it shows itself in actuals as well as in futures, and in all delivery months rather than in a few.

Hypothesis 3. A trend is more dependable when prices have moved within a relatively narrow, tight channel, rather than along a broad, and more loosely defined path.

Hypothesis 4. A trend is more dependable when its slope is steep, rather than shallow; except that (as noted earlier), if a well-established trend accelerates suddenly, this may represent a last wave of liquidation or covering, possibly indicative of an impending reversal.

Like other generalizations about charting and price interpretation, these hypotheses about trend validity are themselves in need of objective validation through precise formulation and testing. We simply wish to point out here that these rather intuitive concepts about trends are widely held and, in our judgment, probably contain significant and correct insights about market action.

The Trend Reversal

Market trends do not continue indefinitely (they only seem to do so). The chartist is always concerned with his ability to recognize the commencement of either a congestion area or a trend reversal. So long as the trendline remains valid and the market continues to trade in a succession of higher tops and bottoms (in an uptrend), or lower tops and bottoms (in a downtrend), the prevailing trend is assumed to be intact. Prices may penetrate the trendline during the session and then close back within it, or they may even penetrate the line for a day or two. Although these minor penetrations do not necessarily presage reversal in trend, they certainly should raise the possibility of such a turn.

The first indication of trend deterioration occurs when prices turn and close through the trendline, without resuming their original course on the following session. Approach this analysis by examining the recent trading tops and bottoms. The downside penetration of an uptrend line would carry a bearish implication if the most recent rally high had failed to surpass the previous high, and if the current reaction had carried below the former trading low. Similarly, an upside penetration would be bullishly construed if the last reaction found support at or near the previous bottom and if the current rally had closed above the recent trading high. The other delivery months (within the same crop year, where applicable) should exhibit the same trend-breaking action. And finally, the presence of unusually high trading volume accompanied by a significant increase in the total open position tends to add credence to an impending trend reversal.

Occasionally, a particularly steep trendline will be encountered, the penetration of which is generally less significant than would be the penetration of a moderately sloped line. The correction following a very steep move may merely alter the chart pattern to a more moderate trend in the same direction. In trying to analyze whether this situation is an impending reversal or merely a broadening of an existing trend, examine the pattern of recent trading tops and bottoms, as discussed above. As a general rule, prices have a tendency to correct about 50 percent following an extended price move (a correction of less than 50 percent is evidence of a powerful trend, while a greater than 50-percent correction is a possible forerunner of a reversal). Furthermore, if a 50-percent correction from a steep move corresponds to a strong support or resistance area (to be discussed later in this chapter), there is a very good likelihood that the correction will be halted at that level.

We can now review and summarize the principal indicators which might lead us to believe that an existing major price trend is reversing. Ideally, we should see all of these elements in the reversal of an uptrend. See Figure 13.

1. The uptrend itself is broad and not very steep.
2. The final stage of the upmove is accompanied by a reduction in open interest, indicating that the market strength may be attributable to short covering.
3. This high fails to top the preceding one.
4. The major uptrend line is broken.
5. The decline penetrates recent support levels.

To this roster of trend-reversal indicators, we wish to add two others, one already familiar to the reader, and the other perhaps unfamiliar. The first refers to confirmatory open interest and volume signals. The major trend reversal shown in Figure 13 is considered to be of particular significance if, at the time it occurs, open interest is running very high, and if activity expands on the decline. The market, as we have intimated earlier in this chapter, is especially vulnerable when there has been a substantial buildup in the speculative long position.

Typically, a steep increase in the open position in the course of a major uptrend may represent a speculative excess, corresponding to an increasing

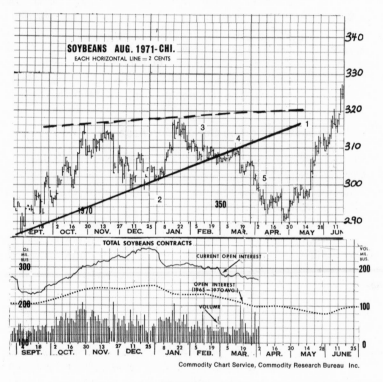

Commodity Chart Service, Commodity Research Bureau Inc.

Figure 13.

euphoria which begins to see the uptrend as invincible. As the "contrary opinionist" points out, markets inevitably appear most bullish at their peaks. This brings us to the second, perhaps less familiar, indicator of a potentially valid trend reversal. That is, evidence that the prevailing body of opinion is overwhelmingly bullish, at a time when the market is beginning to show signs of "tiring," with a major top formation in the making. To judge the consensus of opinion, it may be necessary to subscribe to one of the commodity services which feature a composite analysis, though very often one can sense the same thing from a broad reading of current reports about the commodity under review.

Our review and summary of trend reversal indicators has dealt with a market turnabout starting from an uptrend. It may be constructive to look at an actual case of an upside breakout, eminently illustrated by the action of world sugar in late 1968.

Figure 14 is from a technical report published at the time the breakout occurred.

In this instance, the chart reading proved to be entirely correct, providing an early warning of an impending price rise which, in fact, carried up to over 3.00¢ in the ensuing months. We must caution, however, that similar chart indicators sometimes prove misleading. For example, note the dotted downtrend line (added by the authors). Observe that an upside breakout occurred in May but led nowhere. Anyone who bought on the May signal would probably have been forced to liquidate at a loss sometime later.

Support and Resistance: the Congestion Area

Apart from price trends and trendlines, which clearly lay first claim to the chartist's attention, perhaps the most important technical factors with which the analyst must deal are support and resistance levels. A thorough understanding of these factors, coupled with the ability to recognize and integrate them into an overall trading scheme, will contribute materially to trading success.

Support and resistance levels, basically, help the trader to determine:

1. The likelihood that a price trend will continue or falter.
2. The possible price objective of a given move.
3. Where and when to initiate purchases and sales.

To understand support and resistance, one should first pause to reflect on the way in which price movements develop. The pace of price fluctuation is sometimes sluggish and sometimes rapid. The market tends to alternate between periods of relative equilibrium (when supply-demand forces are comparatively balanced and prices are static) and periods of disequilibrium (when prices are in flux, seeking a new level which will restore balance to the supply-demand structure).

If this alternation were exact and the market able to discount supply-demand changes perfectly, we'd see a kind of "block pattern" on our chart. That is, prices would be absolutely flat for a time, then a perfectly vertical upmove or downmove would occur to a new flatland. As indicated earlier in this chapter, this kind of perfect discounting would mean chart patterns were completely fulfilled at any instant and quite useless in any forecasting

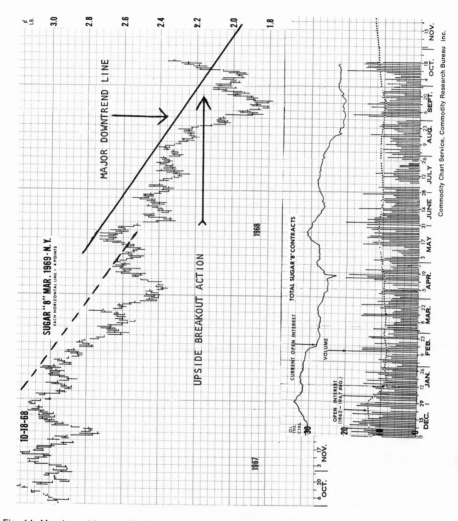

Fig. 14. March world sugar No. 8. Our new long position at 2.15 was purchased this week as the intermediate downtrend line was penetrated and the moving averages developed from a neutral to positive uptrend. We have raised our protective open stops to 2.11 via special wires to offices this week. (Source: Reynolds & Company, "Commodity Scope," Oct. 18, 1968.)

sense. It is the imperfection of the adjustment process (and of supply-demand information and analysis) which allows us to believe that the chart may have some predictive significance, that it may be giving us some indication that prices are moving from one comparative equilibrium condition to a new one yet to be determined.

Let us say we are experiencing a market phase of comparative stability and equilibrium. Prices are moving horizontally, but not in a straight line. Instead, values are fluctuating in a sideways trading zone ("congestion area"). The reason for the price band or zone rather than a straight-line is twofold: (1) traders are unable to interpret the market exactly and (2) their buying and selling ideas differ, even if many agree generally that the price is right.

Given this rather broad underlying agreement that supply-demand forces are in some sort of rough balance, any attempt at price advance or decline tends to be regarded as unwarranted and untenable. Under these circumstances, rally attempts would likely encounter long liquidation and new short selling. This upper level of the congestion area, therefore, would become a "resistance level"; e.g., that price level at which sufficient selling occurs (or can be expected to occur) to contain price advances. On the other hand, price declines would tend to be supported by new buying and short covering. This would establish the lower boundary of the trading range as a "support level"; e.g., that price level at which sufficient buying occurs (or can be expected to occur) to halt price declines. Penciled lines drawn tangent to the top and bottom of the congestion area need not be parallel. These lines may converge or diverge, although in most cases at least one of the two lines will be horizontal.

Sooner or later, a congestion area is fated to have one of its boundaries sundered. That is, new buying or selling forces develop, capable of propelling prices through an existing support or resistance level. An interesting turnabout occurs when prices move out of a congestion area. The market role of support and resistance levels reverses as the trend of the market changes. A support area in an uptrend reverses to become a resistance area in the succeeding downtrend. Conversely, a resistance area in a downtrend will become a support area in the succeeding uptrend. Let us illustrate these concepts.

For the entire month of October, 1966, the January 1967 egg shell future traded within a narrow congestion area between 32.00 and approximately 33.00. During that four-week period, reactions towards 32.00 encountered good buying support and rallies to the 33.00 level were met with heavy resistance. Therefore, 32.00 represented the support level, and 33.00 the resistance level. During the first week of November, demand (buying pressure) finally overcame supply (selling pressure), and prices broke out on the upside, rallying to just above 36.00 before finding any resistance. At that point, the former resistance level at 33.00 became the new support level, which would tend to support any subsequent decline. Why should this be so?

Let us examine the positions of the four classes of traders who had an interest in this market:

1. Those *longs* who had bought in the 32.00 to 33.00 area and who did not sell at the 36.00 rally high (few traders ever sell at the top of a move) should have little incentive to sell as prices react towards 34.00. They still have profits and the major trend is moving in their direction. As a matter of fact, some of these longs would probably be inclined to buy more on the ensuing pullback (measuring 50 percent of the original upmove) to 34.00, providing additional buying support at that level. Those few longs who were fortunate enough to sell near the high would probably consider rebuying as prices react back towards their original purchase price.

2. The *shorts,* on the other hand, who had expected the market to decline from the 32.00 to 33.00 congestion area, realize that they are wrong, and that they are short in a bullish market. An astute short, who had not "stopped out" on the breakout above 33.00, would likely try to minimize his losses by covering on the first substantial price reaction. Experienced traders appreciate that the first loss is usually the cheapest. Therefore, short covering should lend support to the market around the 33.00 to 34.00 level.

3. The *bulls who had missed buying* during the 32.00 to 33.00 congestion area now find another buying opportunity in the current reaction. And why not buy this time? The market is still in an uptrend, and sound trading practice advises buying technical reactions in a major uptrend. Therefore, their bids in the 33.00 to 34.00 area would add market support.

4. Finally, we have the *bears who missed selling* previously. These traders should consider themselves fortunate not to have shorted the market, considering the strong upwards breakout. A sharp trader is not likely to short a market during a technical reaction following a major upside breakout.

Had the market (in Figure 15), instead broken downside from the 32.00 to 33.00 congestion area, the implication would have been distinctly bearish. Furthermore, the 32.00 area, which served as a support level during the entire month of October, would have become a resistance level following the downside breakout, and would have tended to repel any upwards rally attempts. The detailed analysis here would be the reverse of that presented above dealing with the upside breakout.

Validity of Support and Resistance Levels

One basic principle underlies this tendency for a market to "respect" a previous congestion level by pausing, if not halting, in its neighborhood: Even without charts, traders are inclined to take action where they took action before. If a great many traders went long and short at a particular price level, many of them are apt to consider taking action again when the market returns from its roller coaster ride to that same level. Others who do not yet have positions will look back at that price as a focus of earlier activity, and a possible benchmark or decision point for fresh action.

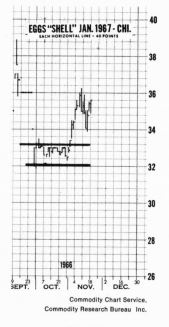

Commodity Chart Service,
Commodity Research Bureau Inc.

Fig. 15.

It follows that a congestion area will exert a more pronounced influence as a support or resistance level if it is comparatively recent (and thus, fresh in traders' recollections); also, if it was the occasion for significant and prolonged trading activity (and thus, is both more memorable and more specifically related to the actual prices at which today's longs and shorts initiated their positions). Recent congestion areas tend to stand up better than older ones, moreover, because a time lapse following the formation of a congestion area permits the introduction of new factors which could exert a more profound influence on the market.

In determining the validity of a particular price zone as either a support or a resistance level, certain other factors should be considered. First, the price activity prior to the formation of the particular congestion area should be scrutinized. At what level did the congestion area occur, and did this price level represent the attainment of the projected price objective? A congestion area occurring at a price level which corresponds to the attainment of a projected price objective would be more apt to represent the end of the move and to presage a reversal formation, than would a congestion area which had attained only part of the projected price objective.

A technical correction following an extended price move tends to retrace 40–50 percent of the previous move. For example, assume a bullish grain market with a major price objective of some 20–25 cents. Let us further assume that the breakout from the original congestion area had carried upwards about 10 cents, followed by a 4-to-5 cent reaction. At that point, assume the market had gone into a sideways price trend, with prices locked within a 2-cent range for a number of weeks. This pattern would probably carry a bullish implication; we would anticipate an eventual upside breakout from the congestion area, with prices likely to surpass the previous rally high. This reasoning is based on the expectation that the major trend (upwards) will likely continue, and that the current upmove had covered less than half of the technically projected price objective. If prices ultimately do break out of the congestion area on the upside, the former overhead resistance level will change into a newly established support level, as discussed earlier in this chapter.

A final clue to the validity of a given support or resistance level would be revealed by an examination of the other delivery months (within the same crop year, when applicable) of the respective commodity. Prices breaking out in just one delivery month may be an advance indication of a forthcoming general breakout. However, this move should be skeptically appraised if it were not soon confirmed by other futures months.

WHY PRICES BREAK OUT OF A CONGESTION AREA

At some point during the period of price congestion (equilibrium), a significant price-influencing development will occur, or will be expected to occur e.g., crop damage, a revised production or consumption estimate, or military action or legislation affecting the particular commodity. This news, if not already anticipated and, therefore, discounted in the prevailing price level, may significantly upset the existing technical supply-demand equilibrium. In the case of a bullish development, buying pressure will overpower selling pressure at the former resistance level (top of the congestion area), and prices will move upwards. Based on similar reasoning, a bearish development would precipitate a downward breakout move.

WHY BREAKOUT MOVES "RUN OUT OF STEAM"

Although the bull move described above will be subjected to periodic minor technical reactions, the basic technical elements of the market situation will tend to determine the extent of the complete major move. On a longer-term basis, this uptrend will continue until prices have advanced to a significantly overbought condition (the technical market condition is too weak to maintain prices at that level). At that point, substantial long liquidation and new selling will come into the market, halting the upward price trend and turning prices sideways or even downward. This new price disequilibrium may be followed by another congestion area, which will again represent the adjustment of the new price level to the existing conditions of technical demand-supply (buying pressure and selling pressure). Ultimately, new forces will develop which will again tip the price equilibrium, creating another imbalance between buying and selling pressure. This will mark the commencement of another major, or at least intermediate, price move.

Reversal and Continuation (Anticipating the Direction of a Breakout from a Congestion Area)

As noted earlier, a congestion area is a formation of lateral price movement which represents the market's adjustment to a close balance between supply and demand at the prevailing price level. Eventually, either supply (selling pressure) or demand (buying pressure) will become dominant, and prices will break out from the confined limits of the congestion area. This breakout will represent either a reversal or a continuation of the precongestion area price trend. How can the probable direction of this breakout be anticipated?

In analyzing such a market situation, begin by studying the major market trend and the major trendline. Is the major trend still intact, or has it been penetrated by the sideways action of the congestion area? If still intact, preliminary evidence would suggest a continuation of the existing trend, primarily because major price trends contain latent momentum and tend to continue in their basic direction. This is particularly true in the case of a major downward trend which, experience suggests, generally takes longer to reverse than does an uptrend.

Secondly, the price level of the congestion area sometimes provides a clue concerning the probable direction of the next significant breakout. If the congestion area occurs at a level which represents the approximate attainment of the major price objective for the prevailing move, the market would be more likely to reverse than if an analysis of the major price objective indicates that, for example, only half of the projected move had been attained.

When the preponderance of trading (market activity) occurs near the bottom of a congestion area, it indicates that offerings are being well absorbed, and that the market is likely to ultimately break out on the upside. Conversely, a market in which the preponderance of trading activity occurs near the upper level of the congestion area is more likely to break out downside. The comparative degree of trading activity within a congestion area is generally easier to analyze on a point and figure chart than on a line chart.

In addition to the foregoing techniques of congestion area analysis, there exists a number of recurring chart formations which serve as useful supplementary tools in technical market analysis.

Chart Geometrics: Analysis of Chart Patterns

In a sky full of celestial bodies, the stargazer sees outlines of big and little dippers, bulls and bears, and gods and goddesses. In a portfolio of commodity charts, the avid technical analyst sees pennants and flags, heads and shoulders, and a host of other part-visionary designs. Whether or not they point anywhere is the question.

Rather than study each individual chart pattern as an independent analytic tool, we prefer to place chart-pattern analysis in its proper perspective—within the broader concept of market trend analysis. This can be achieved through the development of a thorough understanding of the primary components of chart patterns: trends and trendlines, support and resistance, and reversal and continuation. There can appear so many variations of each standard chart formation that the particular pattern may be unrecognizable until it is too late to initiate appropriate market action. It is obviously more important to be able to identify the broad picture and to take a proper position during the beginning of a major market formation than it is to concentrate on recognizing the formation (as being, say, a triple top rather than a head-and-shoulders top), perhaps missing a good market position in the process.

TOP AND BOTTOM FORMATIONS

A great deal has been written about "multiple tops and bottoms." The chartist should become familiar with these formations because they are frequently encountered and are, moreover, found in many other chart formations. It is perhaps useful to think of a multiple top as the upper bound of a congestion area, in which resistance to price advance proves insuperable; and, conversely, to view a multiple bottom as the lower bound of a congestion area in which support on price declines turns out to be unyielding. The problem, of course, is to identify a top or bottom before the ensuing price move is completely obvious and well on its way.

In analyzing a multiple top or bottom formation, the chartist attempts to forecast whether prices will break out of, or be contained within, the formation; and if the technical evidence suggests a breakout—in which direction. This analysis should be initiated with a study of *the separate components of the multiple formation: the trend, the trendline,* and *the congestion area,* as discussed earlier.

In addition, certain technical indicators can be useful in analyzing this formation. First, prices tend to move in the direction of increasing volume (total volume of all delivery months). Therefore, a bullish breakout can be anticipated if trading volume increases on rallies and contracts on reactions. On the other hand, a situation in which trading volume increases on price reactions and contracts on rallies may wisely be construed as bearish. (The relationship between price movements and trading volume will be further discussed in this chapter.)

Another useful technical indicator in forecasting impending breakouts from multiple tops and bottoms is the price level of the multiple formation. Have prices attained their major price objective following their breakout from the previous major top or bottom formation? If not, they are more likely to complete the move than if the major price objective had been attained.

The upside penetration of a multiple top is a bullish technical development; while failure to break through, followed by a price decline below either a support area or an uptrend line, would have a bearish implication. Similarly, the penetration of a multiple bottom would be bearish, while failure to break through followed by an advance above either a resistance level or a downside trendline would be bullishly construed.

Sometimes, with prices locked within a trading range, with the top of the range representing a multiple top (resistance level) and the bottom of the range representing a multiple bottom (support level), the chartist is unable to draw any inference concerning the direction of the ultimate breakout. In such a situation, a sidelines attitude would be indicated, pending an actual breakout and trend commencement. Following the breakout, a market position can be taken with a "stop order" as the trend develops, or on the first technical correction following the breakout.

Of the top and bottom formations generally associated with major trend reversals, it is perhaps pardonable to say that one stands "head and shoulders" above the rest in terms of reliability. That is, of course, the head and shoulders formation. When it occurs, it tends to display a surprising degree of uniformity. Figure 16 illustrates this formation, and very likely suggests

Commodity Chart Service, Commodity Research Bureau Inc.

Fig. 16.

at once the foundation for its corporeal name. The central, high peak represents the "head," while the two adjacent, lower peaks are the "shoulders." Less evidently, the support line which marks the lower bound of this unique type of congestion area is termed the "neckline." It may be a horizontal line, or it may slope either up or down. It is also possible in this formation for one shoulder to be higher or lower than the other.

Let us examine the development of a head and shoulders top formation as it occurred in the March 1967 soybean oil future at Chicago. Between mid-June and mid-July, the market displayed a definite bullish trend, advancing from 10.50 to approximately 12.30. At the 12.30 level, the market encountered substantial offerings, and prices reacted some 75 points, back to 11.55. This reaction corresponded to slightly less than 50 percent of the basic upwards move from the 10.50 area. Following the reaction to 11.55, prices firmed again and advanced to 12.90, establishing a new life-of-contract high, at which point the market again turned down. This decline found good support around 11.70, and prices rallied easily.

It should be noted that, until this point, the market action had conformed to the classical uptrend action with successively higher tops and bottoms accompanied by prices consistently above the bullish uptrend line T_1.

The rally from 11.70 ran out of steam around 12.40, the same level where the original advance had failed seven weeks earlier. This time, however, the decline from 12.40 failed to find any support around 11.60, as had the previous decline from that area, and prices continued their retreat all the way down to 10.70 before any substantial support was encountered.

In analyzing this market, the critical turning point occurred during the week of September 9th, when prices broke below both the 11.60 support level and the major uptrend line. Furthermore, this price decline violated the series of successive highs and lows established up until that time.

With the major top formation completed, the market reacted all the way down to the 10.50 level, although several minor technical rallies were experienced. The first of these occurred from the 11.30 level following the initial breakdown, with prices rallying back up to 11.60. Here, once again, we observe the changing roles of support and resistance levels. Previously, the 11.60 level was referred to as a support level but, with prices having penetrated downwards, the area became a significant resistance level. Following this technical rally to 11.60, prices again broke, continuing their major bearish trend.

The chartist refers to the two intermediate rallies to the 12.40 level as the "shoulders" of the move, while he identifies the major 12.90 high as the "head." The 11.60 support area is known as the "neckline." The bearish implication of this formation was confirmed with the downside penetration of the neckline (at the 11.60 level). An oft-recurring characteristic of head and shoulder reversal formations is that, following the breakthrough of the neckline, prices tend to return to that breakout point before continuing the reversal move. In the March soybean oil market under review, prices broke through the neckline at the 11.60 level, declined to 11.30, and then rallied back up to 11.60 (return to the neckline), before completing the major downside move. As a trading tactic, the return to the neckline in a head and shoulder reversal formation offers the technician an opportunity to enter the market (i.e., in Figure 16, to sell the market at the 11.60 rally back into the neckline). Stop-loss protection can be placed just beyond the right shoulder.

The neckline in this type of formation need not be horizontal and, as a matter of fact, it frequently is not. When downward-tipped, the neckline tends to carry a more bearish implication than it does when it slopes upwards. The two shoulders need not be of identical size, although they should each be smaller than the head. As a variation, the head and shoulders formation sometimes develops with a series of multiple shoulders on either side of the head. This multiple head and shoulders formation is less common than the simple formation, but can nevertheless be treated similarly.

The head and shoulders bottom is the reverse of the formation described above and consists of an extended decline (the left shoulder) followed by a technical recovery (to the neckline), which is then followed by a decline into new low ground (the head). The rally from the low should top out at approximately the same level as the previous rally (the neckline) and be followed by another decline. This decline should find support before breaking the last trading low, and from that point should rally back towards and through the neckline. The uptrend may falter temporarily, just after penetrating the neckline, but should gain momentum from that point and continue upwards.

Trading volume can assist in analyzing the development of head and shoulders reversal formations. The volume on the right shoulder should be light, with a marked increase in volume evident as prices ultimately break through the neckline.

The head and shoulders formation provides the chartist with a fairly accurate indication of the probable span of a forthcoming move. In a great many cases, the minimum move following a major head and shoulders reversal formation will approximate the distance from the tip of the head to the neckline. The slope of the neckline may influence the extent of the price move. A head and shoulders top formation with a downward-slope neckline will likely carry prices lower than would the same top formation with the neckline slanted upwards; this applies inversely for the head and shoulders bottom formation. Adapting this price projection analysis to Figure 16 (p. 129), we find the distance from the top of the head to the neckline is 130 points, which (subtracted from the price level of the neckline 11.60), indicates a downside price objective of approximately 10.30. The market, in fact, declined to the 10.45 level, which is pretty close, considering that the neckline had a slight upwards slant.

In stating our generalizations about head and shoulders formations, we have (as is usual in this chapter) indicated that they represent incompletely validated ideas popular among traders. Although some analysts believe that chart patterns are devoid of predictive significance, we do not share this viewpoint. However, we certainly wish to emphasize again the need for objective, systematic testing of even those chart assumptions which are considered most dependable.

There are infinite variations of chart formations which various technical writers have identified. However, we are not enamored of the idea of classifying and picturing specific formations in such great variety. The analyst or trader, in our judgment, should not be too concerned with specific identification of a prescribed pattern. His primary effort should be devoted to understanding the significance of varying technical activity, with alert response to trends and trend reversals, penetration of support and resistance, considerations of open interest and volume and, finally, the study of crowd behavior (contrary reasoning). Nevertheless, a few of the more popular chart formations are catalogued below.

OTHER TOP AND BOTTOM FORMATIONS

Aside from the head and shoulders formation, the leading top (and bottom) formations are shown in Figure 17.

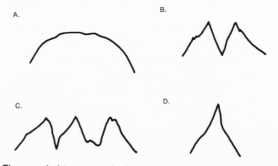

Fig. 17. A. The rounded top, most docile, pleasing, and completely self-described.
B. The double top, also fairly self-evident.
C. The triple top, or more nondescript head and shoulders.
D. The V-top, infrequent and provocatively difficult.

Any of the aforementioned formations may assume more complex configurations. The rounded pattern may be partly fragmented into a series of small arches or saucers and, in its more recondite form, threaten to break down into a multitop formation. Either hump in a double top may verge on division into two narrower peaks. In the same way, the shoulders of a head and shoulders formation may cleave in two.

It may be supposed that the longer a top formation has been building (particularly if the top formation has been accompanied by a significant open interest expansion), the more distinct it will be. Also, the more "work" (price activity) that is concentrated near its upper bound, the more dependable is the prognosis that a downside breakout will have follow-through.

MID-FORMATION PATTERNS

Still refusing to encourage too great a weight for individual price etchings or contours, we nevertheless wish to briefly describe certain other geometric formations commonly discerned by chartists, and to suggest what possible use their recognition might entail. We single out for attention here: rectangles, triangles, flags, and pennants. These formations should be approached deductively, by applying basic chart concepts and analytical techniques (e.g., trendlines, support and resistance, and reversal and continuation).

Rectangle. A rectangle is a congestion area consisting of a combination of multiple tops (resistance level) and multiple bottoms (support level) with prices fluctuating within the confines of the rectangle formation. The chartist is concerned with determining in which direction prices are likely to break and how far the move is likely to carry. Concerning this, the reader should refer to the previous discussion regarding breakout moves from congestion areas. The minimum anticipated price objective from a breakout of a rectangle equals the height of the rectangle. Specific market factors, peculiar to each situation, tend to add to or detract from the total move. The longer the rectangle took to develop and the greater the total number of new positions which were initiated within the congestion area, the more significant will be the ultimate breakout. Neither the top nor the bottom of a rectangle need be perfectly horizontal, although, if either one develops at much of an angle, the formation might more closely resemble a triangle or a pennant (see Fig 18).

Triangles. Triangles are frequently encountered chart formations which tend to occur while a trend is underway. They often mark the mid-point of a move, and *are more likely to represent a continuation pattern than a reversal pattern.* Triangles occur in three variations: symmetrical, ascending, and descending. A symmetrical triangle is a congestion area bounded on top by a downtrend line and on bottom by an uptrend line. Trading activity consists of a number of descending tops and ascending bottoms, with values converging towards the apex of the triangle. Prices are liable to break out of a symmetrical triangle in either direction (see Figure 19)

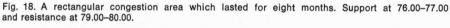

Commodity Chart Service, Commodity Research Bureau Inc.

Fig. 18. A rectangular congestion area which lasted for eight months. Support at 76.00–77.00 and resistance at 79.00–80.00.

Commodity Chart Service, Commodity Research Bureau Inc.

Fig. 19. A symmetrical triangle. This congestion type formation is usually a continuation pattern, with prices likely to break out in the direction of the basic trend.

although, as noted above, this triangle is more likely to represent a continuation rather than a reversal formation—therefore, the bias would favor a breakout in the same direction as the pretriangle trend. Consequently the prudent trader could remain on the sidelines pending an actual confirmation of the breakout trend. A price breakout from a triangle pattern (and this includes any of the three types of triangles) will be more reliable if the breakout occurs before prices get to the apex of the triangle. A breakout from the apex is frequently a false alarm, and must be watched very carefully.

An ascending triangle is a congestion area bounded by a multiple top (resistance area) and an uptrend line (support area). This succession of level tops and ascending bottoms exhibits a tendency to break out on the upside.

The third triangle formation, the descending triangle, is the reverse of the ascending triangle, and consists of a level bottom (support level) and a downtrend line (resistance level). The descending triangle has a tendency to break out on the downside.

Flags and Pennants. These are two other geometrical chart formations which, like triangles, usually occur during the course of a major move and which, not infrequently, are continuation patterns marking the mid-point of the prevailing move. Particularly following a steep, uncorrected price move, a flag or a pennant resembles a "pennant on a pole." In the majority of cases, these two patterns are continuation formations rather than reversal formations. A downward-sloped flag or pennant seems more frequently to break out on the upside (see Figure 20), while an upward-sloped flag is more likely to turn downwards.

Let us stress, once again, that all of these—rectangles, triangles, pennants, and flags—are simply names applied to differently shaped congestion areas. These variations may well have occurred by chance. It seems clear that, if congestion areas were randomly designed, many could be conveniently framed in outline in one or another of the above configurations. We therefore do not place great value on "shape identification" alone. Greater significance attaches to a composite evaluation of: (1) the support and resistance levels of the congestion area; (2) the level and location of activity in this area; (3) the relation of this area to trendlines and channels; (4) chart price objectives.

MARKET GAPS

The final family of chart formations to be discussed is a group notable for its "absence." Although occurring in several forms, "the gap" is basically a price range within which no trading occurred. The gap formation is, obviously, more prominent on a line chart than a point and figure chart, although the point and figurist sometimes places a small dot (rather than the regular "X" or "O") in squares corresponding to a market gap.

In an upside gap, trading will open one morning above the previous day's high, while a downside gap occurs when prices open below the low of the previous session. Some gaps are "closed" during the same trading session, or within a few days, while other gaps may not be closed for weeks or months. Gap openings are usually caused by heavy public buying or selling at the opening of the market, precipitated by some unexpected news

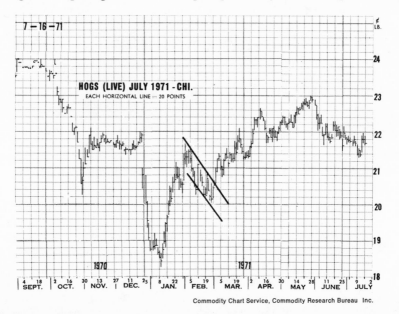

Commodity Chart Service, Commodity Research Bureau Inc.

Fig. 20. A pennant formation. Like the triangle, this formation usually represents a continuation pattern, with the downwards slanting pennant likely to presage an upwards move. The pennant frequently measures the approximate mid-point of the move, as it did here.

or by the execution of heavy stop orders on the opening. A gap caused by stop orders, without the support of substantial follow-through buying or selling, will usually trade back to close the gap after the stop orders have been satisfied. This gap, closed shortly after being formed, is called a "common gap." It is not of great significance, except as a possible forerunner of more volatile impending price action.

A gap which occurs at the breakout of an important congestion formation, and which is not subsequently filled, at least for quite some time, is called a "breakaway gap." This formation frequently marks the commencement of a major move and is usually accompanied by a marked expansion of volume. An upside-breakaway gap is inclined to close at or near the day's high, and a downside breakaway gap at or near the day's low.

After a major move has been underway for some time, prices will sometimes gap in the direction of the basic trend. This may be caused by some unexpected news or by an accumulation of stop or market orders at the opening of the market. This is a "runaway gap," frequently occurring at or around the mid-point of a major move (see Figure 21). The technician may "guesstimate" a price objective for the move on the assumption that the runaway gap represents approximately the half-way point of the entire move.

Even major price trends do not continue indefinitely. An important type of reversal formation, especially following a steep move, is the "exhaustion gap," or "key reversal gap." During the latter stage of a bull move, an exhaustion gap would begin just like a runaway gap, opening higher than the previous session's high. But the day's high would not be sustained and towards the close, prices would begin to decline, closing at or near the lows for the day. This close is frequently, although not necessarily, below the previous day's close. The key reversal from a bear market occurs in inverse fashion. Key reversals are usually accompanied by a sharp increase in trading volume. Unless new trend-continuing incentives come into the market on the following day, the key reversal gap is likely to attract additional liquidation and new counter-trend positions, and will very likely signify the termination of the existing price trend. As noted previously, a major top reversal from a bull market usually takes less time to develop than does a major bottom formation following an extended bear market.

What Do Volume and Open Interest Show?

Technicians and chartists are volatility-seekers. They are ever on the lookout for two inviting omens:

1. A pronounced price change.
2. An indication that the price change in question is significant.

One obvious sign that new forces may be stirring is a quickening tempo of activity. In stocks as well as commodities, traders who watch market action closely always become intrigued with situations in which volume buyers and sellers have suddenly appeared. Where the action is, price movement is apt to be worthwhile. In such circumstances, a dollar ventured may be expanded by a significant multiple—or quickly lost.

For the watchful trader, an ideal situation might be one in which a commodity has been quiescent for many months or years. All at once,

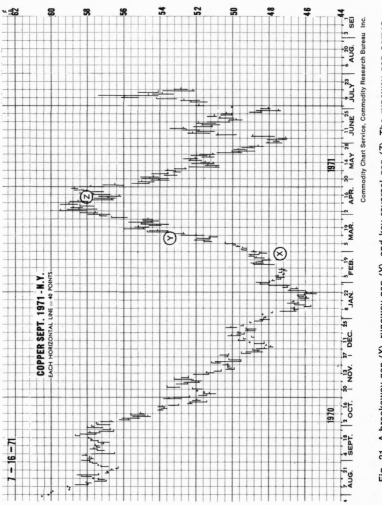

Fig. 21. A breakaway gap (X), runaway gap (Y), and key reversal gap (Z). The runaway gap comes close to measuring the mid-point of the bull move.

volume begins to expand and prices move out of their long-established trading range. The increased trading pace supports the belief that a significant change is brewing and that a market "play" may be imminent.

Examples close to the ideal are not hard to find. Consider the lustrous case of silver which, from late 1963 to early 1967, was static at the U.S. Treasury redemption price of $1.293 per ounce. Treasury sales kept a ceiling at this level despite a widespread belief that the eventual termination of these silver sales would lead to a substantial price rise. In May-June of 1967, futures trading in silver perked up and prices surged above the treasury's $1.293 selling price. Over the ensuing twelve months, the silver market moved up mightily to a new elevation twice that of 1963–1967.

Fig. 22. (Courtesy of Commodity Research Bureau, Inc.)

During the better part of this price rise, activity was expanding, with dips in volume most evident during periods of price reaction (see Figure 22).

From observation of this kind, a theory of volume may be drawn. As usual, however, this theory has not been stated in any exact, verifiable way. Researchers might test the idea that price reversals (defined as a specific change in trend) are more significant when they occur on large volume or that any selected signal of price change has greater validity when it is accompanied by greatly expanded trading activity.

Pending such tests, we maintain the opinion that, in most situations, high volume packs "go-power" and is particularly worth considering as a sign of impending price change. This may be true not only at the beginning of a move, but also at or near its end. Thus, it is a popular hypothesis that: After a sustained price advance, a period of exceptionally heavy volume marked by an inability to advance, followed soon afterwards by a price reversal on high volume, will often portend a significant trend reversal. In the same way, after a sustained steep decline, a high-volume reversal may be climactic.

A coindicator, often interpreted together with variations in volume, is change in "open interest" (number of contracts outstanding). Just before a delivery month commences trading, the open interest in that futures position is zero. Once trading begins, the open interest rises as buyers and sellers come into the market. For each contract outstanding, there exists one buyer and one seller. Thus, if a new buyer and a new seller enter the market, the open interest increases by one contract. When a new buyer replaces an old one (by purchasing a contract from a previous long), there is a change in ownership but no change in the number of contracts outstanding. When an existing long sells one contract and an existing short buys one contract, the pair have liquidated one "lot," and the open interest drops by that figure.

A buildup in open position is most often associated with a rise in the volume of hedge-selling[1] and, on the other side of the ledger, with an increase in the speculative long interest. Ordinarily, hedging is the dynamic element. As a crop movement expands, dealers and processors hedge their purchases of actuals, and prices move to the levels necessary to attract adequate speculative buying demand. However, the situation may be reversed, with an expansion in open interest coming from speculative buying. For example, large-scale speculative purchases of silver futures in 1967–1968 provided trade interests with an incentive to accumulate inventory in silver bullion. That is, the trade was able to buy actual silver and, thanks to dynamic speculative demand, was able to hedge-sell futures at a sufficient premium to pay carrying costs incurred on the purchased silver.

The Commodity Exchange Authority study referred to earlier (see p. 40), indicates that speculators most often trade on the long side of any commodity market. A consequence of this preference is that, once open interest builds up significantly, the number of speculative longs in a market is generally high, often to a degree that technically weakens the market (increases the market's vulnerability to sharp reactions). As long as speculators continue to buy, the potential for market reversal may be obscured. But once new speculative buying falters, weakness can develop suddenly, with prices declining to a degree beyond any apparent fundamental justification.

1. Although the trade is not necessarily net short the market—long hedges may dominate trade positions at times—in most instances, the trade will be net short futures.

The cocoa price downturn in early 1968 affords a particularly good illustration of the vulnerability of a high open interest market, once vast speculative buying diminishes. As shown in Figure 23, the cocoa market (basis the September 1968 future) climbed from a low of about 25.30¢ in July to a high of nearly 30.60¢ in late January. Open interest expanded over most of this price rise, then leveled off as prices proceeded to churn sideways. However, strength seemed well grounded from a fundamental point of view, in that the overall supply-demand position in 1967–1968 gave every evidence of tightening.

Nevertheless, during the end of January, signs of a market reversal began to show. On expanded volume, prices dropped below the established trend (indicated by line T), and open interest began to decline. Thus began the liquidation of a major part of an exceptionally large open position; a position equivalent to over 400,000 tons of cocoa, or one-third more than the annual U.S. cocoa grind. Feeding on itself, this liquidation exerted a depressing influence for months to come, even though no apparent significant change had occurred in the cocoa statistical position.

The lesson of this experience is plain. When open interest stands at a particularly high level, a penetration of an established trend (especially on large volume) should be regarded as a potent warning of an impending price reversal. This warning is not infallible, but experience suggests that it is significant in some probabilistic sense.

Moreover, a large open position may be particularly vulnerable if it is concentrated in a soon-to-expire delivery month. As an example, consider the case of the December 1970 silver future during the last two weeks of November 1970. On November 16th, the December open interest stood at 5,676, a particularly high figure in view of the fact that first notice day was only eight trading days away. The pertinent data for the period was as follows.

Date	Closing Price	Open Interest Dec. 1970 Silver	Total Open Interest All Silver Futures	Transferable Notices Issued
Nov. 16	179.40	5,676	46,558	
17	177.90	5,501	46,836	
18	174.60	5,383	47,000	
19	174.10	5,125	46,409	
20	175.10	5,038	46,476	
23	172.80	4,752	46,362	
24	164.10	4,233	46,466	
25	166.20	4,065	46,535	
27*	164.10	1,487	44,092	2,689
30	159.80	1,097	43,851	582

* First notice day for December 1970 silver.

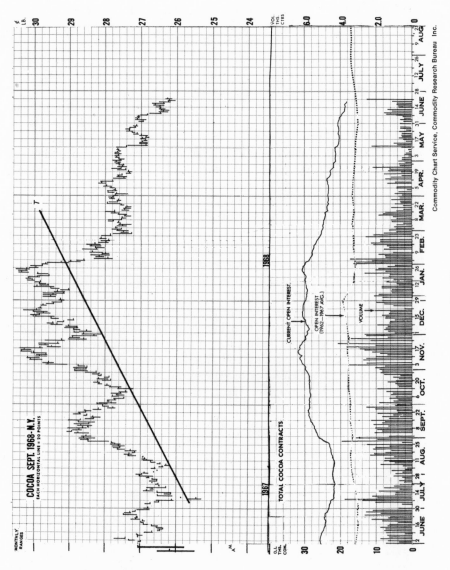

Fig. 23.

Commodity Chart Service, Commodity Research Bureau Inc.

This high open interest in the expiring future contributed to a particularly weak technical market condition. The liquidation of 4,579 December contracts in just ten trading sessions, *resulting in a price decline of 19.60¢ per ounce,* was culminated by the issuance of 3,271 transferable notices (to deliver silver) during the first two days of the notice period. It is interesting to note that, notwithstanding the major decline of 4,579 contracts in the December position, the total open interest for all silver futures declined by only 2,707 during the same period.

The attitude of trade firms concerning the tendering or accepting of delivery against the spot month will depend, to a great extent, on the price differential between spot and various future delivery months. At certain premiums for forward positions, it pays trade houses to take delivery and carry the respective commodity in inventory, subsequently delivering it against a later short futures position. (This will be expanded in Chapter 19.)

In evaluating the significance of changes in open interest, one logical approach is to analyze how any given change is produced. It is usual for analysts to consider four alternative eventualities and their possible significance. These alternatives are as follows:

IF price and open interest change as follows:	THEN the main market influence is judged to be:
Price rises *and* open interest rises.	New buying.
Price rises *and* open interest declines.	Short covering.
Price declines *and* open interest rises.	New selling.
Price declines *and* open interest declines.	Long liquidation.

Recall that every time a futures trade occurs, there is always an equal number of contracts bought and sold. However, when price and open interest rise together, then it seems plausible to regard new buying as the predominant force. Similarly, when open interest is rising and price is declining, we may consider the dominant market influence to be new selling.

Assuming the value of this inference, how does it help us to evaluate the price outlook? The usual hypothesis is that new buying (as indicated by a simultaneous rise in price and open interest) carries a more bullish connotation than short covering (as inferred from a price rise accompanied by a reduction in open interest). We shall see, however, that this invitingly easy concept cannot be applied casually, and requires flexible application.

As a simple modification in evaluating open interest change, it is advisable to consider not just the actual figure of the open position, but the seasonally adjusted data. The need for such adjustment arises from the fact that the open interest in many commodities displays a fairly consistent seasonal variation due to annual marketing and hedging influences. A rise in open interest at a particular time of year when an increase is typical may have less analytic significance than the same open interest rise occurring during a period of normal seasonal open interest decline. Accordingly, it is usual for professional analysts to work with seasonally adjusted open interest figures.

Let us illustrate this with the case of the 1971 corn market. Referring to Figure 24, we note that the open interest "topped out" at 478.1 million bushels on November 19th, with the July future having closed at 1.57. Two months later, on January 22nd, the July future closed at 1.62, with the open interest having declined to 393.0 million bushels. This 5¢ price rise which brought prices back into the resistance area of a massive 6-month congestion area (the formation had not yet been confirmed as a major top formation) was accompanied by a 17.8 percent decline in open interest.

Figure 25 indicates that open interest on November 20th averages 119 percent (of the 10-year average) while, on January 20th, it averages 109 percent.[2] Thus we would normally project a seasonally adjusted open interest decline of 10 percent during the 2 months under review. In this instance, the total corn open interest actually declined by 17.8 percent— representing a 7.8 percent adjusted net decrease.

This seasonally adjusted open interest decrease paired with a price advance back into the 1.62 major resistance area (accompanied, we might add, by a marked decline in trading volume), was a clear indication of the weakened technical condition of the market. This bearish prognosis was subsequently validated, as prices declined by some 15¢ from the 1.62 resistance level.

Technicians generally consider trading volume (in addition to open interest change) in gauging the significance of a given technical formation. Generally, the combined open interest-volume theory has two principal assertions:

1. In an advancing market, rising open interest (seasonally adjusted) and high volume tend to confirm the validity of the uptrend (the market is considered technically strong).

2. Additional charts for other commodities are contained in Appendix A.

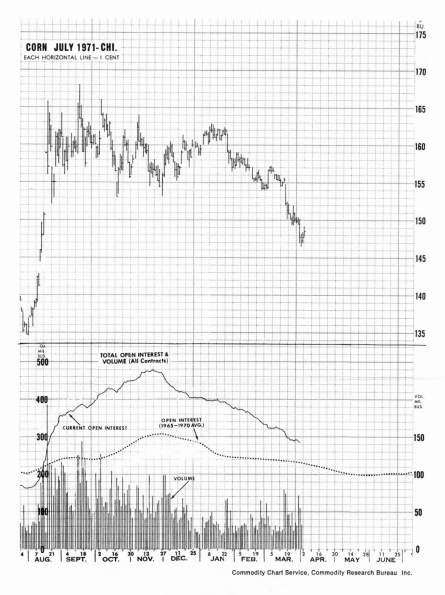

Fig. 24.

2. In a declining market, rising open interest (seasonally adjusted) and high volume tend to confirm the validity of the downtrend (the market is considered technically weak).

As a corollary of the above, it is considered that:

1. A declining open interest in a rising market represents strength primarily due to short covering (the market is considered technically weak).
2. A declining open interest in a falling market represents price weakness primarily due to long liquidation (the market is considered technically strengthening as the open interest is reduced).

In summary, we may state that:

1. When price and open interest move together, the market is considered technically strong and, therefore, either actually or potentially bullish.

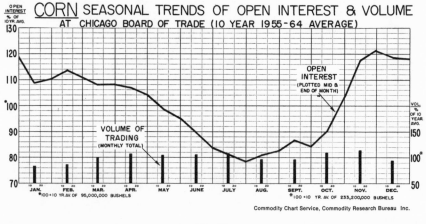

CORN SEASONAL TRENDS OF OPEN INTEREST & VOLUME AT CHICAGO BOARD OF TRADE (10 YEAR 1955-64 AVERAGE)

Commodity Chart Service, Commodity Research Bureau Inc.

Fig. 25.

2. When price and open interest diverge, the market is considered technically weak and, therefore, either actually or potentially bearish.

Critics of this conventional theory point out that it has not been easy to validate it statistically. The relationships involved are probably more subtle and complex than the foregoing hypothesis implies. For example, it is not uncommon for a top or bottom to be made on high volume accompanied by rising open interest. At such times, the combination of an extended price move accompanied by expanded open interest and volume may indicate that the market has become overconfident and is becoming increasingly vulnerable. Whether or not this is so must be judged, in part, from other evidence, including the behavior of the "crowd." That is, one must give consideration to the "contrary opinion" view which holds that a very one-sided public conviction is often the prelude to a significant market reversal.

Taking these criticisms into account, our open interest theory might be stated in somewhat refined form. It now suggests that, in general, a combined rise of price and open interest on high volume has bullish significance in the early stage of an upmove; but this bullish significance diminishes as the open interest further increases and as the speculative public assimilates the bullish factors which fueled the advance.

An excellent case in point was the behavior of the Chicago 1971 corn market, in the wake of severe blight damage to the corn crop. Referring to Figure 24, volume and open interest change seems to particularly warrant the following observations:

1. As the price rise commenced in August, the open interest and volume expanded. This strong technical action confirmed the bullish market trend.

2. In September as the market reached its high, an increase in open interest and sizeable trading volume again accompanied the advance. Note, however, that the rate of increase in the open interest diminished, and prices just churned around static levels, unable to advance any further. Contrary opinionists might have pointed out that bullish sentiment had reached a suspiciously universal level.

3. In October and November open interest increased while prices declined. This bearish signal was eventually vindicated, but not before an interval of unexplained price strength.

4. However, the rising price trend in December and January was not supported by increasing open interest or high trading volume. This technically weak market action suggested an impending price downturn.

5. Thereafter, the dominant technical influence was long liquidation, with open interest continuing to decline with market prices. Although some temporary support was encountered around the 1.55 and then the 1.50 levels, bearish liquidation continued to dominate trading, with values ultimately finding good support around 1.47.

Several conclusions concerning the significance of open interest change seem to be implicit in our discussion:

1. The "rules" regarding open interest and price change do not follow a simple and invariant course. They change at different stages of a market move, and must be considered in relation to other factors, including an evaluation of prevailing market psychology.

2. Rising open interest and heavy trading volume appear to be more significant in confirming a trend at its emergent stage, and of more doubtful meaning later on. In particular, when an uptrend is at a more mature stage,

a sharply diminished rate of open interest expansion may be a harbinger of weakness.

3. Following a period of massive buildup in open interest and great price strength, a downturn may well feed on long liquidation, and no open interest increase on the downturn is needed to validate a bearish signal. Similar reasoning will apply to a market reversal from a downtrend to an uptrend.

Point and Figure Analysis

Point and figure chart analysis provides the technician with more flexibility than any other form of technical analysis. At the option of the chartist, a given commodity future may be scrutinized in minute detail or in summarized broad perspective. In following silver futures, for example, the technician's portfolio may include both a 10-point "jiggle" chart and a 100-point comprehensive chart for both a detailed and overall picture of trading activity.

Figure 26, covering potatoes and soybeans, illustrates this flexibility. (A) and (B) and (C) and (D) each cover the same time period, though from a completely different perspective. (A) and (C) provide considerable trading detail, helpful for short to intermediate-term market timing. (B) and (D), on the other hand, present a rather broad market perspective, useful for longer-term trading decisions.

The theory of point and figure analysis is summarized by Wheelan as follows:

> Price trends and market fluctuations result from the operation of supply and demand in the market. Point and Figure analysis is directed towards the development of good market judgment in estimating the relative strength of Supply and Demand in individual stocks or commodities, to determine when to buy, when to sell, how much of a price movement is indicated and how to appraise and limit risk.[3]

Point and figure analysis embraces the following elements:

CONGESTION AREA ANALYSIS

A congestion area (general sideways price trend) may occur either during the course of a major market trend or at the top or bottom of a trend (the congestion area would evolve as either a continuation or a reversal formation). At some point in the congestion area, prices will break

3. Alexander H. Wheelan, *Study Helps in Point and Figure Technique,* New York, Morgan, Rogers and Roberts, Inc., p. 3.

A

May 1971 potatoes, 5-point, 3-block reversal.

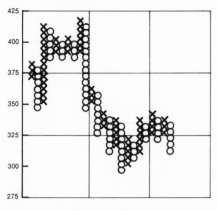

B

May 1971 potatoes, 10-point, 1-block reversal.

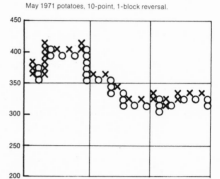

C

August 1971 soybeans, 1-cent, 6-block reversal.

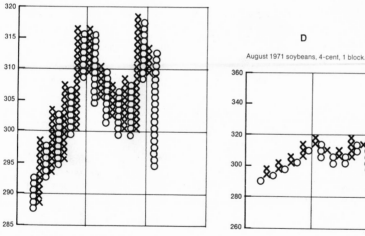

D

August 1971 soybeans, 4-cent, 1 block.

(all courtesy of Dunn and Hargitt Commodity Service.)

Fig. 26.

out; our analysis attempts to project the probable direction of such a breakout. Although it has not been objectively tested, experience has demonstrated that when the majority of trading activity occurs near the top of a congestion area, reflecting the fact that selling pressure (distribution) is handily absorbing buying pressure, the market can be expected to break out on the downside. Conversely, an upside breakout would likely be projected if most of the trading activity within a congestion area were to have occurred near the bottom of the area (pattern of accumulation).

The exact identification of the congestion area may, at times, be obscured by the complexities of trading formations. For example, boundaries of a congestion area may encompass a number of minor subareas, any one of which could be analyzed individually. The entire multiple formation, however, may have to be considered as a single entity in order to reach a meaningful conclusion. Within the confines of such a broad congestion area, the more recent price activity would doubtlessly play a dominant role in the formation of analytic conclusions.

In a particularly detailed chart, a broad congestion area may, in fact, consist of several minor price trends, the total analysis of which may be very enlightening. A series of ascending tops and bottoms within a broad congestion area signifies that offerings are being well absorbed with the implication of bullishness and an eventual upside breakout from the congestion area. Of course, this projection would be invalidated were the market to abruptly reverse course and break through on the downside. Conversely, it may be possible to recognize a pattern of distribution, as represented by a series of minor descending tops and bottoms. In such a situation, the technician would project an eventual downside penetration.

The congestion area in point and figure analysis need not conform to a rectangular shape. It may appear as a triangle, flag, or pennant.

TREND ANALYSIS

Just as it is in a line chart, the market trend will be represented as either up, down, or sideways. Although minor counter-trends are continuously interacting with the major market trend, it is this major trend which primarily concerns us here.

Trendlines in point and figure work are less apt to be perfectly linear than with other types of charts. The penetration of a trendline, particularly if it was steeply drawn, will not necessarily indicate the reversal of the trend. It may be a sign that the trend has merely broadened and that the trendline must be redrawn in a corresponding manner. However, penetration of significant support or resistance levels and development of new trendlines constitute important evidence of trend reversal, and should be carefully scrutinized.

The velocity of a trend may be a useful indicator in projecting and analyzing trendlines. When successive price advances in an uptrend appear to be losing momentum (that is, not carrying as far as the previous advance), it could be an indicator of an impending reversal or, at least, of a flattening of an existing uptrend. The converse reasoning would apply in the case of momentum loss in a downtrend.

At times, a chart will offer very clear trend channels to the astute technician. The projection of a clear trend channel provides the chartist with an effective short-term measuring indicator—one which helps project the possible extent of short-term swings. Once prices get into the channel, they have a tendency to find support at the bottom and resistance at the top of that channel. Sound trading judgment must be applied: We would not necessarily assume a short position at the upper boundary of an uptrend channel, nor would we necessarily go long at the lower boundary of a major downtrend channel. However, when trading in accordance with the prevailing market trend, one can improve market timing by buying at the bottom of the trend channel (support level) in a major uptrend, and by selling at the top of the trend channel (resistance level) in a major downtrend.

When a price trend steepens and moves through the top of an uptrend channel or the bottom of a downtrend channel, the chartist should consider the possibility that the price trend is approaching its final stage. This is not an invitation to trade against the steepened trend, simply a caution to watch it with particular care for possible "blow-off" action.

SUPPORT AND RESISTANCE

The effective zone of support consists of the top half of the support area, while the effective zone of resistance lies in the bottom half of the resistance area. A price decline to the lower half of a support zone could carry a bearish implication, particularly if the congestion area occurred during a mature phase of a bull market. Conversely, a price advance into the upper half of a resistance area could be bullishly construed, particularly if the congestion area occurred during the mature phase of a bear market.

As a general rule, the first uncorrected rally following an extended bear market will likely fail around the level of the first resistance area, particularly if the resistance area was of fairly recent vintage. The same may be said regarding the first decline following a major market top, although not as convincingly. As will be pointed out in Chapter 15, prices are inclined to fall "of their own weight," but it takes buying—usually substantial buying—to significantly advance prices. This is just another way of saying that prices breaking down from a major top area seem to go down faster and further than they go up during an advance out of a major base area.

CHART FORMATIONS

For the most part, chart formations in point and figure analysis coincide with line chart formations. However, the most distinctive and important point and figure pattern is the "fulcrum" (bottom formation) and its counterpart, the "inverse fulcrum" (top formation). The fulcrum is the congestion area which follows a major downmove, and corresponds to a base area of accumulation. The implication of such a formation is almost invariably bullish.

The fulcrum consists of:

1. An extended downmove.
2. Considerable trading activity near the bottom of the formation.
3. A technical rally out of this bottom formation.
4. A reaction testing the recent low but encountering good buying support.
5. A rally back to the top of the formation accompanied by a "catapult" move (upside breakout) from the formation.

Naturally, no two fulcrum formations will develop in exactly the same manner, although the basic elements will be similar. In particular, the fourth item above is subject to one significant variation: The reaction following the first technical rally may not hold at the recent lows. While prices may penetrate support, following the execution of resting stop orders (there are invariably stop orders placed below the trading low of a formation), prices will either rally or churn in a sideways direction. This inability to decline following the making of new lows will likely be followed by a rally, perhaps of significant proportions. This variation of the "standard" fulcrum does not alter the bullish implication; in fact, it may be even more bullish in that it strengthens the technical condition of the market.

The fulcrum formation may be considered most bullish if it occurs: (1) following an extended price decline; (2) at a price level which coincides with a major downside price objective; and (3) in the area of a major support level. As noted earlier, the top formation, or inverse fulcrum, takes the inverse form of the above. We leave it to the reader to reconstruct this formation.

PRICE OBJECTIVES (THE "COUNT")

One of the distinctive features of point and figure analysis is its adaptability to "counting"; that is, projecting price objectives. There is a basic relationship between the breadth of a congestion area and the extent of a price move out of that area. In practice, the technician will count across the number of squares in the congestion area, and then project the same number of squares in the direction of the breakout move. This is obviously not a precise relationship, but one which nevertheless provides guidelines for the prediction of price objectives. Count across the congestion area from the bottom of the sidewalls (in a bottom formation) or from the top of the sidewalls (in a top formation). Calculate across a single price line, and include in your count any unoccupied squares.

At major tops and bottoms, a count analysis may come up with more than one projection; perhaps a major and a minor count, or even a major, intermediate and minor count. All count projections should be penciled on the chart because they may provide additional insight as new formations develop. Note that, in a bull market, upside counts are apt to be exceeded, while major downside counts may not be fully realized. Conversely, in a

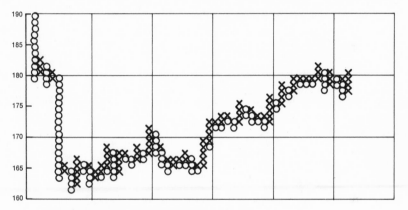

Fig. 27. September 1971 New York silver. Each box equals 100 points.

major downtrend, downside counts are apt to be exceeded, while upside counts may not be attained.

Figure 27 illustrates both the "fulcrum" and the "count." Referring to our description of a fulcrum, we note that this silver chart consists of:

1. An extended downmove to 1.61.
2. Considerable trading activity near the bottom of the formation in the 1.61 to 1.66 range.
3. A technical rally out of this bottom to 1.71.
4. A reaction back to the 1.64 level.
5. A rally to 1.72, followed by a catapult move to 1.81.

Figure 27 provides a particularly interesting example of price movement projection by counting across successive congestion areas, as follows:

a. The major price objective can be projected by counting across the 1.65 level, yielding a count of 25 boxes. Projecting the 25 box count upwards yields a major price objective of 1.90 (1.65 plus .25).

b. Counting across the catapult congestion area which developed in the 1.71 to 1.75 range—our count across the 1.72 level measures 11 boxes— yields an intermediate price objective of 1.83 (1.72 plus .11). It is interesting to note that the subsequent breakout to 1.81 substantially fulfilled this intermediate-term price objective.

c. Counting across the next congestion area, in the 1.76 to 1.80 range— our measurement across the 1.77 level yields a count of 12 boxes—provides a price objective of 1.89 (1.77 plus .12). It is particularly noteworthy that this count, on the third leg of the bull market, confirms the major upside count of 1.90, as developed in point a, above.

TRADING TACTICS

The essence of point and figure analysis involves the ultimate question: Where and when to buy or sell. Wheelan has succinctly summarized the various conditions comprising *the ideal buying point*.

1. The technical position of the general market is favorable for an advance.
2. A broad and unmistakably clear-cut fulcrum occurs following an extended downtrend.
3. The bottom of the fulcrum occurs at a level that represents fulfillment of the maximum count objective from the previous top.
4. The bottom of the fulcrum occurs at a level that constitutes an important support area.
5. A catapult occurs coincidentally with the penetration of a downtrend line established either within the fulcrum or from a previous top made tangent with the mid-fulcrum rally point.
6. The catapult occurs at a price level at which no nearby resistance is indicated.[4]

The development of an ideal selling point proceeds along similar, although converse, lines.

Moving Averages

In Chapter 10, we referred to a 10-day moving average. In practice, the period of the moving average is left to the discretion of the analyst, e.g., 5, 10, 15, or 30 days. Moreover, the analyst may elect to use a "straight" moving average—that is, a straightforward mathematical average of the

4. *Ibid.,* p. 35.

respective closing prices—or a "weighted" moving average, which is worked out on a formula basis to give greater weight to recent price changes than to older changes. For example, in a 40-day weighted moving average, closing prices for the most recent 10 days may be given double the weight of the preceding 30 days' closings.

There are a number of approaches to moving average analysis. First, the technician could regard a direction change in the moving average line itself as a buy or sell signal, that is, he may buy when the moving average line turns to a positive slope, and sell when the line turns to a negative slope. The shortcoming to this approach is that a slope reversal in the moving average line may be too laggard to use as a buy/sell indicator. More often, moving average technicians tend to be guided in their trading decisions by changes in the market price relative to the moving average line. That is, the chartist would buy when the market price crossed above the moving average line, and he would sell when the price crossed below the line. The third approach involves the crossing of two moving average lines, a short-term versus a longer-term line. The chartist, using this method with, for example, 10- and 20-day moving average lines, would buy when the 10-day line crossed above the 20-day line, and would sell when the 10-day line crossed below the 20-day line.

How can moving averages assist in the timing of trades? Our initial problem is to identify the trend; more specifically, to determine at what point the trend has turned up or down. It is here that moving averages may first be of assistance. Clearly, prices must rise above the moving average line (or the short-term line must rise above the long-term line) before the trend, as measured by this moving average, can be said to have turned up. And they must decline below the moving average line (or the short-term line must decline below the long-term line) before the trend, as measured by this moving average, can be said to have turned down. The question is: How much of a breakout above or below the moving average line should be required to trigger a trader's action? Should the requisite breakout be fulfilled on an intraday penetration, or must we require a penetration on a closing basis? This is the same type of problem which we discussed in connection with the simple trading system (described previously); and, again, it may be necessary to strike a balance between a small trigger change (which leads to whipsawing) and a larger trigger change (which may lead one to act too late).

The technician's perennial quest is for a system which will yield substantial profits during periods of broad, trend-following markets, and some profit (or, at least, nominal losses) during dull periods. In attempting to design such a system, the analyst's first step usually involves giving trial consideration to one or more plausible decision rules. Often, it is found

Commodity	Delivery	Computer Trend	Trend Started		Current Computer		Market Risk	Market Close 8/13/71
			Price	Date	Support	Resistance		
Wheat (Chi)	Dec. '71	DOWN	$157\frac{3}{4}$	7/7/71		$148\frac{3}{8}$	$\frac{3}{4}$¢	$147\frac{5}{8}$
Corn (Chi)	Dec. '71	DOWN	144	7/7/71		$125\frac{1}{2}$	$\frac{7}{8}$¢	$124\frac{5}{8}$
Oats (Chi)	Dec. '71	DOWN	$64\frac{3}{4}$	8/10/71		$70\frac{3}{8}$	4¢	$66\frac{3}{8}$
Wheat (Minn)	Sept. '71	DOWN	160	7/9/71		$155\frac{3}{8}$	$1\frac{3}{8}$¢	154
Wheat (K.C.)	Dec. '71	DOWN	$148\frac{1}{4}$	7/7/71		144	$\frac{7}{8}$¢	$143\frac{1}{8}$
Oats (Winn)	Oct. '71	DOWN	$73\frac{7}{8}$	7/22/71		$70\frac{3}{4}$	$1\frac{1}{4}$¢	$69\frac{1}{2}$
Barley (Winn)	Oct. '71	DOWN	$112\frac{1}{4}$	7/22/71		$112\frac{1}{4}$	3¢	$109\frac{1}{4}$
Rye (Winn)	Oct. '71	DOWN	$102\frac{3}{4}$	7/28/71		$106\frac{1}{2}$	$5\frac{1}{4}$¢	$101\frac{1}{4}$
Rapeseed (Winn) #	Sept. '71	UP From Side	314	8/9/71	$298\frac{1}{2}$		$10\frac{1}{4}$¢	$308\frac{3}{4}$
Flaxseed (Winn)	Oct. '71	DOWN	$247\frac{3}{4}$	7/14/71		$243\frac{5}{8}$	$1\frac{3}{8}$¢	$242\frac{1}{4}$
Soybeans	Nov. '71	DOWN	$319\frac{3}{4}$	8/4/71		$324\frac{3}{8}$	$7\frac{7}{8}$¢	$316\frac{1}{2}$
Soybean Oil	Sept. '71	UP	13.97	7/14/71	13.66		9 pts	13.75
Soybean Meal	Sept. '71	DOWN	82.70	8/4/71		86.42	392 pts	82.50
Sugar "11"	Oct. '71	UP	4.39	7/28/71	4.16		35 pts	4.51
Cocoa #	Dec. '71	SIDEWAYS From Up	26.08	8/11/71	24.43	26.91		26.30
Wool (Grease)	Oct. '71	SIDEWAYS	62.4	7/26/71	5.51	6.19		59.5
Cotton #2	Oct. '71	UP	32.10	7/14/71	31.18		72 pts	31.90
Potatoes, Maine	Nov. '71	UP	2.79	7/1/71	2.74		1 pt	2.75
Eggs (Shell) #	Sept. '71	UP From Side	40.60	8/9/71	37.53		62 pts	38.15
Orange Juice #	Sept. '71	UP From Side	63.70	8/9/71	60.81		419 pts	65.00
Broilers	Sept. '71	DOWN	27.05	8/10/71		28.45	115 pts	27.30
Cattle (Live)	Oct. '71	UP	30.87	7/20/71	32.22		63 pts	32.85
Hogs	Dec. '71	DOWN	20.07	7/23/71		19.90	75 pts	19.15
Pork Bellies	Feb. '72	DOWN	29.27	7/27/71		30.00	225 pts	27.75
Plywood (Chi)	Nov. '71	DOWN	88.10	8/4/71		92.36	716 pts	86.20
Lumber	Sept. '71	UP	110.90	7/21/71	107.43		107 pts	108.50
Copper	Sept. '71	SIDEWAYS	48.85	7/20/71	48.63	52.59		50.60
Platinum	Oct. '71	SIDEWAYS	113.50	8/3/71	111.04	117.02		115.90
Silver (Chi.)	Oct. '71	SIDEWAYS	164.60	8/4/71	158.12	165.10		161.50
Silver (N.Y.)	Dec. '71	SIDEWAYS	166.10	8/4/71	160.14	167.12		163.10

#TREND CHANGES   ##TREND REVERSALS   *CONTRACT TRANSFERS

Fig. 28. (Courtesy of Commodity Research Bureau, Inc.)

that the first set of rules "just misses" being significantly profitable over a selected test period. After experimenting with the two variables (period of the moving average and specified trigger price change), the system-designer should obtain a set of rules which works well for that period. However, when this newly adjusted method is tried on another market period, the results may not be so successful. Decision rules which work during one interval may break down in another.

Before a system should be considered usable, it is clear that, once all the adjustments have been made and tests run, the system be retested without any further adjustments. If it continues to work well, and the test period seems reasonably balanced between intervals of wide and narrow price swings, then one can attempt to apply this system to actual trading.

Many variations of moving average trading systems have been devised over the years. One of the pioneers in this field was Curtiss Dahl, who started with a simple 10-day moving average line and adopted trading rules to be used in conjunction with his technical studies. Dunn and Hargitt, Inc., as successor to Curtiss Dahl, has conducted extensive technical research into moving average systems utilizing advanced computer techniques.[5] The results of this research indicate that the market action of some commodities is so random that it appears impossible to construct an effective moving average system. However, in other commodities, the degree of randomness is limited, and the moving average has proven both workable and helpful. Reviewing the moving average line as a trend detection device, Dunn and Hargitt concluded that most of the grains, cattle, and sugar worked well with a 40-day weighted moving average line; pork bellies and silver seemed to produce best results with a line closer to 20 days; and soybean oil and copper with a line near the 60-day period. In all cases, a requisite penetration or crossing of the applicable moving average line (by the market price) by about $150.00 provided optimum results.

One of the more widely known moving average methods is the so-called "Computer Trend Analyzer" published weekly by the Commodity Research Bureau, Inc.[6] The findings of the Analyzer are summarized in a table which indicates the market trend, the calculated values of support and resistance levels, and the estimated risk in following the trend at the prevailing price. Figure 28 is a sample of this weekly tabulation.

The Commodity Research Bureau prudently asserts that the Computer Trend Analyzer is not represented as a trading system, but rather as an objective method of labeling trends and, therefore, "a check on all other methods of analysis that depend on human evaluations which may be partially based on emotions."

5. 124 West State St., West Lafayette, Indiana.
6. 140 Broadway, New York, New York.

CHAPTER 12

The Role of the Computer in Technical Analysis

Trading Systems and the Computer Analyst

Until now, our discussion of the technical approach to commodity price analysis has focused on a subjective, individual interpretation of chart patterns and other technical indicators. This kind of approach permits subtle differences of opinion and, more importantly, may leave room for disagreement as to whether one should buy, sell, or stand aside at any given moment. We now wish to consider more binding types of rules for formulating trading decisions. When these decision rules are obligatory, allowing no latitude for personal judgment, they constitute an *automatic trading system*.

Long before the computer era, trading systems were evolved and utilized by those who sought an unambiguous and consistent path to commodity profits. Like the old gold prospectors, they labored long and hard, and rarely struck rich veins. Today, however, mechanization and automation are becoming commonplace, and it is scarcely surprising that the computer is beginning to take over the task of working out and testing various trading systems, especially those based on purely technical considerations.

The computer's virtue in this respect is obvious. It is a tireless, incredibly fast worker, which obeys instructions to the letter with slavish obedience. It cannot originate concepts on its own, cannot "think" in the more profound sense. But it can perform myriads of mathematical calculations, and carry out trials when labor time and cost would otherwise be prohibitive.

We shall examine first, however, a system which requires no elaborate computation and, hence, no computer aid.

A Simple Automatic Trading System

The simplest automatic trading system may be based on a single decision rule which says: Buy when the price goes up by X number of points, and sell when the price goes down by X number of points, over any specified trading interval (e.g., one day, one week, or one month).

Ideally, we would like to apply this kind of rule to a commodity which shows high trend persistence, and comparatively little erratic price motion. Otherwise, the market's haphazard up and down jiggling will get us in and out too often, with many whipsaw losses. Assume that we find a commodity which is more eligible than others because, for a foreseeable period at least, it seems likely to have sizeable price fluctuations and has, in the past, been less capriciously jumpy than other commodities. We have two further steps: (1) to select the most appropriate price series to use and (2) to decide how large a price change X we should use to trigger action under our trading rule (as stated above).

To illustrate this automatic trading system, we have chosen cash mercury in 1966–1967; the price selected was the weekly spot quotation published by *Metals Week*.[1] This combination (spot mercury on a weekly basis) was selected because it displayed comparatively little erratic fluctuation and therefore seemed unlikely to produce frequent whipsaw losses. To decide on the magnitude X needed to trigger action, we first asked ourselves what minor rallies or reactions seemed to occur with great frequency. We then selected as a trial value a price change a bit greater than these minor variations. Thus, we anticipated that we would not be obliged to trade on random fluctuations.

In the table below, the trading rule we adopted was: Buy when the weekly spot quotation goes up $10.00 per flask; liquidate the long position and sell (short) when the weekly spot quotation goes down $10.00 per flask. The results were astonishingly good for the period shown, because this happened to be a period characterized by extensive price swings with few minor jiggles. It should be noted, however, that in subsequent tests in other periods, the same system resulted in losses.

Even though consistent profits may not be attainable with such a simple system, it does serve to clarify some of the underlying problems involved in setting up any automatic system based on some kind of trend-following rule (i.e., a rule which anticipates buying when prices have turned up by some stipulated amount, and selling when prices have turned down).

One difficulty associated with such a system is of basic importance: If

1. *Metals Week,* New York, McGraw-Hill.

Spot Mercury Trading Results Based on Automatic Trading System, 1965–1967

Date	Action*	Initial Price	Final Price	Profit	Loss
1965	B	485	700	215	
	S	700	600	100	
	B	600	590		10
	S	590	610		20
	B	610	620	10	
	S	620	540	80	
	B	540	530		10
			Subtotal	405	40
1966	S	530	345	185	
	B	345	505	160	
			Subtotal	345	0
1967	S	505	460	45	
	B	460	475	15	
	S	475	490		15
	B	490	495	5	
	S	495	495	—	—
			Subtotal	65	15
		Total 1965–1967		$815 Profit	$55 Loss

* (B: Buy)
(S: Sell)

our decision rule leads us to buy or sell on small price moves X, then we are very likely to be whip-sawed by frequent losses, as shown in Figure 29.

On the other hand, if our decision rule leads us to buy or sell only after large price moves, we shall be spared the whip-saw but we may be too late to profit on all but the most sweeping price moves, and may find that losses on adverse positions are excessive. Thus, in Figure 30, our profit is nil because our trigger price change was too high.

It is clear that, for a trading system of this type to have any chance of being successful, its price trigger magnitude must be neither too small, nor too large, but just right for the respective commodity. Sometimes this quest will appear illusory, but at times systems have been evolved which worked —or so it seemed.

A crucial difficulty with systems of this trend-following variety is the frequent occurrence of erratic and random price moves which trigger premature purchases or sales. To minimize this, we attempt to define a significant price move more precisely. The most popular way to do this is to take a moving average as a base (or reference point) from which to measure price change.

To understand this fully, refer to pp. 112–115. We said that a breakout is significant when it moves far enough away from the trendline to exceed the specified bounds of the channel. In much the same way, a moving average (which we are about to describe) is a kind of fitted trendline, and by theory or by trial and error, we can draw a channel a certain distance away from it. Above the channel, we consider that a buy signal has been triggered and, below it, a sell signal.

This is the essential nature of an automatic trend-following system based

Fig. 29.

Fig. 30.

on moving averages. The most popular types of systems are founded (explicitly or not) on a principle of this kind.

Computer Use in Designing a Moving Average System

When a trading system is based on a calculated moving average and on specific trigger price changes, then a computer is an obviously appropriate tool for conducting the necessary mathematical operations. Today, it is an easy matter to program a computer for this work. The computer can be "asked" to print out one or more moving averages of any desired period and, if we wish, to signal "buy" or "sell" whenever a selected moving average is penetrated by a specified amount. The computer can also "keep score," giving us a running record of profits and losses scored to date based on the assigned decision rules.

It is not just a question of simplifying the burden of mathematical calculations. The computer can carry out repeated trials of different decision rules, involving so many millions of operations that it would not be feasible to do in any other manner.

Let us say, for example, that we have access to 10 years of daily price data for a particular commodity, and wish to design an automatic trading system utilizing this data. Further assume that our initial attempt at system designing specifies a simple system, based on a single moving average and a one-unit trigger price change in either direction. The objective is to determine what period moving average works best, and simultaneously to determine how large a price move above or below the moving average (trigger price change) will most advantageously determine a buy or sell action.

Let us assume that we have access to computer services and are prepared to foot the bill. We can readily present this problem to the computer, and expect it to report the optimum combination of moving average period and trigger price increment. Knowing which method provided the best results profitwise in the 10-year trial period, we can then integrate the system into our trading scheme and apply it in practice.

Anyone can now design his own moving average (or any other technically oriented) system, and check its results over the past decade. This can be accomplished by determining the type of system to be tested and the various alternatives to be considered, and submitting the problem to a computer-oriented service which handles this type of research.[2] Naturally, both the proposed trading system as well as the test results should be thoroughly evaluated with the computer-service company, before you actually take up the market's gauntlet.

Trading systems based on moving averages can be vastly more complex than we have indicated so far. We may employ two or more moving averages simultaneously and be guided by their relationship (for example, a 10-day versus a 20-day moving average). Or we may establish a "trigger rule" which requires prices to be above or below the moving average for any number of days rather than just for one day. Also, our liquidation rule may be different from our initiation rule, calling for us to exit when prices

2. One of the leading proponents of computer-oriented analysis is Dunn and Hargitt, Inc., Lafayette, Indiana. For a fee, this firm will program and test, on their computer, any analytic or trading system, and will provide an evaluation of testing results.

drop back (or recover) to within a particular distance of the moving average.

It is possible to construct systems of impressive complexity. But, of course, complexity is not necessarily an advantage, and it entails evident penalties. As one introduces more elaborate alternatives for the computer to consider, the machine time and cost rise geometrically, and it becomes much more difficult to revise and refine such systems. Thus, except where good reason dictates otherwise, it pays to work as simply as possible.

In any event, experience with trading systems suggests that it may be possible to operate any given system successfully for a period of time, but perhaps the structure of price relationships will change sufficiently to require a modified design. Moreover, the more extensively followed a particular system becomes, the less likely it is to continue yielding profits. For, as more bids are entered at the trigger price, one must pay a greater premium to buy; and, in the same way, more offers at downside decision points mean one will probably sell at lower average levels.

Other Computer Applications

Moving averages, plainly enough, are just one kind of trend-following device. There are a host of other methods of defining the direction of market movement and, in each case, the determination can usually be made most efficiently with the help of a computer.

As noted earlier in this chapter, a computer can fit a straight-line trend and trend channel to price data. It can do this daily, if we so instruct, and will signal us when any designated line is penetrated.

The shape of the fitted trendline need not be straight; however, dependent on our instructions, the computer can fit any one of a large family of mathematical curves to our price data. The essential requirement is that we have some reasonable basis for preferring one particular curve to another. Whatever the shape of the curve we fit (up to a straight line, which retains the virtues of arbitrary directness), we can ask the computer to extrapolate that trend ahead one day, or one week, or whatever we choose, to give us a mathematically projected value. However, a specific projection of this type may not necessarily have any operational advantage over the more general statement that the mathematically computed market trend is up, or down, as the case may be.

A researcher studying price action in a variety of commodities conceivably might find it useful to have the computer print out each day (or each week) a battery of prespecified market indicators. Illustratively, a computer printout (for a hypothetical commodity) might usefully contain the following data.

Date	Closing Price	10-Day Average	20-Day Average	Projected Price 1 Week Forward	
				Linear	Curvilinear
Apr. 1	100	98	97	101	101
2	102	99	97	102	103
3	105	100	98	103	106
etc.					

The printout might also include data on volume and open interest, both in absolute and seasonally adjusted terms.

The Computer as Chart Reader

The output of the modern computer is not confined to numbers. The directed printout may be a chart picture showing the original price data plotted in a conventional way, and also a moving average appropriately drawn on the same scale. In Figure 31, the computer printout also indicates prices at which long positions (marked L) and short positions (S) were initiated, the resultant profit or loss (+13, −6), and then, a "final account" statement.

It is most interesting to consider the extent to which the computer might eventually be able to replace the human technician. Typically, the technician is conscious of the fact that each commodity can display somewhat distinctive patterns. He reviews past charts to consider whether the commodity in question is prone to V tops or bottoms, or doubles or triples, or island reversals. One wonders: Given a highly sophisticated set of programming instructions, could not the computer scan "charts" in similar fashion, identify any recurrent patterns, and match today's market behavior with that of other portentous intervals?

The answer, at least in the purely mechanical sense, would appear to be yes. The computer can be programmed to consider a current commodity chart, to scan all past technical action in that commodity and, if it discerns a technical pattern of a specified degree of closeness, to "tell us" what occurred in the day, week, and month which then followed. In this way, the computer might provide us with a chart forecast. It could also be programmed to consider other technical indicators, such as volume and open interest (either actual or seasonally adjusted).

What the computer probably cannot do is to be cognizant of a subtle spectrum of technical and fundamental influences which the experienced

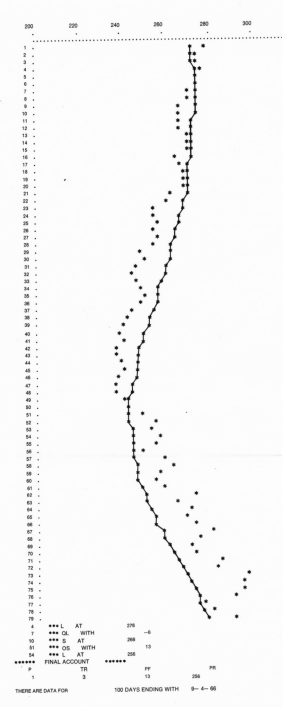

Fig. 31.

human interpreter should be able to absorb. For this reason, the essential role of the computer system—whether applied to technical or fundamental market data—is to systematically analyze that portion of the available information which lends itself to mathematical treatment, because it displays regularity and uniformity.

The Future Role of the Computer

Of one thing we can be certain, and that is the widening role of the computer in tomorrow's commodity research. Increasingly, this instrument will be used to check out many of the trading concepts currently favored. It will expose the weakness of some popular systems, and perhaps elevate others to proven usefulness.

More esoterically, perhaps, we foresee the end of an era—the open bids, cries, and colorful expressions of the floor traders—to be mourned nostalgically by many in the commodity trades. All of this may someday be replaced by the silent movement of electrical impulses and the soft whirr of computer tapes. (In Chapter 13 we shall discuss how computers may be used as an aid to price estimation based on fundamental supply and demand analysis.)

CHAPTER 13 Fundamental Analysis—
An Econometric Approach

While technical analysis is concerned with the market symptoms of a particular commodity situation, fundamental analysis directs its attention to the underlying causes. Which economic factors lie at the root of price change? And how much influence does each of these factors exert?

If our goal is to predict price based on fundamentals, then we must have some idea how much weight to allow each of the different supply and demand factors. Essentially, we estimate these weights from past experience. We may attempt this on a judgmental basis, recalling as best we can how much the price of a particular commodity has responded to past market forces. Or, we may adopt a statistical method, in which we estimate the average influence of different price-making factors.

We call this second, more objective and disciplined approach to fundamental analysis, *econometrics*. As the name implies, it entails the application of a formal metric or measurement technique to economic relationships.

Thus, we might determine that: (1) a 10 percent increase in production of commodity X has typically resulted in a drop of 5 percent in the price of X, or (2) a 10 percent increase in consumer income has historically resulted in a 5 percent increase in the consumption and a 2 percent increase in the price of X.

It is our belief that the evolution of commodity research on Wall Street is in a direction away from the current broad, subjective approach, and towards methods which include a larger proportion of objective econometric analysis.

A principal purpose of this chapter is to introduce the reader to the way in which an analytic approach is formulated econometrically. This introduction is largely nontechnical. It is concerned with basic concepts understandable to a layman or student without substantial mathematical or statistical training.

Let us begin with a tangible example. The following case history in cocoa is intended solely to demonstrate some of the basic principles and problems involved in econometric analysis. It does not illustrate a refined method and is certainly not intended to foster any illusion of econometric infallibility. We will see that reliance on high-powered techniques is no guarantee of forecasting accuracy.

Cocoa in 1967: an Example

In the following table, using 10 years of statistical data, we present an econometric approach to cocoa price analysis.

In setting up this table, we have moved one step in the direction of systematic analysis. We now have a statistical summary or balance sheet of world supply and demand in cocoa during the 10 years prior to our forecast period. It is obvious from the estimates given in this table that, at the time the table was prepared, 1967 production was expected to fall considerably short of grindings (consumption).

What does this statistical summary imply for the price of cocoa? Answers to this question may be reached through different methods of fundamental analysis, ranging from subjective and judgmental to objective and econometric. Let us examine the various interpretations, in order of increasing precision.

1. On a broad, judgmental basis, traders might interpret the available estimates as pointing toward a decidedly short crop in 1967. They might note that this follows on the heels of a very large deficit (stock reduction) in 1966. Therefore, by the end of 1967, cocoa bean inventories might be down to the lowest levels in many years. The situation might well warrant a price in 1967 materially above the average of 24.4¢, basis spot Ghana cocoa in New York, during January-September 1966.[1]

2. Taking a balance-sheet approach, the same viewpoint could be expressed in a more specific way. (Let us examine the first estimate given for 1967, deferring until later any consideration of the second estimate.)

It appears that world production in 1967 will approximate 1,304,000 tons (after a 1 percent weight-loss allowance). This is roughly 75,000 tons below expected use for grinding purposes. In an important sense, this 1967 deficit measures the extent to which the statistical position will be stronger in 1967 than it was in 1966.

1. Average price is used for the period January-through-September rather than for the entire calendar year, because the price in the final quarter strongly reflects new crop developments.

World Cocoa Statistical Position, 1957 Through 1967 (1,000's of long tons)

Crop Year Ending In Yr. Shown*	Beginning Stock A	Production (Net of 1% Wt. Loss) B	Total Supply (A + B)	Calendar Year Grinding C	Ending Stock (and Change from Prev. Yr.) (A + B)−C	Closing Stock as Fraction of Grind (A + B)−C / C†	Supply Ratio A + B / C_{t-1}†	Price Spot Ghana, N.Y. Jan.–Sept.†	Price Spot Ghana, N.Y. 3rd Quart.†
1957	230	887	1,117	910	207 (− 23)	.228	1.35	27.3	32.5
1958	207	763	970	848	122 (− 85)	.145	1.07	45.2	45.9
1959	122	900	1,022	871	151 (+ 29)	.173	1.21	37.4	37.3
1960	151	1,034	1,185	933	252 (+101)	.270	1.36	28.6	28.6
1961	252	1,164	1,416	1,018	398 (+146)	.391	1.52	21.9	21.3
1962	398	1,120	1,518	1,110	408 (+ 10)	.368	1.49	21.0	20.4
1963	408	1,146	1,554	1,144	410 (+ 2)	.358	1.40	25.0	24.5
1964	410	1,192	1,602	1,184	418 (+ 8)	.353	1.40	23.3	23.4
1965	418	1,499	1,917	1,328	584 (+166)	.439	1.62	16.7	14.6
1966	584	1,200	1,784	1,378	406 (−178)	.295	1.34	24.4	25.8
1967									
Estimate 1	406	1,304	1,710	1,378**	332 (− 74)**	.241	1.24	28.5	28.7
Estimate 2	406	1,304	1,710	1,415**	295 (−111)**	.208			

* The cocoa crop year runs from October through September.
** Figures estimated by Mr. Shishko during 1967.
† Computed by the authors.
SOURCE: Gill & Duffus, Ltd., London, monthly report, February 1967, except as noted.

We move closer to an econometric analysis when we ask ourselves: How much premium does this 1967 deficit of 75,000 tons warrant over the average 1966 price of 24.4¢? Our answer, based on experience rather than on any exact method, might take account of the fact that a stock change of 75,000 tons is about midway between the very large stock changes of 1961, 1965, and 1966, and the very small ones of 1962, 1963, and 1964 (see the table). Accordingly, we might expect a medium-sized price change for the year, which our recollection might suggest would be 3¢ to 5¢—in this case, in an upward direction.

3. Finally, we might try to determine, with the help of more specific measuring rules, just what price would be warranted on the basis of the particular supply and demand conditions indicated in 1967. We can do this in a generally more sophisticated way.

Let us start by suggesting a relatively simple econometric approach to estimating a 1967 price, based on the statistics shown in the preceding table.

A Simple Econometric Approach

What forces might we expect to determine the price of cocoa? Each new cocoa season begins with a heritage of the past: a certain rate of world consumption and a carryover from previous seasons. Added to the old supply (carryover) is the level of new-crop production, which starts in October but is usually not estimated very accurately until the following January or February.

It seems reasonable to suppose that, from an economic point of view, the price of cocoa depends primarily on the level of total supply in relation to the level of consumption prevailing at the start of the season. When total supply is large relative to our initial consumption estimate, we may expect price during the new year to be relatively low. Conversely, when total supply is small relative to our initial consumption estimate, we may expect prices to be high.

We can logically translate this theory into a statement which lends itself to predictive use. The price of cocoa depends upon the supply ratio (or, expressing this in symbols):

$$P_c : \frac{S}{C_{t-1}.}$$

P_c is the price of cocoa (Spot Ghana, January-September average)
:   means "depends upon"
S is total supply (carryover plus production)
C_{t-1} is consumption in the year the cocoa season begins

This equation states a basic price-estimating relationship; however, it does not specify the mathematical form which this relationship might take. In practice, the econometrician must decide which form is appropriate (e.g., a linear, semilog, log, log-inverse, or other mathematical function). Here we shall simply consider, by inspection, what sort of curve seems to fit the data.

For reasons which will be clear later, Figure 32 is called a "scatter diagram." Each small circle (or dot) registers a pair of related values: (1) the supply ratio, and (2) the price of cocoa (January-September average price) during a single year (labeled 1957, 1958, or 1959, as the case may be). For example, we see from the statistical table (p. 169) that, in 1957, the supply ratio was 1.35 while the cocoa price was 27.3¢. This pair of values is shown as one dot in Figure 32. You will find this dot where a

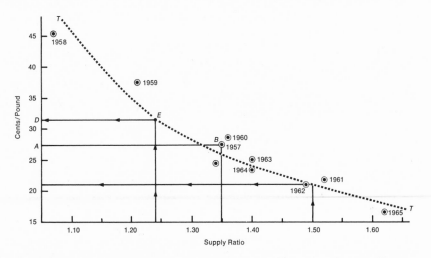

Fig. 32. Scatter diagram showing the relationship between the price of cocoa (January–September average) and the supply ratio for the period 1957–1965.

horizontal line *AB,* starting from 27.3¢, intersects a vertical line *BC* drawn upward from the supply ratio 1.35.

Looking at our scatter diagram we see that the dots (representing yearly observations) conform closely to the curve labeled *TT.* In this case, the curve has been fitted to the dots by inspection; that is, visually and subjectively. To be more precise, the curve could be calculated mathematically. In either case, the line of fit (*TT*) gives us an estimate of the average price to expect for any given supply ratio. For example, if, in a given year, we project the supply ratio to be 1.50, then Figure 32 tells us to expect an average price of approximately 21¢. (To see this, start at a supply ratio of

1.50 on the horizontal axis; follow the arrow up to the estimating line *TT*, then across to a price reading of 21¢.)

Whether the curve is fitted by inspection or by computer, the resulting analysis expresses the simple correlation between two variables: the supply ratio and the price. Given a particular supply ratio, we can estimate the average price, either by a direct reading from the graph or from a mathematical formula which is simply the equation of a line similar to *TT*.

In either case, some of the dots will not lie exactly on the line, either because there are imperfections in our data or, more likely, because some price-influencing forces have not been included in our analysis. The wider the scatter of dots (or observations) around our estimating line *TT*, the less perfect the correlation between the two variables we are including. If the dots cluster very closely around the line, we think we may have explained most of the cause of variation in our dependent variable (in this case, the price of cocoa). We then say the "correlation coefficient" is high.

In Figure 32, the dots are fairly close to the line, and we may therefore suppose that changes in the supply ratio explain a large part of the variation in the price of cocoa (i.e., the supply ratio is highly correlated to the price of cocoa). Let us examine the forecast which this analysis might have yielded in 1967.

1967 FORECAST

We note from the table (p. 169) that, as measured in February 1967, the supply ratio was 1.24. As indicated in Figure 32, this implies a price forecast of about 31.50¢ for spot Ghana cocoa, average January-September. (We read this price estimate by starting at the supply ratio 1.24, and moving along the lines marked FED to the price axis.)

Would a 1967 price forecast of 31.50¢ have helped us to trade cocoa successfully during the crop year 1966–1967? That depends largely upon when we developed the forecast. As we see from Figure 33, a 31.50¢ price estimate would probably have been quite useful if we had it in November or early December 1966. For, at that early time in the season, the prevailing spot price for Ghana cocoa was 6¢ to 8¢ lower than the forecast. Recall, however, that the 31.50¢ forecast was based on Gill & Duffus data published in February 1967. Would our price forecast have been radically different if predicted on data available in November or December 1966?

Assume (as, in fact, was the case) that the estimates of 1967 world supply and demand, published by Gill & Duffus in November and early December 1966, would not have drastically altered the price forecast of 31.50¢ basis spot Ghana. As long as one accepted this data, the analysis would have pointed to a price well above the prevailing market level. The incentive to buy would have been clear.

It is essential to point out, however, that in November-December 1966, some traders were deterred from buying cocoa because their supply estimates were, in fact, different from those published by Gill & Duffus. In some quarters, carryover stocks in cocoa were thought to be well above the levels estimated by Gill & Duffus. In addition, early African crop movement was relatively heavy in 1966–1967, leading some traders to expect a larger production than had been forecast.

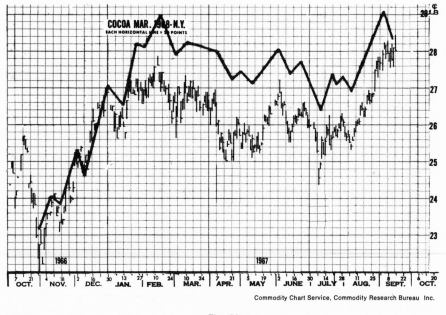

Commodity Chart Service, Commodity Research Bureau Inc.

Fig. 33.

If these other estimates were correct, the supply ratio for 1967 would be higher than was indicated in the table (based on Gill & Duffus data). Accordingly, the price estimate for 1967 would have to be lower. In this case, the price estimate, based on the high supply assumption proved to be 3¢ below that based on Gill & Duffus data—a significant difference.

The moral of this story is plain. The data we use relating to cocoa supply and other key economic variables may well be as important as—or more important than—the type of analysis we use. *Econometrics can only be a useful servant to an enlightened master,* one who has an in-depth understanding of his commodity, good sources of information, and carefully evaluated data.

Let us turn back to Figure 33 and see whether our analysis would have guided us correctly even if we had accepted the higher production and stocks estimates. In reality this change proved to be equivalent to an increase in the supply ratio from 1.24 to 1.29. Even so, the price forecast derived from our diagram turned out to be 28.50¢, which was still some 4¢ above the spot price prevailing in November and early December. It appears, therefore, that even in this instance, a relatively simple econometric analysis may well have led us to initiate a long position just as an upswing was getting underway. Would it also have been helpful in determining when to liquidate this position?

A Problem of Timing

From mid-November 1966 to mid-February 1967, the spot Ghana price climbed from 24¢ to a high of 30.50¢ (as one can see in Figure 33). We recall that, using Gill & Duffus data, our analysis pointed to an average Ghana price of 31.50¢, but, based on higher supply figures, the same analysis yielded a price forecast of 28.50¢. At this point (February 1967), the difference between these two forecasts is quite significant. For, on the basis of the first forecast (31.50¢), it would probably have appeared reasonable to remain long when the spot price reached a high of 30.50¢ in mid-February. On the other hand, using the lower forecast, it might have seemed prudent to liquidate at (or before) the 30.50¢ high.

Even on the basis of the lower price forecast, however, the decision to liquidate would not have been unequivocal. Recall that the projected price—in this case, 28.50¢—represents the anticipated average price for the period January-September. Of course, significant price fluctuations will occur in the course of the year above and below the average price. Thus, if the projected average price is 28.50¢, the market high might well be 31¢ to 33¢. The fact that, in February, the market surpassed the 28.50¢ level would not, in itself, have been a compelling signal to liquidate, although it might have suggested taking partial profits on the rally.

It appears, therefore, that econometric analysis may not provide an entirely satisfactory or definitive rule concerning the timing of purchases and sales. Although subject to errors of its own, technical analysis may offer some assistance on this crucial question of timing. Thus, in following cocoa in February 1967, a technician would likely have been impressed by the very high open interest which prevailed at that time, this open position being heavily weighted with speculative longs. Moreover, the bullish side of the cocoa story had been well known for months and, possibly, had been discounted. To the technician, the market's inability to advance in March might have been construed as a further sign of trouble. Perhaps this technical viewpoint, combined with the econometric price forecast, would have permitted a more correct market assessment than either method used alone.

There are ways to handle this problem of timing without borrowing the technician's tools described in Chapters 10 and 11. The fundamentalist has available the following options.

1. He may combine his annual average price forecast with a separately estimated seasonal index, thus giving him a monthly or quarterly price criterion. This method can only be useful when the seasonal pattern itself is quite consistent; one does not find this to be true very often.

2. Instead of estimating an average price for the season, he may seek to project the high and low points of the price move. Econometricians have employed this approach with some success in the grain markets.

3. Alternatively, the analyst (still using an econometric approach) may adopt a narrower forecast interval. Instead of projecting the price average for the season (or for nine months, as in the above cocoa example), he may develop a price estimate on a quarterly basis.

In theory, we might even hope to develop an econometric analysis which would forecast prices every month, or every week, or every day. If that were possible, we would solve our timing problem altogether. In practice, however, as long as our analysis is based on broad supply and demand statistics, it is usually impossible to narrow our "fine tuning" to below a quarterly time period.

Let us consider briefly how a quarterly analysis might be developed and applied. Since we have already studied cocoa in 1967, it will be convenient to again refer to this commodity and this period.

COCOA IN THIRD QUARTER 1967

Since the cocoa crop year runs from October through September, the third quarter of the calendar year is also the final quarter of the cocoa season. The price in that final quarter may be thought to reflect two main influences: (1) The size of the remaining supply (carryover), measured in relation to the prevailing level of consumption (i.e., the stock ratio), and (2) expectations as to the supply and demand outlook for the approaching season.

The first of these variables—the stock ratio—is already familiar, since it closely resembles the supply ratio which was used earlier to estimate the average cocoa price for January-September. At the end of the season, this stock ratio is a particularly crucial variable in many commodities; in one simple expression, it sums up what is statistically essential about a commodity's supply and demand position before allowing for new crop factors.

In price determination, the future either works or contends with the past. As an old season nears its end, expectations for new crop supply and demand play an increasingly important role. Determining which statistic to use in measuring expectations is one of the more difficult problems of econometrics. For simplicity's sake, we shall assume here that the expectation variable (E) is represented by a trend forecast of new crop production. Our theory for the determination of the third quarter price can be expressed in the symbolic shorthand to which we have become accustomed:

$$P_{III} : S, E.$$

That is, the average spot price of cocoa in the third quarter depends upon the stock ratio (S) and some expectation variable (E).

In our previous example, we had just two variables (P and S), and it was rather easy to show the relation between these variables in one graph or scatter diagram. (We measured this supply ratio on the horizontal axis, and the price on the vertical axis.) As the number of variables increases, it becomes increasingly difficult to apply a graphic method of analysis. Instead, the econometrician relies on a statistical method called "multiple correlation analysis" to estimate just how our dependent variable, price in this case, is determined. (For an explanation of this method, refer to any of the statistics references listed in the Bibliography.)

The result of this multiple correlation analysis will be an equation which, in simple (linear) form, may be stated as follows:[2]

$$P = a - b(S) - c(E)$$

or to illustrate, using numerical values for a, b, and c:

$$P = 145 - 80S - .07E.$$

What our correlation analysis has done is estimate for us the constants: $a = 145$, $b = 80$, and $c = .07$. It is the constants, b and c, which express the average relationship between our variables. Thus, the constant, $b = 80$, tells us how much a change in the supply ratio S will affect the price P. For example, if our stock ratio goes up from one-quarter of a year's coverage (.25) to one-half a year's coverage (.50), the change in this S ratio is .25. Our coefficient, $b = -80$, tells us that the price change will be -80 times the change in the stock ratio, or $-80 \times .25 = -20¢$ (i.e., price will fall 20¢). In the same way, our c (coefficient), $-.07$, tells us how much the price is estimated to change in the third quarter for every 1,000-ton change in expected new crop production. Thus, if this production estimate is raised

2. These values are purely illustrative, having been selected to facilitate an understanding of the kind of calculation involved in the accompanying correlation analysis. To obtain true figures involves elaborating a specific statistical analysis, beyond the scope of the chapter.

10,000 tons, our equation tells us that the price should decline by .07 × 10 = .7¢.

Turning back to the cocoa situation in 1967, we would like to note that an analysis of the kind described above forecast a third quarter 1967 average price of between 27¢ and 28¢, basis spot Ghana cocoa. Appropriately, this forecast projected a downward trend from the prices generally prevailing in the first and second quarter. The point of interest here is that, in actuality, the third quarter started about in line with the projected values, but did not remain so compliant. In August-September, estimates of the new crop outlook took a sharp turn for the worse. As expectations changed, so did the market price.

It would be convenient to say that, by merely "plugging in" new values for E in our equation, we consistently got a forecast price which encouraged us to buy before everyone else did. In this case, we enjoyed no such success. The forecast price and the market price moved up hand in hand, so that there was generally no clear econometric incentive to buy.

It is perhaps some comfort to point out that, in July, when market action seemed very bearish, both the average season forecast (29.50¢) and the third-quarter forecast (27¢ to 28¢) were above the prevailing market price. In this case, econometrics may have helped to prevent the error of going short, even if it did not clearly prescribe buying in anticipation of the August-September price rise.

The first quarter of each new cocoa season (October-December) is usually a period when crop estimates are fickle, changing from one week—or one day—to the next. This is when timely and reliable production information is likely to be more valuable than the most sophisticated price forecast. Econometrics may still provide us with a useful price criterion, indicating whether the market has overreacted or underreacted to a particular supply estimate. However, this price criterion will, of necessity, shift to reflect variations in the underlying crop estimates.

At this time of year, when crop "guesstimating" is a universal and vital sport, we may sometimes advance our forecasting goals by tackling the problem of production before we deal with the dependent variable, price. Econometrics may sometimes be used to analyze weather information, data on crop movement, or other crop news, as an aid to judging the probable size of production. The production estimate derived in this way may then be fed into a price-forecasting equation.

First Lesson Reviewed

So far, this chapter has taken us on the first lap of our excursion into econometric territory. Let us pause now to recall the highlights of this journey, and to review some of the lessons we have learned.

First, we saw that econometrics provides a systematic method of analyzing selected supply and demand fundamentals. Essentially, this approach involves estimating how much weight certain price-influencing factors have had in the past, and applying these weights to project future price moves. This projection can be valid only if the relationships considered in our analysis have not substantially changed.

The starting point of our econometric analysis is a theory of price determination. Good results can only spring from sound theory. But this is only one of many considerations affecting accuracy. Our econometric analysis is not better than the statistics upon which this analysis is based. Major errors in forecasting have often arisen from uncritical acceptance of published data.

Like other types of fundamental analysis, econometrics is best suited to estimating whether a commodity is overvalued or undervalued. It is harder for this kind of analysis to determine whether this over- or undervaluation will increase. A market that is too high today by 1¢ may be too high tomorrow by 3¢ or 5¢. To help decide when to buy or sell, we may fall back on charting or other forms of technical analysis. Or we may seek to "fine tune" our econometric method by narrowing our forecast period from an annual to quarterly basis, or by incorporating a seasonal analysis which estimates the highs and lows of a move.

In any case, it is quite clear that price is not determined solely by the statistical (supply and demand) data. It is also influenced by technical factors, by people's opinions as to what the facts really are and, above all, by changing expectations for the future.

Econometrics enables us to explicitly summarize those factors in a commodity situation which lend themselves to numerical description. The answers provided by econometrics have the virtue of being specific. But they are neither as precise nor as objective as might appear at first sight. For the underlying assumptions (such as the choice of data) have a great influence on the resulting forecast. This choice of assumptions (and data) is, at least in part, subjective. In fact, it is typical that surface exactitude conceals many a coarse approximation, or valiant surmise.

Let us avoid the fallacy of thinking that, because we have put our ideas in mathematical form, and have relied on computer methods of calculation, our results necessarily acquire immunity from error. Whatever form of statistical analysis we use, we are not spared the need to exercise careful judgment. For no amount of statistical refinement can replace a wide and enlightened appreciation and application of all elements in a commodity situation.

Towards a More Advanced Analysis

We have said that a futures market tends to discount all that is known and all that is anticipated about a particular commodity situation. If this discounting were perfect, there would be no need to build an economic model (or analysis) to explain price. The market itself would be acting as a model, and would be telling us exactly what price was justified on the basis of the available information.

In reality the market is not always right. That is, it does not always correctly interpret a situation and register a price equal to that which a theoretically perfect model might yield. Sometimes the market reflects a collective misjudgment; at other times it misses because of technical conditions (such as a chain of liquidation or covering) which displace price from fundamental value.

Essentially, the trader who bases his analysis on fundamental factors is seeking a situation in which there is an error in the collective price evaluation of a particular commodity. He must have reason to think that his model is more accurate than the consensus of all traders as expressed by the market price. This reason is more persuasive if the trader's model (analysis) is built on convincing economic theory, sound data, and good statistical technique.

Our discussion of econometrics, so far, has been based on a simple and largely intuitive approach to explaining price change. To refine our methods, we must go beyond this basic approach. We must examine the contribution of economic theory to that joint economic and statistical undertaking known as econometrics.

What can economics teach us about the way to formulate price analysis? Why might one type of analysis constitute a better market model (explanatory system) than another?

On Model Building

Our goal now is to introduce the reader to more advanced econometric models. The student of commodity markets cannot be a master builder of such models, but he can hope to penetrate the veil of mathematical symbols and to glimpse the logic which underlies them.

To the econometrician, a model is a mathematical structure designed to show how a given economic sector functions. Like a model auto or railroad, the economic model is a replica of reality. Unlike the miniature car or train, the economic model cannot hope to be a perfect or even near-perfect representation of the particular phenomenon which it attempts to portray.

The economic model is, of necessity, an abstraction—confining its attention to those elements of a situation which are judged most important. Further, the economic model includes relationships which do not hold exactly; it must therefore make allowance for errors which may be more-or-less random. (In the econometrician's parlance, his model is "stochastic," that is, it involves chance elements.)

Building a model entails several crucial steps:

1. The first step is to analyze and interpret the situation under review, identifying the main cause-and-effect relationships.

2. Next, this interpretation must be expressed in a set of statements (or equations) which shows the structure of relationships in the way which is most plausible from the point of view of economic theory and experience.

3. Finally, we estimate the constant terms or weights, which indicate the specific links between the different elements in our structure. These weights tell us how much one variable affects another, and they transform our set of structural relationships into a specific working model.

The reader will, no doubt, recognize that we followed these same steps in developing our simple single-equation analysis of cocoa. Thus, in explaining the price of cocoa in the final quarter of the crop year, our procedure was as follows:

1. First, we interpreted the main causal relationships. We decided that the price of cocoa in the last quarter of the season is principally dependent on end-of-season stock coverage and new crop expectations.

2. Next, we expressed this idea in the form of a single equation:

$$P : S, E$$

That is, price depends on the stock ratio (S) and on an expectation variable (E).

3. Finally, we indicated that by statistical procedures, it is possible to estimate the constants a, b, and c in the equation $P = a + b(S) + c(E)$, thus showing how much a change in S or E will affect P.

Typically, an econometric model is expressed in the form of one or more mathematical equations. However, as we observed earlier, a simple model can also be portrayed graphically. Thus, in projecting an average seasonal price for cocoa, we saw that the price estimate could be read directly from Figure 32.

In examining models of greater complexity, we shall of necessity lean increasingly on mathematical formulations. To make these formulations easier to understand, we shall write them as statements in everyday language as well as in mathematical symbols. We shall also make use of graphic analysis where this seems helpful. In short, we shall portray models in symbols, in words, and in pictures.

As noted previously, our model building should be rooted in proper economic theory. It will be helpful in this connection to recall some lessons of elementary economics, and especially to refresh our memory as to the meaning of the supply and demand curves which embellish every economics primer.

Supply and Demand

Typical demand and supply curves are shown in Figure 34 (A and B). In (A), each dot (*a, b, c* . . . etc.) is an estimate of the quantity of a given commodity which consumers are willing to purchase at a given price. Dot *"a"* tells us that, at the price $P = 50$, consumers would buy 100 units of the commodity in question; dot *"g"* indicates that, at $P = 20$, purchases rise to 140 units, and so on. Given estimates of this kind, the economist theorizes that there is a continuous curve D_1D_1 which portrays the demand for this commodity at every possible price. He speaks of this as a "demand curve." (This expression is usually applied to curves of varying degrees of flatness up to and including a straight line.)

It is important to note that the theoretical demand curve shows a complete set of possible price-purchase combinations at one very limited time interval. In practice, however, it is not feasible to measure how much consumers are willing to buy at varied prices in such a narrow interval. The econometrician must estimate this instantaneous demand curve from a series of observations showing how much consumers actually bought at different prices at markedly different points of time. At best, this estimated demand curve is an imperfect rendition of the theoretical or "true" demand curve. This imperfection, one hopes, can be minimized. For, as we shall see later, the accuracy with which we estimate the demand curve is often a critical factor in our price forecasting work.

The demand curve in (A) of Figure 34, like any normal, well-behaved member of its class, slopes downward to the right. In other words, as price declines, the quantity which is demanded increases along the path marked out by the demand curve. This assumes that the demand curve itself is immovable; it does not shift due to any outside factor, such as a change in consumer income or taste, or a price cut or increase in some substitute commodity.

In reality, the demand curve is not inert. Shifts in demand do occur due to factors such as those mentioned above. For example, if consumer incomes rise, the demand curve D_1D_1 in Figure 34 may move to the position plotted as D_2D_2. Such an upward shift means that consumers will

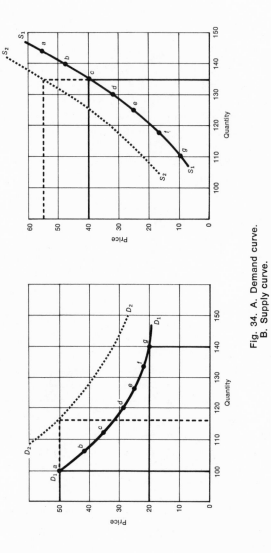

Fig. 34. A. Demand curve.
B. Supply curve.

buy more at any given price. Thus (referring again to Figure 34), the quantity purchased at $P = 50$ rises from 100 to 116 as the demand curve shifts up from D_1D_1 to D_2D_2. When an economist speaks of a rise in demand, he generally alludes to this kind of upward shift in the demand curve, and not to an increase in consumption along the demand curve brought about by a price change alone.

The slope (or steepness) of the demand curve at any point tells us how "price-elastic" demand is, that is, how much demand will change percentagewise for each 1 percent change in price. If D_1D_1 is nearly vertical, then demand is very inelastic; a price change will have little effect on the quantity demanded. On the other hand, if D_1D_1 has very little slope (being nearly horizontal), then we infer that a small price change prompts a large reaction in the quantity demanded.

Economists devote appreciable effort to estimating demand elasticities. The reason for this should now be plain. Let us say that production of commodity X falls and there is a small supply deficit. If demand is highly elastic, it will take very little price increase to bring usage down enough to eliminate the deficit. On the other hand, if demand is very inelastic, it may require a large price rise to evoke the same reduction in demand. Thus, the degree of demand elasticity will, at times, largely determine the extent of a price move.

The supply curve and its properties may be portrayed in a manner quite analogous to that used to describe demand. The main difference, of course, is that the supply curve normally slopes upward; this upward slope indicates that, as the price of a commodity rises, the quantity produced (or offered by sellers) tends to increase also. Apart from any price change, however, the supply curve itself may shift. For example, in (B) of Figure 34, the supply curve S_1S_1 might move up to S_2S_2 if sellers' costs increase, or if higher prices on other commodities divert resources away from production of the commodity in question.

Here again, a very steep supply curve indicates an inelastic response to price change. That is, even when price changes substantially, the quantity offered by suppliers changes little. This inelastic behavior is, in fact, typical of many commodities, particularly "tree crops" like cocoa and coffee, whose acreage and tree population are mainly determined by prices prevailing 5 to 15 years earlier. In such cases, supply mainly reflects lagged prices plus current weather conditions, and is largely inelastic with respect to the current price.

Even in these cases, there is usually some small supply reaction to the current price, since harvesting may vary in thoroughness and completeness according to the prevailing price level. However, to facilitate study of a very simple economic model, we may start with a hypothetical case in which acreage is entirely predetermined by prices from previous years, and crop yield depends on weather. In this case, the supply curve is vertical.

A SAMPLE MODEL

A sample model incorporating this vertical supply curve is pictured in Figure 35, and is also explained in words and symbols. Let us say that the commodity in question is oranges.

Basic Statement	Specific Mathematical Form
Demand is a function of (depends upon) price alone. $D = f(P)$.	THE MODEL (1) $D = 300 - 50P$. (2) $S = k^* = D$.
Supply in this period is "given" at some level "k" (determined by outside factors) independently of the current price. Equilibrium occurs at that price at which all of the given supply is absorbed by consumers.	Derived Equation (3) $P = \dfrac{300 - S}{50}$

* Where k is a level determined by acreage and weather.

Let us look first at the model as it is expressed in Figure 35. It is evident that, if we know production (S), we can at once read off expected price P_1. Thus, if production S_1 at 100 million boxes, moves up line S_1 to the point where it intersects D_1D_1 (at this point, D_1D_1 tells us that 100 million boxes will be absorbed, no more, no less), reading to the left of this intersection, we see the price will be $4 per box. Similarly, if production turned out to be 150 million boxes, we would see (reading along S_2 up and across) that the equilibrium price would be $3.00; or at $S_3 = 50$ million boxes, price (P) would be $5.00. In this simple model, price depends on production alone.

Exactly the same results would be obtained from our mathematical version of this model. Here we start with two equations to express the model:

(1) the demand equation: $D = 300 - 50P$, which is simply the mathematical way of writing "all points along the line D_1D_1."

(2) $S = D$; the statement that in equilibrium, supply (determined from outside the model) equals demand.

Since $S = D$, we can substitute S for D in equation (1), and this gives us a single equation to sum up our model:

$$S = 300 - 50P.$$

By simple algebra this can be rewritten as

$$P = \frac{300 - S}{50}$$

(This is simply our demand equation juggled about a bit and with S substituted for D.)

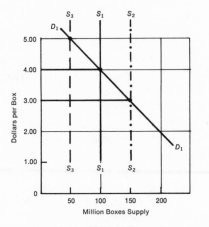

Fig. 35. Vertical supply curve.

Now we can use this single equation to compute an expected price for any given level of supply S. Thus for $S = 100$ we have $P = \dfrac{300 - 100}{50} = 4$.

The answer ($4 per box) is the same as that obtained from Figure 35. Try selecting your own hypothetical supply value and reading the corresponding price from Figure 35; then calculate it from the equation.

In this simple case, we had one statistical problem: that was to estimate the demand curve D_1D_1. Once we accomplished this, the rest was easy. For any level of supply, we could then determine price as that value necessary to bring demand to the indicated supply level.

The problem we have not yet examined is the actual statistical method by which the econometrician estimates the demand equation. How does he know where to draw the line D_1D_1 in the diagram? Or, what amounts to the same thing, how does he know that in the equation $D = a+b\ (P)$, a is 300 and b is 50 as in the case above? We have already suggested the answer while sidestepping the technicalities of statistical method. The econometrician starts with a series of observations: Let us say that in year 1, 100 million boxes were absorbed at a price of \$3.88; in year 2, 125 million at a price of \$3.55 etc. Each of these price-quantity observations may be expressed as a dot on a scatter diagram (as shown Figure 32). The econometrician draws a line of average relationship through these dots (observations) to estimate the demand curve D_1D_1. He may do this by inspection (as we did in Figure 32), or mathematically using simple methods outlined in most elementary statistics books. In either case, he is estimating the simple relationship between two variables, D and P.

SAMPLE MODEL: MODIFIED

We have assumed, so far, that the demand curve D_1D_1, like a fixed star, keeps to one place in its graphic firmament. In reality, we would expect this curve's position to shift in response to certain nonprice factors which affect usage of most commodities. Outstanding among these is consumer income.

Consumer income is really a composite variable—it is the product of population and per capita earnings. The econometrician often prefers to analyze the effect of the two subvariables separately. However, we shall take the liberty, in this introductory discourse, of considering one variable, aggregate income.

The demand curve for oranges may be expected to shift upward each year that consumer income grows. The change this makes in our simple model can easily be shown graphically, as in Figure 36. As income rises from year 1 to year 2, and again in year 3, demand shifts up from D_1D_1 to D_2D_2 and D_3D_3 respectively. For any given supply S_1, the equilibrium price shifts in a corresponding manner from P_1 to P_2, and then P_3. However, without an income scale in Figure 36, it is not so easy to measure just how much any change in income affects price.

There are graphic ways of handling this problem as the number of variables increase, but it is much simpler to rely on a mathematical formulation of the problem. Thus, to introduce the income variable into our mathematical statement, we need only a slight revision in the demand equation from our previous model. This revision expresses the fact that usage depends on income as well as on price. We say:[3] demand depends on price (P) and income (Y)

3. This is another way of saying "demand is a function of price and income."

$$D = f(P, Y)$$

or more specifically (assuming a linear relationship)

$$D = a + b(P) + c(Y).$$

Our statistical task, once again, is to estimate the constants a, b, and c in the demand equation. We may do this by utilizing a procedure for multiple correlation analysis, which we find in a statistical handbook. We apply this technique to yearly observations of income, price, and consumption. For illustrative purposes, let us assume that the resulting equation is:

$$D = 295 - 50(P) + .01(Y).$$

That is, we found that $a = 295$, $b = -50$, and $c = .01$.

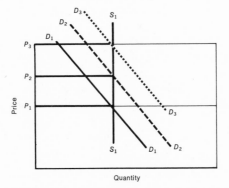

Fig. 36. Upward shifting demand curve.

If, as before, all of the supply S is determined outside the model (S is not influenced by current price or income), and if in equilibrium, all of S is consumed exactly ($S = D$), then the one demand equation is all we need for forecasting purposes. Assume that, in the period under study, we expect supply S to be 100 million boxes and consumer income Y (expressed in billions) to be 500. Then, since $D = S = 100$ (million boxes):

$$D = 295 - 50P + .01(Y)$$
$$100 = 295 - 50P + .01(500)$$
$$50P = 200$$
$$P = 4 \ (\$ \ per \ box).$$

In this example, as in the case of most agricultural commodities, the effect of income change is usually modest. Often, it exerts a small incremental effect each year. For agricultural commodities, in particular, the biggest single source of price change is usually a variation in free supply. (See Figures 35 and 36 for a visual indication of how shifts in S affect price.)

Where free supply variations are effectively dampened, price changes also tend to be narrow. We see this clearly in United States' controlled commodities, such as "domestic sugar" and, to a lesser degree, in world commodities such as coffee, which have been significantly influenced by international commodity agreements.

Although shifts in demand may not cause wide price fluctuations in most agricultural commodities, such shifts are often the prime movers of metal prices. For the metals, shifts in demand mainly reflect variations in the output of metal using products. Therefore, in a metal demand equation, we ordinarily use a measure of output instead of the income variable incorporated in the demand equation for agricultural goods. Often, the output index used to explain metal demand is the Federal Reserve Board Index of Industrial Production.

Business cycles (or the fluctuations which go under that name) usually entail marked variations in industrial output, but much smaller changes (and rarely declines) in consumer income. For this reason cyclical factors exercise a pronounced effect on metals prices while they exert a much smaller effect on most farm prices (especially in an era of agricultural price supports).

In the case of the metals, our simple model, modified to allow for demand shifts, would incorporate an output variable: Demand depends on (is a function of) price and output

$$D = f(P, O).$$

Use of an income or output variable is only one of many variations we must introduce as we seek to make our models more realistic. Particularly in the case of metals, consumption is often less dependent on today's price than on yesterday's price. The reason for this is that consumption habits in metals tend to be established over long periods and to persist as such. If aluminum is cheap relative to copper, the ratio of aluminum to copper use in some applications will tend to rise gradually. This change may be significant if the aluminum-copper price ratio remains low for several years, but the current price ratio may have little effect on today's use pattern.

Our demand equation for metals, therefore, can often be improved by incorporating this "lag effect." We write this revised form as follows: Demand depends on lagged price and output

$$D = f(P_{t-a}, O)$$

where O is industrial output and P_{t-a} is price going back "a" periods of time.[4]

There is yet another important element in our demand equation for metals. That element is the impact of a changing technology on metal use. This is a very hard factor to quantify; it often makes demand analysis for metals more challenging than for those agricultural commodities which enjoy relatively stable use patterns.

Economists sometimes handle this technology factor by assuming that there is a regular trend in technology which, each year, adds to or subtracts from use of the metal in question. This may be expressed mathematically by incorporating a time-trend variable "t" in the demand equation. Very much like an index number of income or population, t is even more invariant in its growth. We could let t be 100 in year 1, 101 in year 2, 102 in year 3, etc.

In a rare instance, growth of demand for a particular commodity may be extremely regular. It is not influenced by price, nor by income or output. It increases by a constant amount (or percentage) each year. In this case, we say that demand is a function of time alone, or $D = f(t)$. This is merely the formal way of saying: "To explain demand, just look at its trend and forget everything else."

It would be more usual, however, to assume that a trend factor (perhaps due to technological innovation) operates together with other factors causing demand change. Thus, in the case of metals, we might write:

$$D = f(P_{t-a}, O, t).$$

Demand depends on lagged price, (P_{t-a}), some output index (O), and a time-trend variable (t).

Let's make this a bit more explicit by looking at a simple version of a copper model.

ILLUSTRATIVE MODEL: COPPER

As we suggested earlier, copper demand may depend not only on the price of copper but also on the price of aluminum, which is substitutable for copper in certain applications. However, it may take several years for the copper-aluminum price ratio to exert any appreciable effect on copper demand. We may incorporate these ideas in a copper model, as follows:

4. The subscript t in P_t represents time. $t-o$ means the current period; $t-1$ means 1 period back; $t-2$, two periods; and $t-a$, "a" periods back.

Mathematical Form	*Basic Statement*
$$D = f\ (Pc, \sum_{t-a}^{t-b} \frac{Pc}{Pa}, O, t).$$ $$S = D.$$	Demand for copper depends on the current copper price (Pc), the copper-aluminum price ratio in past years ($\frac{Pc}{Pa}$), output of copper-using industries (O), and a trend variable (t). Supply is assumed to be determined outside the model and equilibrium occurs where supply and demand are equal.

You will notice that we have introduced a new symbol in the demand equation, the symbol Σ. By itself, Σ means "summation"; $t-a$ and $t-b$ refer to a period of time going back "a" to "b" years. In other words, the price which is relevant to determining copper demand is the price ratio of copper-to-aluminum summed up over a period of "a-to-b" years ago.

The major oversimplification in this copper model is on the supply side. We have assumed (above) that supply is given independently of price, and also that total supply may be considered to have a single uniform origin.

In copper and other metals, however, our analysis is complicated by the existence of two distinct supply sources: one, new production; the other, the return flow from metal of scrap origin. In a more complex model, we might wish to evaluate each of these supply streams separately. For example, in dealing with supply of newly mined copper, our equation might include two main variables: (1) mine capacity, and (2) current price, where price is considered as the determinant of rate of capacity utilization. Even with a sophisticated model, we shall probably have to make separate allowance for changes in supply brought about by strikes, wars, or other unpredictable events affecting mining activity.

In our pursuit of increasing realism, we must also consider some neglected complications affecting our demand analysis. First, we have assumed throughout that it is possible or desirable to consider consumption of each commodity as if it were a single monolithic entity. This may be entirely satisfactory with a single-use commodity like coffee, but it has shortcomings in a commodity like copper, in which uses are very clearly differentiated. One approach is to set up separate demand equations to analyze consumption in each major end-use area (e.g., electrical, construction, aircraft, and military, etc.). Alternatively, one might adopt an input-output approach, in which the amount of copper moving as an input to each user-industry is measured in relation to the output of that industry.

A second complication in our demand analysis is as pertinent to coffee as it is to copper. This concerns the twofold character of demand. A commodity is bought for direct use or for consumption. But it is also bought for storage (except in the case of highly perishable goods). Variations in storage demand largely reflect changes in price expectations. As we suggested earlier (in our discussion of cocoa), a realistic model must pay heed to the persuasive role of changing expectations. This influence can be taken into account by incorporating a storage-demand equation in our model.

A Universal Model

Our concept of model building has now advanced in several significant respects. We have seen that:

(1) Demand (or supply) may be determined by lagged prices as well as by current prices.

(2) Consumption may depend on the price of competing commodities as well as on the price of the commodity in question.

(3) Consumption also is a function of income/output variables and, possibly, of trend factors which may or may not fully express substitution technology.

(4) In addition to demand for use, allowance must be made (wherever carryover supplies exist) for storage demand.

(5) Supply may sometimes be treated as predetermined. However, it may also be necessary to incorporate a supply equation in which production is seen to depend upon price, capacity or acreage, and other variables such as weather.

Utilizing these concepts, we can build an archetypical or "universal" model as a guide in analyzing a variety of commodities.

This universal model might have the following form:

Mathematical Statement	*Verbal Statement*
(1) $$Dc = f\ (P,\ P_{t-a},\ Z,\ P_r,\ t).$$	Demand for consumption purposes (Dc) depends on the current price of the commodity, lagged price (P_{t-a}), an output or income variable (Z), the price of some rival good (P_r), and a time trend variable (t).
(2) $$Ds = f\ (P_{t+1} - P).$$	Demand for stocks (Ds) depends on the extent to which the expected price next year (P_{t+1}) exceeds or falls short of the current price (P).

(3)
$$P_{t+1} = f(P, E).$$

As one hypothesis, the expected price depends on current price and on some expectational variable (E) such as the first estimate of next year's production.

(4)
$$S = f(P, A, W).$$

Production (S) depends on the current price (P), acreage or capacity (A), and on weather or some other variable (W).

(5)
$$Ds_{t-1} + S = C + D_s.$$

This last equation is an identity, or exact relationship. It says: beginning stocks plus production equals consumption plus ending stocks.

Let us say we have 10 years of data covering all of the variables shown in the above model for commodity X. Let us further assume that we have a competent statistician to help us fit the model. Our statistician applies a statistical method which considers all of these equations simultaneously, and then estimates the a's, b's, and c's (the average weights) in each equation which levels all of the variables together. Although the detailed statistical method is beyond the scope of this discussion, there is no reason why the reader cannot understand the basic structure of the model.

This model is more than just a specific tool for estimating supply, demand, and price; it is also a general guide to objective economic thinking about a commodity. It leads one to organize one's concepts, and provides a logical framework for considering what omissions or conceptual inadequacies can affect our fundamental interpretation of a commodity situation.

We should note that this complete set of equations includes two kinds of variables:

(1) Variables whose values are determined by the operation of the model itself. We call these "endogenous" (or inside) variables. The endogenous variables in the above model are P, D_c, D_s, P_{t+1}, and S.

(2) Variables whose values are determined from outside the model: "exogenous" variables. The exogenous variables in this model are Z, P_r, t, D_{st-1}, A, W, and E.

Let us look further at the endogenous variables. Notice that there is one equation for each. And so there will always be in any model which lays claim to being complete. You will observe that our model includes both current and lagged values of these endogenous variables. The lagged values have been determined before the model goes to work generating current values. Because these lagged values of endogenous variables have been set beforehand, they resemble exogenous variables. The econometrician usually groups these two kinds of variables—lagged endogenous and exogenous variables—together under the heading "predetermined variables," that is, variables whose values have been determined before our model grinds out its latest results.

Why is this important? The answer is that all of the current endogenous variables are linked together by the model in a kind of mechanical way. Within the structured framework, it is no more accurate to say that consumption determines price than to say that price determines consumption. More correct is the statement that the values of price, consumption, and all other current endogenous variables are dependent on the values of the predetermined variables—values set outside or before the period of analysis.

Mathematically speaking, we can solve these five equations to express any one of the endogenous variables as a function of all the predetermined variables in the model. Thus, if we wish to derive one price equation from the universal model, it will have the following form:

$$P = f(P_r, D_{s_{t-1}}, Z, A, E, W \text{ and } t).$$

The equation, then, states that the price of commodity X depends on the price of a rival commodity (P_r), beginning stocks (D_{st-1}), a weather variable or other production variable (W), income-or-output (Z), acreage or capacity (A), an expectation variable (E), and a time trend variable (t).

As a matter of fact, we can use our model as a heuristic device or guide to help us identify the main predetermined variables. We could then use these variables to explain price in a single equation multiple correlation analysis. In such an analysis, it is usual for some of the variables shown in the price equation to "drop out," that is, to show no significance by statistical tests.

Although we have permitted outselves to call the above model "universal," it falls short of universality in some important respects. For one thing, it makes no allowance for the role of government support action. Such allowance might be made in various ways. For example, it might be appropriate to add a sixth equation which says that the size of government stocks (G_s) depends on the difference between the prevailing price (P) and the loan level (P_t), that is, $G_s = f(P - P_t)$.

Our universal model also does not take into account qualitatively distinct supply sources (e.g., new mine production and scrap), or distinctly different demand outlets. Let us consider now one case in which it is appropriate to give separate consideration to different end-uses of a single commodity. Our illustrative commodity will be a major U.S. price-supported grain: wheat.

A WHEAT MODEL

The reader will recall that the first step in building any model is an analytic study of the relationships which are most important for the respective commodity. It is often useful, at an early stage, to draw a kind of economic roadmap to point up the main cause-and-effect relationships.

The U.S. Department of Agriculture has prepared the following (Figure 37) to portray the principal economic relationships and the main variables in the complex wheat economy.

Let us first note the special signs or designations the USDA uses.

Direct economic forces are shown in circles; items that are essentially physical are shown in boxes; and government factors are shown in broken circles.

The heavier lines connecting the various items indicate the more important factors; the lighter lines indicate factors that are relatively minor or operate only occasionally.

Arrows indicate the principal direction of the causal effects. Where arrows are double-pointed, a simultaneous relationship is believed to exist.

Other simultaneous relationships grow out of circular processes indicated in the diagram and the fact that the total quantity demanded for domestic use, exports, and carryout must equal total supply at the beginning of the marketing year.[5]

The letter symbols in the various boxes and circles are, of course, simply names for different variables. Most of these symbols are used in the equations which we shall include in our wheat model.

While Figure 37 may look formidable, it should not be difficult to understand if we examine, one at a time, relationships which are actually operating simultaneously.

The upper part of Figure 37 shows the forces which affect wheat production. We see that acreage and yield are both affected by physical factors—mainly weather—and by economic factors such as price in the preceding year. In the main, wheat production is predetermined and can be treated in our model as a given quantity.

Total domestic supply S_d includes carryover and domestic production (adjusted, in this case, to exclude use for seed and alcohol manufacture). Out of this adjusted supply total must come consumption for export (C_e), label this exports; consumption for stocks (C_s), label this ending stocks; and domestic consumption of two principal types: (1) household use (C_h), and (2) feed use (C_f).

5. *The Demand and Price Structure for WHEAT,* Technical Bulletin 1136, Washington, D.C., U.S. Department of Agriculture, 1955, p. 11.

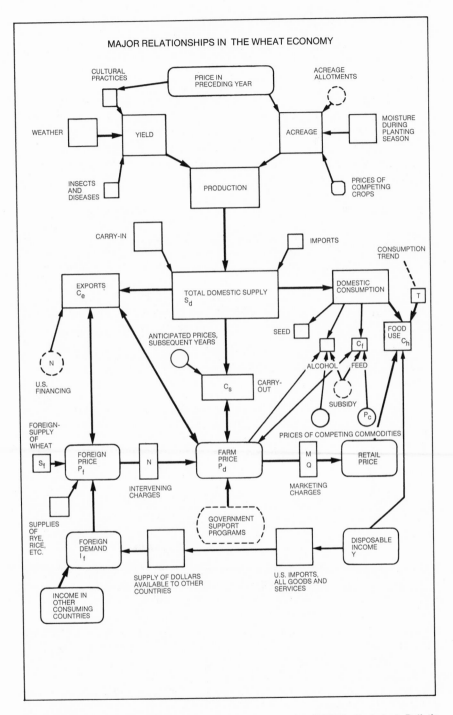

Fig. 37. (Courtesy of *The Demand and Price Structure for WHEAT,* Technical Bulletin 1136, U.S. Department of Agriculture, 1955, p. 12.)

This allocation of total supply is explained in the following six-equation model, adapted from an analysis developed by USDA economists.

Mathematical Statement	*Verbal Statement*
(1) $$C_h = f(P_w, M, Y, T).$$	Household consumption of wheat (C_h) depends on the price of wheat (P_w), marketing costs (M) to bring this price to retail level, consumer disposable income (Y), and a trend factor (T).
(2) $$C_f = f(P_w - P_c, A).$$	Feed consumption of wheat (C_f) depends on the difference between the domestic wheat and corn prices $(P_w - P_c)$, and on the number of animal units (A) to be fed.
(3) $$C_e = f(P_w^L - P_w - F).$$	Consumption for export (C_e) depends on the incentive to export as measured by the difference between the wheat price in Liverpool (P_w^L) and the wheat price here (P_w) with allowance for freight costs (F).
(4) $$C_s = f(P_w, E).$$	Demand (or consumption) for stocks (which equals ending stocks) depends on the domestic wheat price and some expectation variable (E) (early new crop estimate, change in loan level, etc.).
(5) $$S_d = C_h + C_f + C_e + C_s.$$	Total domestic supply[6] is allocated to consumption by households (C_h), feed (C_f), export (C_e) and ending stocks (C_s).
(6) $$P_w^L = f(S_w, P_L).$$	The world price as measured by the price in Liverpool (P_w^L) depends on world carryover plus production (S_w), and also on the general level of all goods as measured by a wholesale price index in Liverpool (P_L).

This is a complete model because we have as many equations (six) as we do endogenous variables. Let us assume that we have decided on the mathematical form of the equations,[7] and have estimated all the constants which bind the variables together.

Our model does not allow for government support operations. During years in which supports are nonexistent, this model can be used to estimate

6. Adjusted to exclude use for seed and alcohol manufacture.
7. That is, whether each of the relationships is linear, or nonlinear, and what sort of curve should be used.

the level of domestic and world wheat prices, and the amounts which will be used in each of the four major demand outlets: exports, carryover, food, and feed. In order to make this estimate, we have to "feed" our model assumed values for all of the predetermined variables. In other words, the price and demand estimates our model gives us will depend on what we "tell" it about the total domestic supply, the income of consumers, the number of animal units to be fed, marketing costs, the general price level, etc.

Since the above model does not take government supports into account, one may raise the question: Is it of any use in a situation in which supports are operative? Yes, in various ways, depending on the situation and the character of government supports. With the help of the above model, we can estimate utilization in each of the four major channels. In turn, these demand estimates may be used in a separate analysis aimed at telling us how much wheat must go into loan to create early season tightness, or how much must come out later in the season to satisfy all requirements.

Formally, this separate analysis may take the form of another model, one designed to forecast price under conditions in which farmers can put wheat into loan. A simple, single equation model of this sort might have the following form:

$$P_{w2} - L = f(R_2).$$

The premium (or discount) of the second-half wheat price (P_{w2}) over the loan level (L) depends on the amount of redemptions (R_2) (or withdrawals) from the loan needed in the second half of the season.

The problem, in this case, would be to estimate R_2, the quantity which must be withdrawn from the loan. This estimate, in turn, might be derived from a balance-sheet analysis which incorporates the consumption estimates obtained from the model.

As always, the science (or art) of model building requires us to imaginatively adapt to the character of the problem. However universal our model, it is never more valid than our insights, and it is always subject to the limitations of our data and the caprice of fate.

On Fundamental Analysis: A Final Remark

Our purpose in this chapter has been to point the reader towards an objective, systematic approach to analyzing the fundamentals of supply and demand.

This systematic approach can, advantageously, take the form of a complete mathematical model. Alternatively, a careful balance-sheet analysis may disclose the regularities we are seeking. Our goal, in either case, is to find in a world of wild flux and interaction, relationships which seem to hold up with relative consistency and which therefore can be a forecasting aid.

As suggested earlier, we have consciously tried to be as explicit as possible in our analysis. We seek to formulate our ideas in a way which is consistent with economic theory, and which is subject to statistical verification or rejection.

While valuing systematic methods as an aid to forecasting, we appreciate the fact that some factors—occasionally decisive—will remain outside the scope of our analysis. We cherish no illusion that computer exactitude is, in itself, necessarily endowed with prophetic significance. Fundamental analysis is ultimately a matter of wide knowledge and subtle understanding, and we fully endorse the continuing study directed towards refining and improving this approach to commodity price analysis.

PART V
_____

SPECULATIVE TRADING

CHAPTER **14** Trading Preliminaries

Buying, Selling, and Delivering

A trader who is bullish on a commodity can buy one or more futures contracts. Purchase of a futures contract obligates the "long" to do one of two things: He may accept delivery of the actual commodity, paying for it in full at the time of delivery at the then current price.[1] Or he may close out (offset) his long commitment prior to receiving a "delivery notice" by selling a like quantity of the same future.

If a trader is bearish on a commodity and sells one or more futures contracts, he obligates himself to either deliver one of the tenderable grades of the actual commodity sometime during the delivery period, or to close out (offset) his short commitment prior to the last trading day in the respective delivery month by purchasing a like quantity of the same future. For example, a trader who is long 5,000 bushels of Chicago March wheat and who does not want to take delivery, would close out his long position by selling 5,000 bushels of Chicago March wheat. He could not close out his "long" position by selling any other month of Chicago wheat, nor by selling March wheat on any other grain exchange.

A futures transaction, therefore, either establishes a new position or liquidates an existing position. Thus, the "open interest" for any given

1. Although he pays for the new actuals position at the then current price (delivery price), his open long futures position is simultaneously "closed out" at the same (delivery) price. Thus, a trader who buys 5,000 bushels of March wheat at 1.60 (per bushel) and who takes delivery at 1.70, actually must pay 1.70 for his cash wheat. However, his long 1.60 March futures position is also "closed out" at 1.70. In summary, he pays an extra 10¢ per bushel ($500.00) for his cash wheat (he originally bought the position at 1.60, but he must pay 1.70 when he takes delivery). However, this $500.00 "loss" is offset by a corresponding "gain" of 10¢ ($500.00) registered in the close out of his long March futures position.

commodity designates the size of the total open commitment—the total number of "long" contracts open, which is also the number of open "short" contracts. For example, in February 1971, the open interest in New York silver, traded on the Commodity Exchange, Inc., was 38,700 contracts; meaning 38,700 long contracts *and* 38,700 short contracts. The size of the open long position, by definition, equals the size of the open short position.

Very few speculators are disposed to deliver or accept delivery of a commodity. The fact that traders are able to offset (by liquidation) their futures commitments, eliminating the necessity of making or accepting delivery, encourages the broad speculative participation without which futures markets could never function. As mentioned earlier, only about 1 percent of the total volume of futures transactions is normally settled by delivery of the actual commodity.

Deliveries against futures contracts are made during the final month of trading. Delivery is at the option of the short, who may deliver any tenderable grade during the delivery period at any of the designated locations. Delivery is effected through the short (seller) passing to the clearing house, who passes to the long (buyer), a negotiable warehouse receipt which is accepted as evidence of title to the specified quantity and grade of the commodity. In some commodities, such as cocoa and silver, the warehouse receipt represents a specific lot of a commodity, identified by number. In other commodities, grains being the most prominent, the warehouse receipt merely represents a quantity and quality of the commodity commingled with other grain of like quality.

Since delivery is at the option of the short, longs who are not in a position to accept delivery of the actual commodity should either close out or switch their position into a more distant month prior to first notice day.

Differences Between the Commodity and the Securities Markets

There exist a number of interesting and important distinctions between the operations of the futures and the securities markets. Futures traders should have a complete understanding of these features.

As futures contracts have a limited term, usually not more than 12 or 18 months and are never paid for in full until delivery, traders cannot establish futures positions and just "sit with them" as they can do with securities. Also, complete price cycles are sometimes compressed into the relatively short life of a futures contract. As a consequence, futures usually offer more extensive and broader short-term price movements than do securities.

Futures have maximum daily trading limits, whereas no trading limits exist in securities markets. In lieu of trading limits, securities exchanges may suspend trading for short periods in any security where there exists such an imbalance of buy and sell orders that it is impossible to maintain an orderly market. However, no such potential restraint exists in the over-the-counter market, where trading is conducted without recourse to trading limits or intraday suspension of trading.

Each commodity delivery month eventually becomes the "spot" or "cash" month. Long positions in the "spot" month involve the additional risk of receiving delivery, while short positions involve risks of a tight situation due to a possible shortage of deliverable supplies. These two important risks are peculiar to the futures markets. The securities trader does not face them, except in the rare instance where "short" stock cannot be borrowed and is called in by brokers.

During recent years, security margins have fluctuated between 50 and 100 percent. In contrast, futures margins have rarely exceeded 15 percent. Therefore, with a given amount of capital, a futures trader can take a position involving a much greater market value than can a securities trader.

There is no distinction between a new short sale and a liquidating sale in the futures market, nor between a new or a short-covering purchase. For round-lot orders in listed securities, short sales must be made on either an "uptick," or on an unchanged "tick," following an uptick. This means that in a weak market, an order to sell short a round-lot of a listed security may not be executed until the price ticks up. This sometimes results in a delay, or an execution at a lower price than anticipated. In summary, a futures trader can more easily effect a short sale than can a securities trader.

Futures trading requires the knowledge of much more specific detail than does securities trading. For example, commodities vary with respect to where they are traded, hours of trading, size of contract, magnitude of price fluctuations, maximum trading limits, margin, commissions, first notice day and last day of trading, and so on. The securities trader is concerned with fewer details.

For any security, the short interest is just a small fraction of the long interest (total amount of stock outstanding). Hence, most investors profit when stocks go up, and few when they go down. In futures markets, the long and short interests are always equal, so that the same amount of money is always made and lost, regardless of which direction prices move.

Commodity margin deposits are technically "earnest money," held by the commission firm as a guarantee that the customer will meet his contractual obligations (as discussed in Chapter 2). There is no debit balance in a commodity futures account, hence no interest is charged. Interest charges are incurred only if the trader accepts delivery of the actual commodity (during the delivery month) and does not pay for it in full. In the securities market, on the other hand, the margin-account investor is charged interest on his debit balance (money owed the broker).

There is no organized specialist system in futures trading. Commodity pit brokers trade directly with each other and execute all buying and selling orders entrusted to them, including stop orders. In contrast, securities trading on the listed exchanges involves the use of the "specialist" system. Specialists are stock exchange members who are designated by the exchanges to maintain an orderly market in specific securities and to execute orders for other brokers.

Many commodities have reduced day trade or spread (straddle) commissions and reduced spread (straddle) margin requirements. There are no reduced day trade commissions in securities trading, although lower margin is required on day trades.

In futures trading, a position must be closed out at the brokerage firm where the position was initiated, and on the same exchange. In the securities market, an investor may order his stock broker to deliver his securities position to another broker (even if it is held on margin), and he may liquidate his position at the new broker. Also a security bought on one exchange may be sold on any other market which lists that particular issue.

Selecting an Account Executive

A futures trader should be very selective in choosing an account executive.[2] Many futures traders have few direct dealings with the futures commission firm; it is through their account executive that business is conducted. Not only does the client-account executive relationship involve mutual trust and confidence, it frequently involves transactions representing substantial sums of money. Therefore, futures traders should not be reluctant to meet and talk with commodity account executives of several commission firms before opening an account.

A commodity account executive should be experienced, knowledgeable, and should have a keen sense of responsibility for his clients' accounts. He should be available during trading hours, and must be quick and accurate in entering orders. He should be capable of answering, or at least obtaining the answer to, all inquiries, should provide his clients with necessary price quotations, and should be able to advise them concerning significant news events as they occur. It is important that the client and the account executive develop a close working relationship.

Although the client should make his own trading decisions, the account

2. Also referred to as customers' man, registered representative, and in the Chicago grain trade, commodity solicitor.

executive should, when asked, provide trading suggestions and should be willing and able to discuss the client's ideas. If the client is a "chartist," the account executive should be chart-oriented and should either keep his own charts or have access to charts.

A commodity account executive should be associated with an experienced, reputable commission firm holding memberships on the principal futures exchanges and providing such essential facilities as an electric board or ticker tapes serving the active futures markets, commodity news broad tapes, and trade or floor contacts. The Commodity Exchange Authority, the individual futures exchanges, or any commercial bank can provide information concerning established futures commission firms.

Most commodity account executives are busy and have neither the time nor the facilities to conduct their own private research work. They should be backed by a firm which reviews basic commodities and offers trading suggestions covering interesting market situations. The commission firm must maintain adequate physical facilities to handle all orders, floor executions, and reports with speed and accuracy. In a rapidly moving market every second is important, and the speed and efficiency of the futures commission firm can make the difference between executing an order or missing the market. One means of determining a commission firm's efficiency is to time how long it takes to receive floor quotes, or to execute market orders.

OPENING AN ACCOUNT

Once you have selected an account executive, you must open an account. You will be asked to divulge some basic items of personal information and bank references, just as when you open an account at a bank or at a retail store. Since nearly all buy and sell orders are accepted by the account executive verbally, commission firms must assure themselves that their clients are reputable individuals of high personal integrity. Commission firms must also inquire into their clients' financial circumstances to ascertain that they can afford the risks associated with futures trading.

Upon opening an account, a commodity trader is required to sign a "customer's agreement" (see Figure 38), the exact title and provision of which may vary from one commission firm to another. Basically, this agreement states the mutual obligations of both the client and the commission firm, and provides the firm with financial safeguards.

In addition, the commission firm will ask for a margin deposit before accepting orders. Some firms stipulate the mimimum size commodity account which they will accept, such as $2,500 or $5,000. This is a safe-

BACHE & CO. INCORPORATED	ACCOUNT NAME (HEREIN REFERRED TO AS I)	OFFICE	ACC. NO.	R.R.	DATE
CUSTOMER'S AGREEMENT					

1. I agree as follows with respect to all of my accounts, in which I have an interest alone or with others, which I have opened or open in the future, with you for the purchase and sale of securities and commodities:

2. I am of full age and represent that I am not an employee of any exchange or of a Member Firm of any Exchange or the NASD, or of a bank, trust company, or insurance company and that I will promptly notify you if I become so employed.

3. All transactions for my account shall be subject to the constitution, rules, regulations, customs and usages, as the same may be constituted from time to time, of the exchange or market (and its clearing house, if any) where executed.

4. Any and all credit balances, securities, commodities or contracts relating thereto, and all other property of whatsoever kind belonging to me or in which I may have an interest held by you or carried for my accounts shall be subject to a general lien for the discharge of my obligations to you (including unmatured and contingent obligations) however arising and without regard to whether or not you have made advances with respect to such property and without notice to me may be carried in your general loans and all securities may be pledged, repledged, hypothecated or re-hypothecated, separately or in common with other securities or any other property, for the sum due to you thereon or for a greater sum and without retaining in your possession and control for delivery a like amount of similar securities or other property. At any time and from time to time you may, in your discretion, without notice to me, apply and/or transfer any securities, commodities, contracts relating thereto, cash or any other property therein, interchangeably between any of my accounts, whether individual or joint or from any of my accounts to any account guaranteed by me. You are specifically authorized to transfer to my cash account on the settlement day following a purchase made in that account, excess funds available in any of my other accounts, including but not limited to any free balances in any margin account or in any non-regulated commodities account, sufficient to make full payment of this cash purchase. I agree that any debit occurring in any of my accounts may be transferred by you at your option to my margin account.

5. I will maintain such margins as you may in your discretion require from time to time and will pay on demand any debit balance owing with respect to any of my accounts. Whenever in your discretion you deem it desirable for your protection, (and without the necessity of a margin call) including but not limited to an instance where a petition in bankruptcy or for the appointment of a receiver is filed by or against me, or an attachment is levied against my account, or in the event of notice of my death or incapacity, or in compliance with the orders of any Exchange, you may, without prior demand, tender, and without any notice of the time or place of sale, all of which are expressly waived, sell any or all securities, or commodities or contracts relating thereto which may be in your possession, or which you may be carrying for me, or buy any securities, or commodities or contracts relating thereto of which my account or accounts may be short, in order to close out in whole or in part any commitment in my behalf or you may place stop orders with respects to such securities or commodities and such sale or purchase may be made at your discretion on any Exchange or other market where such business is then transacted, or at public auction or private sale, with or without advertising and no demands, calls, tenders or notices which you may make or give in any one or more instances shall invalidate the aforesaid waivers on my part. You shall have the right to purchase for your own account any or all of the aforesaid property at any such sale, discharged of any right of redemption, which is hereby waived.

6. All orders for the purchase or sale of commodities for future delivery may be closed out by you as and when authorized or required by the Exchange where made. Against a "long" position in any commodity contract, prior to maturity thereof, and at least five business days before the first notice day of the delivery month, I will give instructions to liquidate, or place you in sufficient funds to take delivery; and in default thereof, or in the event such liquidating instructions cannot be executed under prevailing conditions, you may, without notice or demand, close out the contracts or take delivery and dispose of the commodity upon any terms and by any method which may be feasible. Against a "short" position in any commodity contract, prior to maturity thereof, and at least five business days before the last trading day of the delivery month, I will give you instructions to cover, or furnish you with all necessary delivery documents; and in default thereof, you may without demand or notice, cover the contracts, or if orders to buy in such contracts cannot be executed under prevailing conditions, you may procure the actual commodity and make delivery thereof upon any terms and by any method which may be feasible.

7. All transactions in any of my accounts are to be paid for or required margin deposited no later than 2:00 p.m. on the settlement date.

8. I agree to pay interest and service charges upon my accounts monthly at the prevailing rate as determined by you.

9. I agree that, in giving orders to sell, all "short" sale orders will be designated as "short" and all "long" sale orders will be designated as "long" and that the designation of a sell order as "long" is a representation on my part that I own the security and, if the security is not in your possession that it is not then possible to deliver the security to you forthwith and I will deliver it on or before the settlement date.

10. Reports of the execution of orders and statements of my account shall be conclusive if not objected to in writing within five days and ten days, respectively, after transmittal to me by mail or otherwise.

11. All communications including margin calls may be sent to me at my address given you, or at such other address as I may hereafter give you in writing, and all communications so sent, whether in writing or otherwise, shall be deemed given to me personally, whether actually received or not.

12. No waiver of any provision of this agreement shall be deemed a waiver of any other provision, nor a continuing waiver of the provision or provisions so waived.

13. I understand that no provision of this agreement can be amended or waived except in writing signed by an officer of your Company, and that this agreement shall continue in force until its termination by me is acknowledged in writing by an officer of your Company; or until written notice of termination by you shall have been mailed to me at my address last given you.

14. This contract shall be governed by the laws of the State of New York, and shall inure to the benefit of your successors and assigns, and shall be binding on the undersigned, his heirs, executors, administrators and assigns. Any controversy arising out of or relating to my account, to transactions with or for me or to this agreement or the breach thereof, shall be settled by arbitration in accordance with the rules then obtaining of either the American Arbitration Association or the Board of Governors of the New York Stock Exchange as I may elect, except that any controversy arising out of or relating to transactions in commodities or contracts relating thereto, whether executed or to be executed within or outside of the United States shall be settled by arbitration in accordance with the rules then obtaining of the Exchange (if any) where the transaction took place, if within the United States, and provided such Exchange has arbitration facilities or under the rules of the American Arbitration Association as I may elect. If I do not make such election by registered mail addressed to you at your main office within five days after demand by you that I make such election, then you may make such election. Notice preliminary to, in conjunction with, or incident to such arbitration proceeding, may be sent to me by mail and personal service is hereby waived. Judgment upon any award rendered by the arbitrators may be entered in any court having jurisdiction thereof, without notice to me.

15. If any provision hereof is or at any time should become inconsistent with any present or future law, rule or regulation of any securities or commodities exchange or of any sovereign government or a regulatory body thereof and if any of these bodies have jurisdiction over the subject matter of this agreement, said provision shall be deemed to be superseded or modified to conform to such law, rule or regulation, but in all other respects this agreement shall continue and remain in full force and effect.

DATE _____ CUSTOMER'S SIGNATURE _____ _____

Fig. 38.

guard used by firms to discourage individuals of inadequate means from speculating in futures.

There are certain forms which commission firms mail to their clients every time a trade is made, an open order is entered or canceled, an open position is closed out, and an accounting period (usually a month) is completed. Upon receiving any of these forms, the client should verify it for accuracy and should immediately report any discrepancies to his account executive.

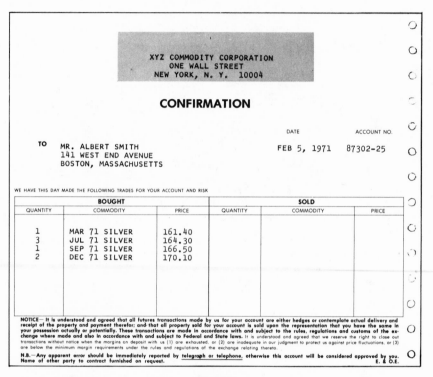

Fig. 39.

A *trade confirmation* is mailed to each client every time he makes a trade (see Figure 39). This confirmation contains the client's name, address, and account number, the trade date, whether it was a purchase or sale, the commodity and the market, the number of contracts (or bushels of grain) involved, the delivery month, and the price. This confirmation usually does not indicate the total money value of the entire transaction, or the profit or loss realized on a liquidating trade.

For every liquidating trade the client receives a *purchase and sale* (close-out) form (see Figure 40). This form recaps both the purchase and the

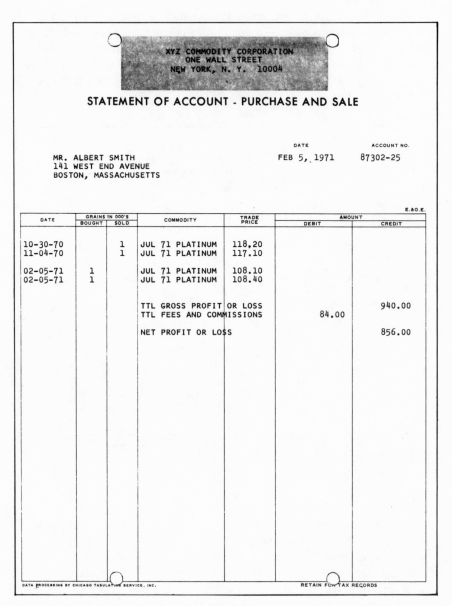

Fig. 40.

sale, the round-turn commission, and the net profit or loss. All purchase and sale forms should be retained for future use in preparation of tax returns.

Every time an open order (good till canceled or good through a certain date) is entered or canceled, the client is mailed an *open order confirmation* (see Figure 41). Open order confirmations contain a statement advising the client that he is responsible for canceling all "in-force" orders when superseding them with other orders. Traders should be certain that all

XYZ COMMODITY CORPORATION
ONE WALL STREET
NEW YORK, N. Y. 1004

Date____FEB 5, 1971_____

Dear Sir(s):

We confirm that we have ENTERED   OPEN ORDER(S) for your account as follows:

TO BUY	TO SELL
	30M BUSHELS JUL SOYBEANS @ 314 1/2
	15M BUSHELS MAR WHEAT @ 173 3/4

MR. ALBERT SMITH
141 WEST END AVENUE
BOSTON, MASSACHUSETTS

As the responsibility for failure to cancel a former order when entering a substitute therefor rests upon the customer, transactions resulting from the execution of both old and new orders will be entered in the client's account.

Fig. 41.

superseded open orders are properly canceled, in order to avoid the costly error of executing an order twice.

At the end of each month commission firms mail out *monthly statements* to each of their clients whose accounts showed any activity during the month, or contained any open cash or futures positions as of the close of the month (see Figure 42). The "monthly statement" is divided into two sections: one for commodity open positions as of the last day of the month; the other indicating all "money" entries (cash deposits and withdrawals, and profits or losses on closed-out trades) during the entire

XYZ COMMODITY CORPORATION
ONE WALL STREET
NEW YORK, NEW YORK 10004

STATEMENT OF ACCOUNT - OPEN TRADES

DATE   ACCOUNT NO.

MR. ALBERT SMITH   2/26/71   87302-25
141 WEST END AVENUE
BOSTON, MASSACHUSETTS

* GRAINS IN 000'S   E.&O.E.

DATE	POSITION * LONG	POSITION * SHORT	COMMODITY	TRADE PRICE	SETTLEMENT PRICE	OPEN TRADE EQUITY DEBIT	OPEN TRADE EQUITY CREDIT
02-01-71			BEGINNING LEDGER BALANCE				20,560.22
02-05-71			P & S 2 JUL PLATINUM				856.00
02-09-71			CHECK RECEIVED				2,000.00
02-11-71			P & S 2 MAR SILVER			291.20	
02-16-71			P & S 4 JAN PLATINUM			468.00	
02-19-71			P & S 4 SEP SILVER				2,217.60
02-23-71			CHECK DISBURSED			1,500.00	
02-25-71			P & S 3 DEC COCOA			1,155.00	
02-26-71			ENDING LEDGER BALANCE				22,219.62
			OPEN POSITION				
06-25-70		4	JUL 71 COCOA	27.56			
01-25-71	8		SEP 71 COCOA	25.94			
01-11-71		10	JUL 71 COPPER	45.60			
02-05-71	1		MAR 71 SILVER	161.40			
02-05-71	3		JUL 71 SILVER	164.30			
02-05-71	1		SEP 71 SILVER	166.50			
02-05-71	2		DEC 71 SILVER	170.10			

DATA PROCESSING BY CHICAGO TABULATING SERVICE, INC.   RETAIN FOR TAX RECORDS

Fig. 42.

month. The cash balance as of the first and last days of the month is also included. All monthly statements should be retained for preparation of tax returns.

Who Trades in Futures?

In the broad, actively traded futures markets, orders originate daily from throughout the world. The two basic classes of futures traders are "speculators" and "hedgers." The speculator is motivated solely by his desire to make a trading profit. He buys in anticipation of a price rise and sells in anticipation of a price decline, risking his own capital on his ability to accurately forecast price movements. The hedger, on the other hand, trades primarily either to establish his commodity prices, or to reduce price risks on commodities owned and not yet sold, or on commodities sold ahead for later delivery and not yet owned. He is concerned with the changing price spreads between cash and futures, or between different futures months, rather than with the actual price or its fluctuations.

There are two broad classes of speculators: "public speculators," who usually are not members of futures exchanges, and "professional speculators," who generally enjoy exchange membership privileges. The public speculator trades through a commission member firm. Public speculators are usually engaged in businesses unrelated to the commodity trades, although occasionally one of them becomes so absorbed in futures trading or so successful at it that he becomes a full-time trader. Many professional traders are "floor traders," that is, as members of one or more futures exchanges, they conduct their trading directly from the "pits" or "rings" of an exchange.

One class of professional traders which is instrumental in maintaining an orderly trading market is the "scalper." He is an "in and out" trader who is almost always willing to buy at a small fraction below previous transactions, or sell at somewhat above the previous price. Price fluctuations between trades are minimized due to the buying and selling of these scalpers. An adept scalper in an active market may trade into and out of several positions within an hour, being satisfied with a profit on minimum fluctuations. Since he is willing to accept small profits, he must close out or even reverse his position at the first sign of a loss. Except in unusual circumstances, the scalper will "even up" his positions prior to the close of each trading session.

Two other classes of professional traders are "day traders" and "position traders." They differ primarily in their time approach to trading. A day trader is a speculator who, although not trading for as quick a "turn" as a scalper, will generally not carry open trades overnight. He may "scalp" trades, but more frequently will try to trade with the trend when he senses a turn developing in the market. Position traders, on the other hand, many of whom do not trade from the exchange floors, but from locations with the quickest services to the pits, or rings, can be either long- or short-term traders. They will carry open positions over a period of time when they consider the trend as favorable.

The fourth class of professional floor trader is the "spreader" or "arbitrageuer." He is constantly watching price relationships between different futures and will buy one future and sell another any time he feels that the price differential between the two futures is temporarily distorted. Some spreaders scalp trades, while others take a longer-term position anticipating a trend in spread differences between futures, between markets, or even between two related commodities. Spreading is an extremely complex form of futures speculation, requiring a great deal of knowledge and experience, but the astute trader will come across many excellent spread opportunities.

How Futures Prices Are Disseminated

The rapid, accurate and widespread dissemination of futures prices is a vital factor in the efficient operation of modern futures markets. Within seconds after each price change on a major futures market, traders throughout the world can see the price change recorded on either a "ticker tape" or an "electric board." Each futures exchange prints a ticker tape, and firms or individuals desiring to subscribe to this service must make application to the exchange whose ticker they want. If approved, they contract to have the necessary equipment installed on a fee basis.

In addition to the ticker tape, commission firms and trade houses can subscribe to a private service, available throughout much of the world, which provides continuous electronically operated price data, displayed on either a wall-size board or on desk-top machines, or else post futures prices on large chalk boards in their offices or boardrooms.

Nonprofessional traders, without access to the ticker tape, electric board, or chalk board, will find a daily financial newspaper to be the primary source of their futures price information. The leading financial dailies, in addition to providing futures prices, volume of trading, and open interest figures, sometimes include a daily column discussing the important features of the previous day's trading in leading futures.

Futures prices are disseminated in the following ways:

NEWSPAPER PRICE QUOTATIONS

A comprehensive futures price reporting section is included in many of the major daily newspapers. For each future, the opening, high, low, and closing prices are provided daily, plus the net price change from the previous trading session, as well as the life of contract high and low prices. Figure 43 summarizes New York silver and Chicago corn trading for February 3, 1971.

The opening or closing price for a future may be printed as a range of two prices, for example 1.53¼ –½, indicating that when the future opened or closed, trades had occurred within that range.

The letters "b," "a," and "n" frequently appear in futures prices. The letters "b" and "a" indicated respectively a "bid" price which a specific buyer is quoted as willing to pay, and an "offer" (asked price), the price at which a specific seller is quoted as willing to sell. The "b" and "a" quotations indicate that buyer and seller are not in agreement and, of course, that no trade has occurred. Prices may be quoted as "bid" or "offered" during the session, or at the opening or close of trading, and may be quoted for those futures which have not opened or traded. The "n" refers to a "nominal" price, the price agreed upon, on the trading floor, as the likeliest

NEW YORK—SILVER							
Feb	162.00	162.00	162.00	162.00	+ .80	165.60	155.00
Mar	163.00	163.40	162.40	162.90	+ .80	230.80	154.10
May	165.20	165.60	164.50	164.90	+ .70	223.50	158.20
July	167.20	167.50	166.40	166.90	+ .60	221.80	158.20
Sept	169.50	169.80	168.50	169.00	+ .50	206.00	160.30
Dec	172.60	172.90	171.60	172.20	+ .40	210.00	163.50
Jan'72	173.70	173.80	173.20	173.20	+ .30	210.80	164.60
Mar	175.80	176.10	175.00	175.30	+ .30	204.80	167.00
May	177.90	178.10	177.30	177.30	+ .30	191.30	169.70
Sales: 1 599 contracts.							
CORN							
Mar	154½	154½	153¼	153½-⅝	−⅞to¾	165	120⅜
May	156⅞	157⅛	155¾	156⅛-156	−⅞to1	167½	128½
July	158⅞	159	157¾	158-158⅛	−⅞to¾	168	134½
Sept	157½	157⅝	156⅝	156¾	−⅞	165	151⅛
Dec	154½	154⅝	153⅝	153¾-154	−⅞to⅝	160⅛	150
Mar'72	159	159⅛	157⅞	158-157⅞	−1¼to1⅜	164¾	154½

Fig. 43. (Courtesy of *The Wall Street Journal.*)

price at which a future might be traded although, in fact, no trade has occurred nor have bids or offers been made.

TICKER TAPE

It requires some degree of experience to "read" a commodity ticker tape, because the information is abbreviated and the tape is continuously printing new prices. A ticker tape presents four basic items of information: the commodity, the delivery month, the price, and the time of the transaction. In addition, some ticker tapes record volume of trading. Figure 44 is an example.

ELECTRIC BOARD AND CHALK BOARD

Both the electric board (and desk unit) and the chalk board present similar information. Their price presentation is similar to price quotations in a newspaper. The principal differences between chalk boards and electric boards are that price changes on an electric board are actuated by computer-directed signals, while with the chalk board, board markers record price changes manually. In addition to presenting the full price range, the chalk board also presents a number of prices preceding the "last sale." This can be helpful in following short-term swings. Instead of erasing each "last sale" upon recording the current one, the board markers record each "last sale" beneath the previous one, erasing the column only when it begins to run off the bottom of the board.

AW	BOH	SWN	B	SWN	BOK
935.00	1233	7965		7970	1217

BOK	SWK	SWK	SIW	CK
1216	7895	7900	1710	1526

SWH	WK	WK	SK	BOK	WN
7860	1608	1601	3088	1215	154

Fig. 44. Chicago Board of Trade ticker tape. This tape contains letters on the upper half (first letter[s] designates the commodity and the second letter designates the delivery month), and numbers (the times of sales, and prices) on the lower half. The following abbreviations are used:

Commodity		Delivery Months			
BO	Soybean oil	F	January	N	July
C	Corn	G	February	Q	August
O	Oats	H	March	U	September
S	Soybeans	J	April	V	October
SI	Silver	K	May	X	November
SM	Soybean meal	M	June	Z	December
W	Wheat				

The letters designating delivery months are standard for all commodity exchanges. However, each exchange will "code" its own commodities, e.g., on the Commodity Exchange, Inc., C designates copper and S designates silver; on the Chicago Board of Trade, C designates corn and S designates soybeans.

Sources of Commodity Information

Data concerning every aspect of the commodities business is continually collected, compiled, and disseminated by various government and private units. With the exception of the advices from private commodity advisory services, this data is available free, or at low cost. Futures traders should take full advantage of the wealth of information available from the following sources:

U.S. DEPARTMENT OF AGRICULTURE

This agency is the principal source of official statistical information concerning grains, other domestically produced commodities, and certain imported commodities. Most government reports are released at scheduled times, so that traders can anticipate those releases which are of particular interest. Important government reports include the monthly *Crop Production* (not published in January and February); *Weekly Grain Market News* which presents grain statistics and information; *Monthly Situation Bulletins* which survey supply and demand factors for various commodities; and the monthly *Commitments of Traders Report.* This last report indicates the composition of the open interest with respect to the size of the large (by reporting traders) hedging, speculative, and spreading interests, as well as the small interests collectively in all categories.

U.S. GOVERNMENT PRINTING OFFICE

Located in Washington, D.C., this office makes available at low cost pamphlets on many subjects relating to commodities, agriculture, and marketing. A listing of this material is available upon request.

U.S. WEATHER BUREAU

The U.S. Weather Bureau prepares and disseminates daily and long-range forecasts for various parts of the country. This information is available through newspapers and radio broadcasts, or directly from the Weather Bureau on a subscription basis. Also, data is collected on a weekly basis, in cooperation with state statisticians, on the conditions of all important crops in each of the major agricultural states.

COMMODITY FUTURES EXCHANGES

Most of the major futures exchanges publish literature concerning their exchange, as well as the individual commodities traded. The exchanges also offer, some on a subscription basis, daily or weekly reports concerning futures prices and significant supply and demand developments for each commodity. Requests for information can be addressed directly to the exchanges:

Chicago Board of Trade, 141 W. Jackson Blvd., Chicago, Illinois 60604
Chicago Mercantile Exchange, 110 North Franklin St., Chicago, Illinois 60604
Commodity Exchange, Inc., 81 Broad St., New York, New York 10004

New York Cocoa Exchange, Inc., 92 Beaver St., New York, New York 10005
New York Coffee and Sugar Exchange, Inc., 79 Pine St., New York, New York 10004
New York Cotton Exchange, Inc., 37 Wall St., New York, New York 10004
New York Mercantile Exchange, 6 Harrison St., New York, New York 10013
New York Produce Exchange, Inc., 2 Broadway, New York, New York 10004
West Coast Commodity Exchange, Inc., 643 South Olive St., Los Angeles, California 90014

FUTURES COMMISSION FIRMS

Many of the major commission firms issue daily or weekly futures market letters, as well as frequent "special situation" reports. This literature is distributed to the firms' clients, and is generally available to prospective clients. Traders can secure this literature by writing or visiting the office of any major futures commission firm.

PRIVATE ADVISORY SERVICES

There are a multitude of private commodity advisory services which offer their market letters and chart services for fees ranging from a $2 trial subscription to several hundred dollars per year. In general, commodity advisory services can be classified by their analytical approach to price forecasting and by the type of service offered. There are technically oriented (charting) services and fundamentally oriented (supply and demand) services. Some services provide specific buy and sell recommendations, while others furnish charts and/or fundamental information, leaving the trading decisions up to the subscriber. The choice between these types of services depends upon the trader's individual preference and on how much he is willing to pay. Sample literature is usually available from commodity advisory services.

FINANCIAL NEWSPAPERS

As noted previously, the leading financial dailies, in addition to carrying futures prices, volume, open interest figures, and cash commodity prices, sometimes include a daily column discussing the important features of the previous day's trading. A good financial newspaper provides a convenient, inexpensive means of following commodity developments. Traders should be cautioned, though, against initiating trades on the basis of information or gossip contained in these public columns. In most cases, news has already been acted upon and discounted by the time it appears in the public press.

BOOKS

There are available a number of books discussing agriculture, commodities, the futures market, charting, and other related subjects (see the Bibliography). The public library may have some of these volumes. Book stores and the publishers can provide the rest.

TRADE PUBLICATIONS

The commodity business is represented by a number of trade associations which publish pamphlets describing their commodities, as well as periodic newsletters and magazines discussing the latest developments within each industry. For the most part, these publications tend to be technical in nature since they are intended for people within the trade. Many experienced futures traders, though, find these publications extremely informative and helpful. A list of some of the more active trade associations can be found in Appendix C.

Commodity Margins

Margin is technically "earnest money," a deposit which a futures trader must make as a financial guarantee that he will fulfill his contractual obligations. The "short" must either cover his short position by buying back a like amount of the same future, or deliver the actual commodity during the specified delivery period. The "long" must either liquidate his long position by selling a like amount of the same future, or accept delivery of the actual commodity when tendered to him during the specified delivery period.

There are initial and variation (maintenance) margin deposits. Initial margin is deposited when the futures position is established. Subsequently, if the market moves against a trader's position by a specified amount (to be discussed later in this chapter), the commission merchant (broker) will call for additional margin funds. This additional deposit is called variation, or maintenance, margin.

A futures exchange establishes minimum initial margin requirements for each commodity future traded on its "board." This is a fixed sum of money per contract, rather than a specific percentage of the total cost, as with securities trading. In setting margin requirements, futures exchanges consider both the price level and the volatility of the commodity future. Since these two elements can change rapidly, exchanges reserve the right to change their minimum initial and maintenance margin requirements at any time. Margin changes usually become effective the day following the announcement by the exchange. Increases in initial margin requirements generally apply only to new business subsequent to the change; lowered rates apply to all contracts.

Margin requirements may vary from one commission firm to another, as brokers sometimes call for a higher margin than the exchange specified minimum. However, competitive pressures within the industry tend to keep margin requirements fairly uniform. Traders should not select a commission firm on the basis of lower margin requirements, as this is one of the least important differences between firms.

Margin for each commodity varies, depending on whether the transaction represents speculative or trade hedging business, and whether it is a net (outright long or short) or a straddle position.[3] A straddle position involves concurrent long and short positions in the same or related commodities, i.e., July versus December cocoa, Chicago wheat versus Kansas City wheat, or, within the same grain exchange, one grain versus another grain. Lower margins are required for straddles than for net positions, inasmuch as a straddle position is considered to be less risky than a corresponding outright long or short position. Furthermore, established trade firms engaged in bona fide hedging operations are carried on reduced margins or, in certain commodities, on a limited line of credit.

Margin requirements are so mercurial that any listing soon becomes obsolete. Nevertheless, in order to illustrate margins and to ensure a thorough understanding on the part of the reader, the following tables are presented.

Exchange Minimum Initial Margin Requirements
(as of December 1, 1971)

	NET POSITIONS		STRADDLE POSITIONS	
	Speculative	Trade Hedge	Speculative	Trade Hedge
Cocoa	750.00	*	300.00	same as net
Cotton	800.00	275.00	100.00	55.00
Pork bellies	750.00	750.00	400.00	300.00
Potatoes (N.Y.)				
up to 3.00	200.00	200.00	150.00	150.00
up to 3.50	250.00	250.00	150.00	150.00
over 3.50	300.00	300.00	150.00	150.00
Sugar No. 11	500.00	200.00	200.00	100.00
Silver (N.Y.)	1,000.00	1,000.00	150.00	150.00

* Credit to $300.00 per contract—maximum $10,000.00.

3. In the grain trade, the term "spread" is used.

**Chicago Board of Trade Commodities,
Minimum Initial Margin Requirements (as of December 1, 1971)**

	NET POSITION		SPREAD POSITION		
	Speculative	Hedge	Same Grain Same Market	Different Grain Same Market**	Same Grain Different Market**
Corn	400.00	300.00	*	400.00	400.00
Soybeans	750.00	500.00	*	500.00	500.00
Soybean meal	500.00	400.00	*	400.00	400.00
Soybean oil	500.00	400.00	*	400.00	400.00
Wheat	500.00	400.00	*	500.00	250.00

* To the market (no margin required, although customer must deposit funds to cover any debit in the account). In practice, however, most firms require around $100.00 per spread, to eliminate frequent small margin calls.
** The higher of the two.

In margining a straddle, each side of the straddle is called a "leg," and margin is required on only one leg of the position. In the case of grain spreads, where the spread margin on each of the two legs is different, margin shall be the higher of the two legs. As an example, spread margin on corn is $400.00 (see above table), with $500.00 the spread margin on soybeans. Therefore, a corn versus soybeans spread would require $500.00 margin (higher of the two legs).

A thorough understanding of margin will be of great assistance to both speculators and hedgers in their market operations. The components of a futures margin account are: requirements, realized profits and losses, paper profits and losses, ledger balance, equity and excess.

REQUIREMENTS

This refers to the total amount of initial margin required by the commission firm. For example, the minimum speculative requirements as of December 1, 1971 (see above table) for an account long (or short) two contracts each of cocoa, corn, pork bellies, and silver is $5,800.00. Changes in market value of the open position have no effect on requirements. Requirements increase only when additional positions are established or when one leg of a straddle is lifted; they decrease when existing positions are closed out or when a net position is straddled.

REALIZED PROFITS AND LOSSES

There is an important distinction between realized and paper profits and losses. A profit or loss is *realized* only after a position has been closed out. If the net difference between the selling price and the purchase price (including commission) is a plus figure, the account has realized a profit. If the net difference is a minus figure, the account has realized a loss.

PAPER PROFITS AND LOSSES

On the other hand, paper profits and losses apply only to positions which are still open. A futures position will reflect a paper profit if the future is trading at a higher price than the original purchase price, or at a lower price than the original sale price. In figuring paper profits and losses, deduct the entire round-turn commission on the open position (even though the commission is not charged until liquidation). It makes more sense to conservatively value an account rather than overstate it.

There is a latent relationship between realized and paper profits and losses. Within minutes after a position has been established, in even a moderately active market, the market price will probably have changed. This price fluctuation gives rise to a paper profit or loss. During the entire period that the position is kept open, every different price from the original trade price causes the position to reflect a changed paper profit or loss. When the position is ultimately liquidated (assuming delivery of the actual commodity is not involved), the paper profit or loss which existed at the moment the position was closed out, is realized. In summary, the paper profit or loss which applies to an open position becomes a realized profit or loss when the position is liquidated.

LEDGER BALANCE

One item on the customers' Monthly Statement, the ledger (cash) balance, frequently causes confusion among traders, many of whom incorrectly assume that it reflects the *equity* (worth) of the account. The ledger balance is simply a statement of the account's cash position as of the close of business on any given day. It is calculated by taking the closing ledger balance from the previous month, adding all deposits and realized profits during the current month and, from this figure, deducting all withdrawals and realized losses. The reason that the ledger balance does not reflect the real worth (equity) of an account is that it does not consider paper profits and losses (on the open positions). This may represent a considerable difference. The ledger balance will coincide with the equity of an account only when all open positions are trading at their original purchase or sale prices, or the net of them (a very unlikely circumstance).

EQUITY AND EXCESS

Equity represents the cash value (worth) of an account if all open positions were to be liquidated. It can be calculated by adding all paper profits to the ledger balance, and deducting all paper losses and round-turn commissions.

After determining the requirements and equity of an account, the trader is able to calculate his *excess* by deducting the total margin requirements from the equity. For example, if an account had equity of $8,000.00 and requirements of $6,300.00, the excess would be $1,700.00. Excess represents *buying power* with which to margin additional positions, or cash which may be withdrawn from the account. Commission firms "price" (calculate requirements and equity) each customer's account daily (more frequently in hectic market situations) so as to note margin deficiencies as they occur.

A futures trader should know, at all times, the current financial condition of his account. He will thus know whether he can add to his position without being called for initial margin; he will also be able to anticipate variation margin calls. *Variation (maintenance) margin* is a sum which the trader is required to deposit if the market moves adversely to the extent that his initial margin deposit is impaired, usually by about 25 percent (whenever equity is reduced to 75 percent of requirements).[4] As an example, an account with initial margin requirements of $8,000.00 and equity of $9,000.00, has an excess of $1,000.00. This $1,000.00 may be used to margin new positions, or may be withdrawn from the account. If the market should move against the trader to the extent that the account sustains paper losses of $3,000.00, the equity would be reduced to $6,000 (with requirements unchanged at $8,000.00). Since equity is now 25 percent less than requirements, the trader is required to deposit $2,000.00 to bring his equity up to the required $8,000.00.

Many traders do not understand how they can receive a sizeable variation margin call, when just the previous day, with the market at almost the same price level, there was no margin call. Let us consider the case of the above account, with requirements of $8,000.00. With an equity of, say, $6,100.00 there would be no margin call. However, if the equity in the account were to be reduced by just $100.00 (a very minor adverse move),

4. The 25 percent variation margin figure may vary somewhat, depending on the exchange and on the firm's "house requirements."

the trader would be called upon to deposit $2,000.00, to bring the equity up to $8,000.00.

Sophisticated traders, closely scrutinizing their accounts, can anticipate and sometimes eliminate variation margin calls, by reducing positions or by depositing just enough cash (at the close of a given trading session) to maintain equity slightly above requirements.

The margin required on futures positions generally represents about 8 to 15 percent of the market value of each commodity. However, many adept traders speculate on 4 percent or less. As noted previously, straddle positions enjoy reduced margin requirements, because they generally involve less risks than do outright net long or short positions. This is based on the assumption, generally valid, that a price move in one delivery month of a commodity future will be accompanied by a like move in another delivery month, with the possible exception of straddles involving the spot month or two different crop years of the same commodity. Unfortunately, reduced risks generally involve reduced profit potential. However, there exist reduced margins for spread positions involving two different grains creating, at times, trading situations on reduced margin, limited neither in risk nor in profit potential. For example, a net position in Chicago wheat calls for margin of $500.00, with $750.00 required for a net position in Chicago soybeans. However, a position involving long wheat and short soybeans (or vice versa) would require just $500.00 to margin the entire position. Both the risks and the potential rewards of such high-leverage trading are substantial.

Commissions

Minimum commission rates, established by each exchange for the commodity futures traded on its "board," fall into three categories: a "regular rate," for a position kept open for more than one day; a "day trade rate," for a position opened and closed during the same trading session; and a "straddle (spread) rate," assessed when both a long and a short position in two different delivery months of the same commodity are simultaneously initiated and liquidated.

No commission is charged upon the initiation of a position, with the full "round-turn" commission (covering the entire transaction) being charged upon liquidation. For example, see the following table.

**Selected Round-Turn (Nonmember) Minimum Commission Rates
(as of December 1, 1971)**

	Regular Rate	Day Trade Rate	Straddle Rate*
Cocoa	60.00	30.00	66.00
Corn	30.00	20.00	36.00
Cotton	45.00	22.50	54.00
Pork bellies	45.00	27.00	48.00
Potatoes (N.Y.)	30.00	15.00**	36.00
Sugar No. 11			
to 5.49	42.00	21.00	42.00
over 5.49	62.00	31.00	62.00
Silver (N.Y.)	45.00	22.50	63.00
Soybeans	30.00	20.00	36.00
Soybean meal	33.00	22.00	44.00
Soybean oil	33.00	22.00	44.00
Wheat	30.00	20.00	36.00

* Straddle commission rate covers all four "legs" of a straddle.
** Minimum of two lots.

A futures position is normally liquidated at the same firm where it was established. If the customer desires to transfer the position to another commission firm he will be charged an extra round-turn commission for the transfer. This procedure differs from the securities market, where an individual may order his stocks delivered to another broker, or registered in his own name and delivered to him (the stocks must be fully paid). He may then sell the stocks through another broker, without incurring any extra commission expense.

Commissions on straddle positions are sometimes misunderstood. Generally, both "legs" of the straddle must have been initiated, maintained, and finally closed simultaneously, in order to qualify for the reduced straddle commission. However, a straddle may be "walked forward" (one "leg" may be "lifted" and shifted into another futures month) and, provided that the straddle is always maintained, the reduced commission will still apply.

It should be noted that a reduced straddle margin does not necessarily imply a reduced straddle commission. For example, a spread involving two different grains is eligible for a reduced spread margin, but the full round-turn commissions still apply.

CHAPTER 15 Trading Technique

In our excursion into the mysterious and sometimes misunderstood economic realm of commodities, we have sought to provide practical guidelines to those who venture to trade in this often traumatic area. It seems useful and appropriate, as we approach the final lap of our journey, to discuss those "decision rules" which may help a commodity trader to join the winning minority.

Trading decision rules are essentially of two kinds:

1. *Budget concepts:* designed to carefully control one's risk-taking, and properly husband one's capital.
2. *Trading concepts:* designed to determine what position to take, in which commodity markets, and when.

Let us examine some salient suggestions and cautions in each of these two categories.

Budget Concepts

"Budget," in the sense used here, is concerned with the basic problem of allocating and protecting capital. How much available capital should be allocated to commodity trading in general, and what portion to each specific market? How to prevent spilling too much down the seemingly bottomless hole of persistent error? How to be sure of maximizing those favorable returns which come our way?

This constitutes the area of capital planning and management, and there are certain principal elements to keep in mind:

1. One's capital should be properly divided between uses which vary in degree of likely risk and rewards. A complete strategy of personal finance necessarily involves a choice; or rather, a weighted participation in real

224

estate, bonds, stocks, commodities, *objets d'art,* and other assets. As a prospective commodity trader, you ought to determine in advance what portion of your capital you are prepared to allocate to the "high-risk money game"—commodity trading. This portion should be low enough to preclude your mental or material ruin even if the preassigned capital is entirely depleted. The ultimate means of limiting losses—if your capital is infringed by a previously stipulated amount—is to merely stop trading. Or, as one old-time sage remarked: "When a market position becomes too large, sell down to a sleeping level."

2. It is suggested that the capital which you have allocated to commodity trading be divided into four or five equal portions: one as a reserve, and the remaining portions as "speculative units," each one to be assigned to a selected commodity trade. In effect, this means diversifying to a modest degree, and keeping a portion of your trading capital to cover unforeseen exigencies.

3. For each commodity trade which you are considering, there are two sets of odds which should be estimated ahead of time:

a. *The apparent profit/loss ratio:* that is, the ratio of the gain you are targeting relative to the loss-limit you plan to enforce.

b. *The likelihood of success:* your subjective estimate of the odds that the market will attain your profit objective before it reaches your loss limit.

It is sensible to favor those trading possibilities in which both odds seem exceptionally high. As a rule of thumb, consider only those trades in which you envision a profit at least three times greater than your loss limit and also in which your subjective estimate of the potential for success is markedly greater than 50:50. The higher your "confidence index," based on value analysis and technical measurements of potential, the more you can logically risk.[1]

4. At the moment you initiate a trade, decide as fully as possible what your course of action will be if the market does, or does not, conform to your expectations. Your plan should include a predetermined point at which you will stop your losses by liquidating an adverse position. You should also predetermine an acceptable target price at which to accept profits or to protect those paper profits against a market reversal. This price objective is, of course, subject to continuous review and revision.

5. Your objective in employing speculative capital is to achieve a higher annual rate of return on this capital than on lower-risk investments. Accordingly, you must be concerned not only with profit objectives but also with anticipated "time rates of gain," that is, the speed with which a return on capital is realized. This points up the need to concentrate on markets in which action seems somewhat imminent. It also argues in favor

1. As discussed in Chapters 10 and 11.

of closely watching those technical indicators which might suggest when a move is starting.

6. For the same reason (and exclusive of tax considerations), you should be willing to accept a more modest profit in a few days or weeks than might be considered satisfactory in six months or a year. In short, the time factor should be considered in determining each trade and deciding on price targets.

7. Keep "value" in mind as an important, although not exclusive, consideration. There is an imperfect tendency, in the very long run, for a market to reflect "cost of production," or some other refined measure of inherent worth. Remember, however, that in the brief time it takes for your highly leveraged commodity position to achieve a substantial profit or loss, a commodity may trade far above, or below, its "true value."

Accordingly, any impulse to buy scale-down "below value," or to sell scale-up, when the price is "too high," must be carefully controlled within the framework of "budget" principles for conserving capital. To illustrate, assume you are allocating one trading unit of capital to silver. Let us say, in this case, that the amount assigned to this silver venture is $10,000, out of a total trading capital of $50,000. Assume further, that original margin is $1,500 per contract, and that you have some grounds for entertaining a "floor concept"; you feel silver will not go below around $1.50 per ounce. Thus persuaded, you plan a scale-down purchase program, buying one contract at $1.80, one at $1.65, and one at $1.50. Your intention may be to hold "indefinitely," if possible. To accomplish this goal, you prudently decide to commit only $4,500 out of the $10,000 assigned to silver trading. The remaining $5,500 has been put aside to meet "variation" margin calls. Therefore, if a precipitous market decline claims most of that margin (should prices unexpectedly drop well below $1.50), you may feel obliged to abdicate your position, acknowledging that your underlying assumptions have been challenged, and that high confidence is far from certainty.

For this type of scale-down position to make sense, a trader must conclude initially that the chance of an advance to well over $2.00 per ounce far outweighs the possibility of a decline to under $1.50. Notwithstanding this, the possibility of a totally unforeseen mishap must be considered in the original budgeting.

An alternate tactic can often be employed advantageously when a market has begun to seem fundamentally attractive. Divide one's assigned unit of trading capital into three portions. Buy the first increment when there is reason to believe that the price is untenably low, if possible, near an indicated "floor" or support level. Buy the second unit when acceptable technical indicators have signalled a trend reversal from down to up. And finally, buy the third unit when profits have begun to be manifest on all previously purchased contracts. (Of course, the same logic—and a corresponding one-two-three selling program may be appropriate when a market appears overpriced and near some definable upper limit, e.g., a CCC selling price, when CCC stocks are ample, and when the technical analysis agrees with the fundamental conclusion.)

On occasions, a bullish or bearish straddle looms as an attractive alternative to an outright long or short position. In general, a straddle is to be preferred when it seems likely to reduce the risk inherent in an outright net position without comparably reducing the profit potential of that position.

Trading Concepts

To be successful, detachment and objectivity are two crucial attributes. As a commodity trader, you must be faithless and irreverent. You do not worship silver and gold, regard lead as base, or sugar as sweet. You have passionate conviction in no market, and believe in no "sure thing." You have no predilection for either the long or short side of a market. And any market view which you may assume today is based on a tentative estimate of likelihood, subject to change tomorrow, or on the very next "tick" in the market price.

Our second set of decision rules is concerned with the problem of detecting potentially profitable situations, and deciding when to initiate and close out positions. As commodity market analysts and price forecasters, we must discover: Which markets are interesting? Where may they be heading? And when?

The ultimate decision to buy or sell is a complex amalgam of fundamental and technical factors:

1. *Fundamental analysis:* oriented, above all, to determining when a market is undervalued or overvalued, based on economic factors related to supply and demand.
2. *Technical analysis:* geared to seeking clues—in the action of the market itself—to its probable future course and to the likely extent of a projected price move. It is a most important tool in recognizing "key" turning points (reversals) in price trends.

Sound fundamental analysis is a key to profitable position taking, although positions initiated on the basis of fundamental analysis should be undertaken with one eye on the technical picture. For example, if corn appears fundamentally strong, one should watch the technical situation within that market with particular care, for a chart buy-signal. It is most important, particularly when one trades with relatively limited capital, that the many "tools" of fundamental and technical analysis be combined into a practical, reliable trading technique.

Acknowledging the importance of fundamental analysis, major technical indicators which run counter to fundamentally oriented conclusions should be seriously heeded. Experience has shown that significant fundamental market changes frequently remain obscure until after the market price has already discounted the change. Stubbornly maintaining a position based on a fundamental analysis, in the face of adverse technical indicators (and an adverse price trend) constitutes a quick method of running up substantial trading losses. In short, do not ignore the technical action of the market, no matter how fundamentally oriented a trader you may be.

Whenever possible, it is helpful to buy or sell in line with an observable seasonal pattern. For example, if soybean meal prices have advanced during the fall and early winter for eight of the past ten years, and if there is reason to believe this pattern may be repeated, then one has a supporting argument for purchases indicated by technical analysis. It is suggested, however, that the "seasonal" itself not be viewed as a completely independent basis for trading.

Whenever forward contracts trade at substantial premiums over nearbys, then such premiums may appear to offer an extra incentive to sell. Whenever forward contracts are at sizeable discounts under nearbys, then such discounts may appear to constitute an extra incentive to initiate forward purchases. However, premiums or discounts are not in themselves sufficient justification for trading. The logic of purchase or sale must be justified on additional grounds, particularly on technical considerations.

Remember that support and resistance levels are often useful guides to buying and selling points. Support may exist at a particular price level either for technical reasons (i.e., because a heavy volume of trading occurred at a particular level at some significant time in the past), or for fundamental reasons (i.e., a prescribed government support or sales level). In the same way, resistance may be anticipated at a particular price level for fundamental or technical reasons.

Let us now relate technical analysis to trading technique in specific terms. In so doing, we shall divide the approach to technical analysis into two significant areas: *identification* and *tactics*.

I. Identification
    A. Identify both the major and minor price trends.
    B. Identify the major and minor support and resistance levels.
    C. Identify the trend channel, if there is one.
    D. Identify both the short- and long-term price objectives, based on:
        1. Support and resistance levels.
        2. Pattern count or other chart projection.
        3. 40–50 percent retracement and other chart patterns.
        4. Long-term (continuation) chart analysis.

II. Tactics
  A. Absolute Rules
    1. Do not initiate or hold a position which is counter to both the major and minor trends. *No exceptions.* The violation of this elementary maxim probably constitutes the largest cause of speculative trading losses.
    2. Limit the risk on every position. Do not permit a good profit (40 percent of margin requirements) to turn into a loss; liquidate the position just ahead of the break-even point. If you have closed out prematurely, you can always reenter the market.
    3. On profitable positions, liquidate 40–60 percent of the position at the indicated price objective, and protect the balance of the position with stops (either chart or "money" stops).
    4. Have all orders scaled and entered in advance. Use m.i.t. (market if touched) orders when necessary.
    5. Do not initiate or liquidate a position due to impatience or boredom.
    6. As the equity in an account increases, do not commensurately increase the size of the position. Diversify into other markets and take advantage of other trading techniques, i.e., straddles and options.
  B. Conditional Rules
    1. A major problem in trading involves the correct timing of trades. The solution lies in being more accurate in initiating positions, so that your percentage of correctly timed trades is greater.
    2. Seek to establish positions which are in the direction of both the major and the minor trends. If the major trend is sideways and the major price objective has been substantially attained, trade with the minor trend. (In a major sideways trend, initiate a position on a minor trend signal, with close stop protection.)
    3. The major trend invariably persists longer than anticipated. If you miss the first reversal from a major trend, you will usually get a second chance to catch the new trend (particularly in an upside breakout from a major bottom area). Do not chase a market.
    4. A market will rarely penetrate an important overhead resistance level on the first attempt. Even if it does go through, it should pull back at least to the breakout point. Seek to sell on this rally if the other technical indicators support the sale.
    5. In a major downtrend, sell on a minor rally into overhead resistance, or on a 40–50 percent retracement of the last down-leg. In a major uptrend, buy on a minor reaction into support, or on a 40–50 percent retracement of the last up-leg.
    6. The minor trend rarely lasts more than seven trading days. Seek to buy downflags in a major uptrend, and to sell upflags in a major downtrend, especially if the flag is five or more days old. Do not buy an upflag in an uptrend, especially if near the top of the up-

trend channel and/or near the major upside objective—seek to unload some longs on this type of rally.

7. A major move frequently runs three "legs" (Elliott Wave Theory). Start looking for a major top formation on the third major up-leg of a bull trend; look for a major bottom formation on the third major down-leg of a bear trend.

8. Important crop and statistical reports will usually be supportive of the existing major price trend (an important report is likely to continue the major market trend rather than reverse it). Accordingly, when trading with the minor trend, against the major trend, lighten up or go flat before such a report.

9. As a general proposition, avoid averaging a position when previous trades are held at losses, except if the other technical indicators strongly support the added position, and efficient stop-loss protection is maintained for the entire position.

In connection with the above trading identification and tactics approach, it may be useful to introduce Figure 45. Although this trading form obviously cannot ensure successful trading results, it can materially assist the trader in objectively viewing and analyzing the technical condition of a market, and in timing his trades. When used in conjunction with sound trading principles, perhaps such as those presented herein, it should substantially improve overall trading results.

On Initiating a Position

In analyzing the technical condition of the market, one should look beyond price, trading volume, and open interest. Consider also a psycho-technical approach, based on the market's response to fundamental events, as follows:

A market can be considered *technically strong* if it rallies on bullish news, but does not decline (or declines minimally) following bearish news.

A market can be considered *technically weak* if it declines on bearish news, but does not rally (or rallies feebly) following bullish news.

Traders all too frequently buy at the top of a move and sell near the bottom. Common to most traders and analysts is a major emotional weakness: sentiment invariably turns bullish on rallies and bearish on declines. A more practical (and generally more profitable) approach, which admittedly requires considerable discipline and courage, involves buying on declines (into support), during a major uptrend, and selling on rallies (into overhead resistance) during a major downtrend.

Should one initiate a position on a breakout from an existing trading range (congestion area), or wait for a pullback following the breakout? This depends on several factors, including where in the overall price level

COMMODITY	TREND		SUPPORT		RESISTANCE		TREND CHANNEL		PRICE OBJ.		COMMENT	TAKE ACTION
	MAJOR	MINOR	MAJOR	MINOR	MAJOR	MINOR	TOP	BOTTOM	MAJOR	MINOR		
CATTLE (LIVE)												
COCOA												
COPPER												
CORN												
COTTON												
PORK BELLIES												
SILVER												
SOYBEANS												
SUGAR #11												
WHEAT												

Fig. 45. Trading form.

the market is trading, what type of technical patterns exist, how the open interest recently changed, what the technical action looks like, how large a position one desires to accumulate, and past experience with this commodity on previous breakout and trading situations.

As a general proposition, one can be more aggressive in selling a reversal from what appears to be a major market top, than in buying what appears to be the reversal of a major downtrend. As noted previously, if one misses the exact reversal from a major downtrend, one usually gets a second "shot" at buying. Not necessarily so, however, with breakdowns from major tops, as prices tend to fall more rapidly and surely than they do when reversing from down to up. It has been said that "markets can fall of their own weight, but it takes buying—and lots of it—to put prices up." A bit oversimplified, perhaps, but it does summarize a generally valid phenomenon.

Initiating a market position on a stop order will tend to ensure that you remain uncommitted until a trading range breakout occurs. You will frequently observe a chart formation developing, and may be then inclined to take a position in anticipation of an impending breakout. In too many situations, the expected breakout does not occur. Those eager speculators who prematurely initiate positions in order to save a few extra points, frequently end up losers. (This is one of the reasons that so many traders find themselves buying at the tops of trading ranges and selling at bottoms.)

Speculators frequently buy (or sell) a commodity merely because it seems to be priced too low (or too high) on fundamental grounds. A prime example of this was the world sugar market in 1964 which attracted widespread buying support around the 3.00¢-per-pound level (prices had just completed a huge decline from the 13.00¢ level), because this 3.00¢ level was "even below the cost of production." Many analysts were referring to the fact that, at that depressed level, the value of the bag and the labor involved in bagging the sugar exceeded the value of the sugar itself. Incredibly, the "value" buyers at the 3.00¢ level saw, in short order, their "investment" continue its rapid tumble down to 1.33¢. Needless to say, many speculators capitulated below the 2.00¢ level.

Noting this example, it is logical to conclude that, when a commodity sells at an "illogical" price level (one which appears to be completely out of line with economic realities) there is probably a valid underlying reason for the apparent discrepancy. Inconveniently, though, the explanation may not become apparent until much later. It may require considerable patience and self-control, but successful trading calls for attention to sound trading principles based on technical factors, particularly when prices are illogically "too high" or "too low."

There are certain types of markets which should generally be avoided by all but very experienced traders. These include:

1. Markets where prices can be determined, or even be largely influenced, by an arbitrary decision or action of an individual, organization or government. It may not be possible to realistically analyze a market under these circumstances, since even the fundamentals can be changed at any time. Charts are of limited help, because trend changes can occur so rapidly and unexpectedly that they are virtually impossible to anticipate.

2. Very thin, volatile markets. It is frequently difficult to get in—and even more difficult to get out—of these markets without sacrificing a substantial "breakage," particularly if trading units are large. In addition, these markets are more likely to become distorted (usually to the public speculator's disadvantage) than are the broader, more heavily traded markets.

Closing Out a Position

The timely decision to close out a position is at least as important, if not more so, than the decision to initiate a position. Successful trading requires that you limit losses and allow profits to run. By so doing, you can make money even though you may lose on the majority of your trades. This trading maxim is elementary. It is emphasized in every book and trading primer ever published, and one wonders why it is hardly ever followed. If the reader has traded in futures previously, it is suggested that he review his trading record in the light of this particular advisory. Note how the trading results would have been improved if this tactic had been followed.

After establishing a position, you may be deluged with conflicting stories, rumors and tips. Many of these items have already been discounted, some are exaggerated and some may even be spurious. Therefore, do not permit yourself to be dissuaded from your position. Stand by your commitment as long as the trend continues to move in your direction, but never hesitate to abandon the position if the price trend reverses. If you do trade with stop protection, try to place the stop close enough to the market to close out the position if the trend reverses, but not so close that a purely random fluctuation can set-off the stop.

CLOSING OUT A POSITION AT A PROFIT

Never be reluctant to accept profits, or at least to very closely protect a position, when it appears warranted. There are two approaches to managing a position with a paper profit:

1. Place a stop order below the uptrend line and the significant support area (in the case of a long position), or above the downtrend line and the significant resistance area (in the case of a short position). As the market continues to move favorably, follow each technical rally or reaction and continue to raise your stop (for a long position) or to lower it (for a short position). Ultimately, a correction will continue to move against you, penetrating the trendline and either the support or the resistance level. At that point, the stop will close out your position.

2. From your charts, establish a price objective (below the current market, if you are short; above the current market, if you are long) and liquidate the position when the market moves to that level.

One practical approach to the problem of closing out a profitable position is to close out half the position based on chart price objectives (as discussed in paragraph 2, above), and to close out the remaining half position on stop only in the event that the market reverses course (as noted in paragraph 1, above).

Is it necessary to point out the folly of waiting for a position to become long term, when market analysis and judgment would otherwise dictate closing it out for a short-term capital gain?

When the market begins to reverse direction, one constructive tactic is to hedge a position either by initiating an opposite position in a different future, or by buying an option (a call option hedges a short position, a put option hedges a long position) in the same future. However, if the reversal appears to be a major development, it is probably advisable to liquidate the position. If subsequent trading proves that you prematurely closed out, and your analysis indicates that you should reinstate the position, you have lost only the cost of a commission. This can be considered cheap insurance while you were waiting for the market to indicate the direction of the next move.

CLOSING OUT A POSITION AT A LOSS

A certain percentage of your positions are bound to go against you. Do not procrastinate in taking a loss; the first loss is usually the cheapest. As a famous cotton trader said some 70 years ago, "Run quickly or not at all."[2]

Be objective and honest with yourself. If the market is moving adversely, do not search out reasons to support a losing position. The market will show you when you are wrong; just be humble enough to heed the warning.

Do not straddle to avoid taking a loss. Locking-in a loss by hedging a position necessitates your lifting one leg of the straddle at a later date. You are very likely to lift the wrong leg; what do you do then?

2. Authors' note: we advise running quickly.

As a general rule, avoid meeting a margin call. Instead, close out the position. You have probably already erred by allowing the position to have gone so far against you. Putting up additional margin merely compounds the error.

Anticipating the Unexpected

The market can trade at your limit (or even through your limit on openings and closes) and you may not receive a "fill."

The market can gap, either on the opening or even during the session, filling stop orders at adverse prices, and leaving stop limit orders unfilled.

If you have an order open to initiate a position on either a limit or a stop order, and include a contingent protective stop-loss order, an unexpected market gap on an opening could fill your order and stop you out simultaneously.

Limit-bid or limit-offer moves may prevent you from closing out a position, even where you are willing to do so "at the market." Furthermore, the market could open on subsequent days limit-bid or limit-offer.

Resting stop orders may be "cleaned up," after which the market may resume its original course.

Trading in the Spot Month

The spot month is invariably more volatile and less predictable than distant futures. Prices for spot futures can move out of line with other futures.

Nontrade speculators should, under normal conditions, be out of the spot month before first notice day. Positions can be maintained by switching into a more distant future.

Trading rules can be changed for the spot month: (1) certain types of orders, such as stop orders and contingent orders, may not be accepted; (2) regular trading limits are usually revoked during the spot month; and (3) if trading gets too "hot," margin requirements for the spot month may be arbitrarily increased. At times a brokerage house may accept only liquidating orders for the spot month.

Factors to consider if you do have a spot month position: (1) Who are the long and short interests in the market? (2) What is the size of the open position, and how has it been changing during recent sessions? (3) Size of the deliverable or certificated stocks, and the extent of deliveries thus far in the delivery period. (4) Spot month price as compared to prices of distant futures. (5) History of previous spot month contracts for the same commodity.

Unless you are prepared to take exceptional risks, do not short the spot month if it begins to widen its premium over distant months. Spot month squeezes may persist until the final minutes of trading, or even as the commodity goes off the board.

The "Don'ts" of Trading

Thus far, our counsel has stressed the "do's" of commodity trading. It may be prudent, in parting, to emphasize the "don'ts," even at the risk of some redundancy.

1. Above all, do not allow your losses to run, in the hope that tomorrow you will be right. There should be no tomorrow beyond your pre-assigned risk limit.
2. Do not hide losses by straddling. If the position has soured, the prudent tactic is to get out. Enter straddles on their own merits only.
3. Do not trade without a plan, which encompasses profit objectives as well as loss limits.
4. Do not neglect either the fundamental or the technical side of the market.
5. Do not overlook those seasonal patterns which have had a high frequency of success in recent years.
6. Do not allow a few successful trades to build overconfidence and undermine meticulous care with respect to profit/loss ratios and likelihood estimates.
7. Do not solicit or accept "tips" from brokers or other traders. Do be ready to learn from all qualified sources, however, including a broker with solid research material.
8. Do not permit widely held bullishness or bearishness to dominate your view. Give credence to the "contrary opinion" doctrine which says: "Watch out when the overwhelming majority sees things one way."
9. Do not maintain a position when the trend of the market has reversed adversely.

As commodity traders, one commitment is central. That commitment is to a rational strategy—one whose key objective is to limit one's losses in some predetermined manner and, with equal foresight and decisiveness, to allow profits to run. This involves the necessity of preventing a good profit from turning into a loss. Success in commodity trading is not easy, but it is perhaps more attainable for those who have maximally absorbed, and will practice, the tactics and techniques surveyed herein.

CHAPTER 16   Straddles and Spreads

In preceding chapters, attention was focused on price relationships between cash and futures. We saw that interpreting these differences and seeking to profit from their variations is a core objective in the dealer business. In this chapter, we wish to consider other ways of trading price differences, methods available to anyone in or out of the relevant trade or industry. We refer to "straddles" or "spreads," involving the simultaneous purchase of one delivery position versus the sale of another, based on some reasonable supposition that price differences will change in the desired direction.

The term "straddle" is commonly used in the New York and London markets, while in the Chicago grain trade, the term "spread" is more widely used. In a more restricted sense, straddle may be used to designate a simultaneous purchase and sale in different delivery months of the same commodity (e.g., buy July cocoa and sell December cocoa). The term spread may then be confined to those simultaneous trades which arch across two different markets (e.g., buy July wheat and sell July corn). In this book, we shall take the convenient liberty of using straddle and spread interchangeably.

The kinship between straddle-or-spread trading and hedge transactions, which will be discussed in Chapters 18–20, is obviously close. In fact, a hedge can be viewed as one important member of a great family of straddle transactions, keyed to changing price differences. The economic forces which shape each member of the straddle are often similar. That is, changes in the price differential between different futures generally arise for the same sort of reasons as do changes in the "basis" (cash versus futures price difference). *The principal sources of change are the "dynamic three-some": quality, time, and place.* In other words, one position or contract

237

may be stronger than another because it calls for delivery of an increasingly scarce or preferred quality, or because it requires delivery at a specific time or place at which need is most pressing.

Our attention in this chapter will be confined to straddles between futures contracts, although the alert reader may easily extend the analysis to straddles between actuals and futures or between different actuals positions.

Straddle positions may be classified as follows.

I. Uni-Commodity Straddles
  A. Time Differential
    1. *Intracrop straddle:* purchase of one future versus the sale of another future within the same crop year, or where no distinction exists between crop years (as in silver futures).
    2. *Intercrop straddle:* purchase of a future in one crop year versus the sale of a future in a different crop year (i.e., the purchase of May wheat versus the sale of September wheat).
  B. Place Differential
    1. *Domestic straddle between two locations:* purchase or sale of a silver future in New York versus the opposite position in Chicago silver.
    2. *International straddle between two locations:* purchase or sale of March sugar in New York versus the opposite position in London sugar.
  C. Quality Differential
    1. Price variations between futures markets for the same commodity, arising from different delivery specifications. For example, the purchase or sale of May Chicago wheat (based on soft red wheat delivery) versus the opposite position in May Kansas City wheat (based on hard winter wheat).

II. Multicommodity Straddles
  A. *Straddle based on different stages of processing:* purchase or sale (in equivalent quantities) of January soybeans versus the opposite position in January soybean oil and January soybean meal (the joint products of soybean crushing).
  B. *Straddle between two completely different commodities:* purchase or sale of a Chicago wheat future versus the opposite position in a Chicago soybean future.

It should be clear that the types of straddles defined in the preceding classification need not be mutually exclusive. Overlapping may occur in a variety of ways. For example, when one purchases London cocoa against the sale of a corresponding position in New York, changes in price relationships may occur in response not only to locational factors and to changes in exchange parities but also to differences in delivery specifications. Thus, supply-demand factors may strengthen or weaken a type of cocoa commonly delivered in London (Lagos) more than it affects a common type of delivery in New York (Sanchez).

Purpose of the Straddle

The purpose of a straddle is to make a profit by correctly anticipating variations in the relative market strength of the two positions involved, as expressed by a favorable change in the price differential between the two "legs" of the straddle.

To illustrate: Assume that March wheat is trading at $1.30 and March corn at $1.20. A trader who believes that a wider wheat premium is justified (or will be justified prior to the expiration of the March contracts) may buy March wheat and sell March corn at the prevailing 10¢ per bushel differential. If, sometime later, the March wheat versus March corn differential widens from 10¢ to 20¢, the straddle can be liquidated at a 10¢-per-bushel profit, less commissions. If, on the other hand, the differential ultimately narrows to even money (both futures contracts trading at the same price), the position will be closed at a 10¢-per-bushel loss, plus commissions.

It should be emphasized that the straddle trader is not concerned with the absolute price change in either March wheat or March corn. He is solely concerned with the relative price fluctuation between the two futures, that is, with changes in the differential between the two legs.

When to Straddle

The trader's objective is to successfully predict the direction in which price differences will change, and to select those straddle opportunities which seem likely to undergo the projected difference changes. It will probably be helpful, in this connection, to review case histories which cast light on the more important types of straddles. But before proceeding with this survey, a bit more may be said about what a straddle is, what it is not, and what its possible advantages are as compared to a position involving a net long or short commitment.

Clearly, if we are to favor being long one contract and short another, we must have reason to suppose that the forces affecting the two differ. It is perhaps slightly less obvious that these forces should not differ totally. For if the separation is complete, we have two distinct outright trades and not a straddle at all.

To buy wheat and sell silver simultaneously has, in general, no significance as a straddle; it merely suggests that two unrelated trading positions were simultaneously initiated. On the other hand, the purchase of wheat versus the sale of corn (or vice versa) has true straddle significance because, while there are forces tending to make these two markets act differently, they also enjoy a common bond to the livestock feed economy and may (for this reason or for other reasons) be affected by identical forces as well as by totally distinct ones.

Similarly, if one could buy XYZ futures for delivery this season and sell new crop XYZ for delivery sometime next season, the position would only qualify as a straddle if the two seasons were linked to some degree by supply carryover or other elements. If XYZ was completely perishable, carryover nonexistent, and the two seasons totally separate, the position (long XYZ in one season, short in another) would, in a true economic sense, constitute two independent positions and not a straddle at all.

When does it make sense to consider a straddle in lieu of an outright long or short position in a particular market? The answer, interestingly enough, appears not to have been sufficiently clarified in Wall Street commodity circles. Sometimes it is suggested that there is less risk in a straddle position. This is not necessarily the case. One should consider risk in relation to profit potential and also to margin required, and these may at times be greater in a straddle than in an outright long or short position. Where there exists a choice between a straddle and an outright position, we must determine on a case basis what the profit-loss ratio seems likely to be. We must, further, take into account any difference in the degree of confidence we place in our estimate.

If we are hunting for the ideal case, our keenest straddle preference arises when one leg of the straddle seems likely to respond most if the market goes the way we expect, whereas both legs (long and short) seem apt to move together if the market moves contrary to our expectation. In short, our straddle preference is at its peak if the straddle seems to reduce the profit potential of an outright long or short position far less than it curtails the loss potential in time of error.

So far, we have considered the case in which a straddle may be viewed as an alternative to an outright long or short position. The purest form of straddle, however, is the one which stands fully on its own, having no alternative of a nonstraddle variety, and therefore requiring acceptance or rejection solely on its own terms. Purity of this sort is rare. It may exist where one has no knowledge, interest, or desire to predict the behavior of one leg of a straddle, yet has some confidence in anticipating a change in price differences. Let us say, for instance, that one wishes to speculate on a possible devaluation of the pound sterling and, in order to do so, buys

London cocoa and sells New York cocoa.[1] The speculative interest in cocoa price movement itself may be nil. The critical assumption is simply the notion that, if the pound is devalued, the sterling price of cocoa in London is apt to rise in response to that monetary event, while the New York price will not. To minimize risk, one would hope to enter such a straddle at a price difference which is modest under normal currency conditions. This type of "devaluation straddle" has been employed by many speculators in periods when sterling was on the defensive; it brought notable gains when devaluation followed, while exposing traders to modest losses during periods when the pound remained firm.

Selecting Straddle Possibilities

Apart from the possible virtue of simplicity, what canons and procedures might guide us in selecting promising straddle possibilities? In general, we think the following sequence of exploratory steps might be usefully observed by the straddle hunter.

Study a Particular Commodity Situation in Depth. Often the soundest straddle ideas evolve out of an appreciation of fundamental or technical forces affecting nearby and distant or new and old crop positions, in a commodity under scrutiny. By all means, use commodity brokers and advisory services to help find straddle ideas, but check out the ideas thoroughly yourself.

Review the past behavior of selected straddle possibilities. After deciding that two delivery positions might diverge or converge in the period ahead, study their behavior in comparable past intervals. What has been the typical range of behavior of their price differences? Is this typical behavior likely to recur, based on similarities and differences between the current situation and previous market situations?

Use charts of price differences to help get ideas and to visualize past market behavior. Plot straddle trends with a view towards projecting current price differential formations into probable future trends.

In particular, look for any seasonal regularities in the behavior of the price spread under consideration. But do not assume that such regularities are invariant. Ask yourself whether similar circumstances apply. Remember, too, that the more unfailing a seasonal pattern seems to be, the more likely that it will be discounted in advance. (In straddles, as in outright position trading, there exists a well nigh divine commodity "law" which states that the more popular a "play," the less likely that any profit resides in it.)

1. Chapter 17 discusses an alternative approach to speculating on anticipated currency devaluations, using put and call options.

Finally, estimate as objectively as possible the risks which seem inherent in the straddle. As in an outright position, evaluate the two key sets of "odds": (1) The chance of failure or success, of being right or wrong on the anticipated direction of change in the price differential, and (2) the estimated magnitude of gain if correct, versus the possible loss if wrong.

The Loom of Carrying Charges

When a straddle is primarily concerned with differentials over time[2] then an especially relevant consideration is the magnitude of the premiums or discounts which exist in forward positions.

As noted in Chapter 7, a market in which distant futures are at premiums over spot and nearby values is commonly termed a premium (contango) market. On the other hand, a market in which forward futures (distants) are at discounts, is described as "inverted." (We assure the reader that this second designation carries no imputation of psychiatric or economic inferiority.)

It is of considerable importance that, in a so-called inverted market, there is no set limit to the premium which may prevail on nearby deliveries. On the other hand, in a premium market, the premium of successive delivery months is limited more or less strictly by the magnitude of carrying charges.

Why does this limit exist? The answer is: When a distant delivery trades at anything over a carrying charge premium to a nearby, it immediately becomes profitable for some eagle-eye dealer to buy the near position and to sell the distant one. Having done so, our alert dealer can (if need be) take delivery on the nearby position when it matures, and later retender (redeliver) on the distant (short) position with all his carrying costs paid and with a sure profit on any slight margin above carrying costs.

A premium market is essentially one in which a large supply (i.e., of newly harvested crop) must be carried over a particular period. When this large supply is "looking for holders," there is a tendency for nearby futures to decline relative to distant futures, until the distant futures are at premiums which pay full (or close to full) carrying charges. At this point, trade people are in a position to carry any surplus above immediate requirements. They can purchase the spot commodity and hedge-sell futures at a sufficiently high premium to return their carrying costs (on the actual commodity).

Thus, the activity of the hedger becomes critical in determining the carrying charge relationship between contract months. The short hedger, who is selling futures against his long actuals position, will generally sell

2. Type A in the straddle classification on p. 238.

that future which best reimburses his carrying costs. If December and March wheat sell at the same price, the hedger does not benefit from carrying the wheat from December to March. He is therefore apt to place his sell-hedges in the December future. Typically this causes December to decline in price relative to March and reestablishes a more normal price relationship. If, on the other hand, March sells over December by more than the cost of carrying wheat for three months, the hedger may find the sale of March much more enticing. In effect he is paid a bonus over cost for holding wheat an extra three months. Or, if he markets the wheat sooner, he enjoys a very favorable basis against which to sell his cash wheat.

Although there is a tendency toward full carrying charges when spot supplies are burdensome, spreads will often fall short of that theoretical price differential. One reason is the large incentive which the speculator has to buy spot or nearbys and sell futures at close to carrying-charge differences. Under this circumstance, there is small risk in the spread, since there is very slight scope for the forward contract to widen its premium above the spot or nearby. As discussed above, carrying charges tend to establish a limit, albeit an imperfect one, on forward premiums. That is why buying a nearby and selling a distant future at around full carrying costs is a highly popular low-risk spread.

A qualification of the low-risk exists when (as in silver) varying interest costs constitute the predominant carrying cost factor; carrying charges themselves may then fluctuate rather widely not only with the price level but also with variations in interest rates.

The actions of the larger commercial firms represent, at times, a major influence over changes in price differentials of nearby futures positions. If, in the period shortly before a future expires, trade interests note that nearby futures are selling at less than full carrying cost discounts to distant futures, they may sell (short) the spot month and purchase a forward future. They can then deliver actuals from their inventory position, with the intention of standing for delivery against their long futures position. In effect, this type of transaction enables a firm to maintain ownership of a commodity during the straddle interval (via a long position in futures), without paying the full costs of carrying the commodity.

A trade firm engaging in this transaction will not necessarily wait until its long futures position becomes current in order to take delivery of the actual commodity. Let us assume that the firm has tendered delivery against the short leg of its straddle and that other trade firms have done likewise. As a consequence of this action, speculators holding long positions in the spot future are faced with heavy deliveries of actual commodities and, if these speculators are not in a position to accept delivery (which they are usually not), they must liquidate (sell) their long positions in the spot month.[3] This concentrated selling of the spot month sometimes depresses that future relative to distant futures. If this occurs, commercial interests may begin to advantageously undo their straddles. That is, they may find it profitable to repurchase contracts sold in the spot month, and liquidate their long positions in the deferred months at favorable price differentials. The transaction is completed when they take delivery against their newly assumed long positions (in the spot month), thus restoring their basic inventory position to that which existed prior to the entire transaction.

These transactions are extremely important. They hold the key to the weakness which often occurs in the spot month in carrying-charge markets. They also explain the heavy deliveries which frequently appear on the first delivery day of an expiring contract. This is the time when the speculator may pay the penalty for being long the spot month. Of course, in situations in which a shortage arises, this downward price adjustment in the spot position need not occur; in fact, prices may advance relative to deferred futures. Thus, ever-changing circumstances may account for divergent finales in successive expiring spot months.

With this background in mind, it is now appropriate to examine some of the principal straddles presented in our classifications on p. 238.

Intracrop Spread—Low-Risk Variety

First, let us look more closely at the speculator's "favorite" straddle—a position in which one is long a nearby and short a distant future at as close to a carrying-charge premium as possible. By way of example, we may consider the varying fate of the November soybean contract versus a later delivery month, say January. Let us recall, in this connection, that soybeans are harvested in late September, in October and, most voluminously, in November. Usually there are enough new-crop soybeans harvested by November 1 to make deliveries on the Chicago Board of Trade and also to take care of November crushing requirements. However, rainy weather in September and October can delay the harvest, prompting supply limitations in November. As a general rule, therefore, November soybeans do not sell at a full carrying-charge discount to January beans until it is evident that supplies will be ample in November. This may seem clear during the summer if the supply carried over from the previous harvest is large.

---

3. In practice, speculators liquidating long positions in the spot month frequently reinstate these positions in more deferred futures, thereby maintaining their long futures commitments. Despite this "shifting forward" of positions, there may be a tendency for the spot month to weaken relative to deferred positions.

However, if there appears to be scant carryover, then the situation can remain in doubt until the expiration of trading in November beans. On rare occasions, November beans may trade at a premium to January because of an unexpected weather-induced scarcity.

Normal carrying charges between November and January should be about 5¢ per bushel. In late October, if November beans are selling 3½¢ under January, an elevator operator with newly harvested beans might sell November and buy January. The pattern may now follow that which we discussed earlier. The operator is likely to deliver beans on November 1, thus closing out his short position. The weight of deliveries may well cause November to decline to 5¢ under January. The elevator operator may then buy November and sell January, closing out his long position in January. His position is now long November, and he takes delivery on this position. He thus retains his original position long actual beans, but he has at the same time made a gross profit of 1½¢ per bushel from his straddle.

Assume, in late October, a speculator anticipates an inversion in spread differences. If he buys November and sells January, his risk is limited by carrying charges and by hedgers' willingness to keep them in line. Under ordinary circumstances, the speculator may lose 1½¢ plus commission. On the other hand, if a shortage develops and November climbs to 5 or 10¢ over January, the speculator's profit could be substantial.

As suggested earlier, the carrying-charge straddle can limit risk. However, its gains—though sometimes appreciable—are apt to be infrequent. Led by an "invisible hand," commodity markets tend to balance profit and loss potentialities as weighted by their relative frequency of occurrence.

It should be noted that the speculator often faces a measurable handicap compared to the larger trade firm, since the latter (if an exchange clearing member) need not pay commissions. The cost difference is substantial. For example, the commission on a grain straddle is $36.00 or about ¾¢ per bushel. An elevator or large "commercial" may be happy to undertake straddles that yield ½¢ per bushel profit, whereas the speculator will lose unless he makes ⅞¢ per bushel. A speculator should not enter trades promising only a small gain, which merely pay commissions and do not afford a reasonable return on capital and risk. The speculator must pursue situations in which the probability and magnitude of gain appear to exceed the probability and magnitude of loss.

Intercrop Spread—High-Risk Variety

Where the risks are high, the rewards are apt to be commensurate. When a speculator takes a straddle position involving a short in the nearby position versus a long in the distant, the potential risk has no set limit. In other words, while carrying charges limit premiums on distant contracts, there is no comparable restraint on the discount to which a far-off month can decline. Thus, a short nearby versus long distant position is a high-risk straddle, except to the degree that the prudent speculator limits his possible equity loss with a protective stop. For most traders, we strongly urge such stop-loss protection.[4]

To gain protection against extreme capital loss, we sometimes must pay the penalty of being stopped out of an ultimately correct position. An interesting example in this connection is a cocoa straddle which was widely recommended in August 1954, just as cocoa futures neared an all-time historic peak. At that time, the cocoa market was extremely volatile and the risks inherent in an outright short position seemed high. Many traders felt that the profit-risk ratio might be more favorable in a "bearish" straddle involving the sale of the last old crop future (September 1954) against the purchase of a new crop future (March 1955). Because the old crop position was then extremely tight, the premium of September over March was exceptionally wide—800–900 points (8–9¢ per pound)—reflecting the possibility that, after the old crop position had expired, the cocoa market would experience a downwards price reversal. In the course of this advance, old crop September widened its premium over new March to about 10¢. For stop-loss reasons, the straddle (short September, long March) was sadly abandoned. Too bad! In the five or six weeks after this position was closed out, the cocoa market plunged, and the September premium plunged with it, dropping from 10¢ to around 1¢ over March, and affording a very large return on investment to anyone who had the wit and fortune to stay with it.

We may draw two lessons from this experience: First, a correct analysis is in itself no guarantee of a trading profit. One may easily "pluck failure from success" by an error in timing. In retrospect, it is clear that the above straddle should have been placed at 8 or 7¢ after the trend of the price differential had already turned down. Secondly, a straddle may sometimes return as much or more on capital invested than an outright position.

In all cases, however, the straddle only has meaning if both legs are related pricewise. If the new crop position is governed by economic forces which are completely distinct from those shaping the old crop, then the "straddle" is largely mythical; it is virtually equivalent to two separate outright positions.

When the old crop future is volatile, and the new crop future inert, the principal lure of a straddle as an alternative to an outright position is the lower margin it affords the trader. The old crop versus new crop straddle

4. Or less formally, a preassigned liquidation point.

has other winning applications. As an example, consider a wheat situation in which nearby supplies are ample, so that old crop futures are selling below new crop months. Assume that the possibility exists that some dramatic event could tighten up the old crop position. However, the event which might evoke this change (e.g., a massive wheat shipment to Communist China or the Soviet Union) is problematical. An outright long position in old crop wheat may seem quite vulnerable, given a continued situation of oversupply. The straddle—long old crop and short new crop—may then be an appropriate play. Any developing supply tightness would cause the spread to be profitable while, failing such tightness, straddle differences may change little so the risk may be small.

Clearly, the two-season (intercrop) straddle is a time straddle in which a key event, a new harvest, occurs during the straddle interval. This event abruptly changes the supply situation. It signals an end to a period of depletion of old crop carryover and production, and may in time transform the statistical position.

The concept of an intercrop spread is applicable not only to crops grown in the ground. Pig crops, for example, move in phases rather like field crops. There are into-storage periods and out-of-storage periods. The start of a large marketing season is akin to the harvest of a crop, with expanded supplies becoming available. Frequently, August pork bellies sell at large premiums to the following February, since marketings during the late fall and winter (after expiration of the August future) are heavy.

Introducing Perishability and Its Perils

If the commodities involved in a "time straddle" are perishable, the rules of the game change perceptibly, and the perils may increase.

This perishable category involves two actively traded commodities: potatoes and eggs. Potatoes delivered in one month may be redelivered in the succeeding month provided that they pass inspection. If they do not pass inspection, a large loss may be incurred. They are distressed merchandise and sell at a substantial discount. The threat of cash potatoes falling out of grade can cause premiums on distant futures to exceed the actual carrying costs. The amount by which these premiums exceed the cost of carrying the potatoes will depend on the anticipated storability of the particular year's crop. It will also vary with the price of the potatoes. The premium over carrying costs is actually a form of self-insurance for the man who carries the potatoes from one month to the next. He is risking more with higher priced potatoes so the amount of the "self-insurance" premium is larger.

Because of this perishability factor, there is no well-defined carrying charge limit on forward contracts, and hence no "low-risk" straddle in potatoes comparable to that in nonperishable commodities. Nevertheless, it is fairly popular for potato traders to initiate "bullish" or "bearish" straddles in lieu of outright positions. Does this make sense? Often, the risk reduction achieved by the straddle, as opposed to an outright long or short position, may be relatively small in relation to the cost and profit potential. In potatoes, straddle commissions are substantially the same as on outright long or short positions. Since an outright position is generally more volatile, a smaller number of outright positions can accomplish the same profit goal as a greater number of straddles.

Fresh eggs are subject to still greater perishability limitations than potatoes. Under prevailing futures contracts, the eggs must be freshly laid, and eggs delivered in one month may not be redelivered in any succeeding month. Since the product cannot be stored, carrying charges are not a factor. Egg futures are highly volatile, reflecting changes in the number of layers on farm, in weather and rate of lay, holiday consumption, government purchases, etc. Spreads also vary dynamically, with price relationships between delivery positions affected by seasonal influences and other time-restricted variables.

One classic example of a fresh egg straddle is keyed mainly to seasonal factors. The heaviest hatchings typically occur during the spring months. Six months later the new birds go into production, and gradually the eggs they lay increase in number and size. It is uncertain just when a heavy spring hatch will begin to have marked impact on fall egg prices, perhaps by October, possibly not until November. A common straddle involves September and November deliveries, ordinarily with September selling at a premium to November. The size of the premium will vary according to the confidence the trading public has in the tightness of supplies in September, the relative abundance anticipated for November and—especially—whether new birds begin laying sooner or later than expected. Thus, this straddle can be approached from either side depending on one's market point of view.

While straddles of this kind offer opportunities to egg-wise traders, they are susceptible to very sharp fluctuations once the nearby contract becomes the spot month. Deliveries must be made quickly, and here again members of the egg trade are at an appreciable advantage over the public speculator. In a period of oversupply, excess stocks may be delivered, depressing prices. On the other hand, in time of shortage, a tight situation can run the spot month to lofty premiums. (Most eggs produced in this country are contracted to various supermarkets or other outlets, and in periods of tightness deliverable supplies are apt to be meager.)

It is good general practice for speculators to liquidate any futures position before the first delivery day. In the case of a perishable commodity such as eggs, this rule should be particularly heeded.

Location Straddles

A straddle based on location differences is distinct from but kindred to arbitrage, another member of the great family of price-difference oriented trades.

As commonly defined, arbitrage is the purchase and sale of an identical article in two different locations. Examples of arbitrage are: the purchase of British pounds in Zurich versus the sale of pounds at the same time in Paris; or the purchase of General Motors stock on the Pacific Coast Exchange versus its sale on the New York Stock Exchange. The hallmark of this sort of transaction is its comparative safety. Typically, the arbitrager is prepared to accept delivery in one location (if that becomes necessary), cover all costs, and redeliver in another location, at some predetermined price differential.

Unfortunately, this type of ideal arbitrage situation is a rare phenomenon. First, we do not usually have an identical article in both locations. Although the same commodity may be traded, delivery specifications usually differ in the two locations. A commodity grade or type delivered in one market may not be tenderable in the other. Even if it is, the cost involved in shipment (say from London to New York) may make this procedure uneconomical unless differences are unusually wide. Buying futures in London and selling futures in the same commodity in New York (or vice versa) is, of course, a common operation. But it is not arbitrage in the sense we have defined it. The London delivery may not be exactly identical to the New York delivery, and the purchase of one versus the sale of another does not guarantee a profit based on acceptance of a tender and subsequent redelivery.

To explore the ideal case, we might assume a situation in which an identical commodity is traded in London and New York. Differences in supply-demand conditions may tend to foster price disparities between the two markets. However, as long as it is possible to freely ship the commodity in question from London to New York or vice versa, price disparities are limited by transport costs, and affected (in this international case) by currency rates of exchange and tariffs, if any.

Where the commodity originates in a third country (i.e., Ghana cocoa), then the transport factor also involves the comparative cost of shipping from that source to each of the market areas. To the extent that transportation costs are primary, discrepancies in price differences tend to be corrected quickly. Big firms with open wire communications are operating constantly to take advantage of any price differences which are out of line. These firms are often members of exchanges in both locales and can operate profitably on narrower margins than public traders.

In practice, international straddles in cocoa, sugar, copper, or silver between London and New York are also affected by factors which affect the supply and demand of each commodity in the given locale. This impact may be particularly significant in the spot month. In the fall of 1967, the nearby cocoa position in London sold at a premium to forward deliveries, while the nearby position in New York was at a discount. In the case of London cocoa, warehouse stocks were meager. In New York, although the overall market was tight, ample cocoa stocks existed in relatively undesirable grades. Spot-month disparities can exist when there is not enough time to transport commodities from one locale to another before contract expiration. In the long run, these price differences will be resolved. If London is priced too high relative to the New York market, African cocoa which will normally go to New York will be diverted to London, or vice versa.

As noted earlier, changes in currency parities can be of vital importance in international straddle transactions. For example, in November 1967, the British pound was devalued by 14 percent. Because the price of cocoa, sugar, copper, and silver did not change appreciably in dollar terms, the British price in pound sterling expressed the devaluation almost entirely, increasing nearly 14 percent. A long position in London profited accordingly, while a short position in London showed a corresponding loss. Roughly speaking, each £100 worth of commodity became worth £114.

Clearly, the trader who expects a currency to strengthen or weaken, has the option of going long or short in the foreign exchange market itself. He should not enter an international commodity straddle unless it has added appeal on noncurrency grounds. Summarizing, in terms of commodity dealing, an interesting "play" to consider under these circumstances involves taking a long position in a commodity in the country with a relatively weak currency, and a short position in the country whose currency seems strong.

Straddles Based on Differences in Delivery Grade

Quite often, the difference between two futures markets is primarily a matter of deliverable grades, and/or differentials specified on the respective contracts. The greater this disparity, the more analogous the position is to a straddle in two wholly distinct commodities.

If one has reason to suppose that Sanchez cocoa (commonly delivered in New York) will be harvested in abundance this year, while Lagos (often tendered in London) will be in short supply, then there is *prima facie* reason for considering the purchase of London cocoa versus the sale of New York cocoa.[5] Similarly, if it appears that soft red wheat production will be low and hard wheat production more ample, one may favor purchases of Chicago wheat (based on soft red) versus sales of Kansas City (hard wheat). For example, relative tightness in soft red prevailed in early 1970 and was mirrored in the spread variations shown in Figure 46.

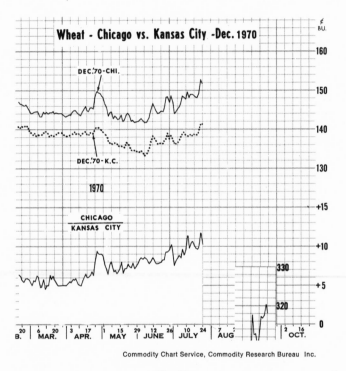

Commodity Chart Service, Commodity Research Bureau Inc.

Fig. 46.

Multicommodity Straddles

As was suggested earlier, all sensible straddles involve some logical relation between the different delivery positions involved. In general, two commodities may be straddle candidates if: (1) they are, to some degree, substitutes for each other (e.g., corn and oats); (2) they complement each

5. In an international straddle of this kind, one must also consider whether the possibility of a change in currency values exists, and whether it supports or discourages the intended trade.

other's use, or are coproducts (e.g., sugar and molasses); or if (3) one commodity is another form of the other (e.g., fresh eggs and frozen eggs).

Two exchange-traded commodities which are to some degree substitutable are corn and oats. Both are used primarily as animal feeds, and their food value per pound is almost identical. Corn weighs about twice as much per bushel; hence there may also be a price disparity about 2:1. Straddle positions involving two bushels or contracts of oats for every one of corn are commonly taken. The incentive to straddle may lie in a relatively short supply or surplus in one or the other grain.

It should be recalled that corn and oats are not always substitutive. True, an animal can eat either, and gain weight. However, animals do not respond well to abrupt changes in diet, and farmers do not react quickly to minor changes in price differences. Their animals are on a feed formula which they are reluctant to change unless the economic factors become extremely persuasive. Therefore, the exact 2:1 ratio between corn and oats prices does not exist often; nor is the prevailing price ratio necessarily stable.

A most interesting and popular straddle is wheat versus corn, notwithstanding the major difference in their use patterns. Wheat is typically priced well above corn so that it is used primarily for human consumption, with very little going into animal feed. However, wheat is superior to corn as a feed if the two are priced evenly. If wheat in Chicago is only 10¢ per bushel over corn, there will be many rural areas where, owing to dislocations or abnormal transportation cost, the two will sell at parity. Therefore, some wheat will go into feed channels. However, the incentive may not develop at every rural area. Furthermore, (as noted earlier) farmers are reluctant to alter the diets of their animals in the short run to achieve modest savings. However, a low wheat/corn price difference early in the season can encourage feeders to substitute wheat for corn; this will induce the price of wheat to rise relative to the price of corn. In this instance a spread (long March wheat versus short March corn) may be reasonable because of the significant and dependable relationship between the two commodities. The straddle will be profitable if farmers make appreciable substitution, and if no extraneous factors affecting either wheat or corn enter the picture. (A disturbing influence might be the cancellation of a large export order by Communist China for Canadian wheat, or a drought in the month of August in the corn belt.)

An excellent example of a wheat-corn straddle which worked out successfully is the accompanying analysis presented in a commission house study.[6]

6. *Wheat and Corn—The Tortoise and the Hare,* New York, Reynolds & Company, August 1969, pp. 14–15. By permission.

Wheat vs. Corn

As an alternative to an outright purchase of wheat or corn, it may be appropriate at this time to consider a straddle position, involving the purchase of December, March or May wheat vs. the sale of the corresponding month in corn. Such a straddle, in our judgment, has appeal at around recently prevailing differences of 10–11 cents in the December and March delivery months, and 7 to 8 cents in May (in each case, wheat premium over corn).

In the late 1950's and early 1960's, this straddle performed very well, widening appreciably in 7 out of 8 years between July and December or January. However, since 1964, the seasonal action of this straddle has been poor, for what we believe are two main reasons:

1) Wherever there is a clearcut seasonal pattern, the futures market tends to discount it out of existence.
2) More important, in this case, the successive reduction in wheat support price established a trend towards narrowing of wheat/corn differences. Beyond that, until recently, wheat was hampered by a static demand picture, and the influence of very poor world market conditions. We think this situation is now changing, mainly due to the fact that wheat has come to be priced at a demand-stimulating level relative to corn.

Other factors which seem to favor improvement in wheat vs. corn in the next few months are:

1) Seasonally, wheat marketing pressure is at or near its peak, whereas the corn harvest should be gaining in the coming months, tending to weaken corn prices while wheat steadies.
2) The stocks-in-all-positions report pointed to a decrease in corn consumption in April/June. Until the facts became known about usage in July/September, the last quarter of the 1968/69 corn year, traders must be concerned about the possibility of a further drop in estimated corn consumption.
3) Unlike wheat, open interest in corn is well above recent year averages, and the number of small speculator longs now concerned over losses is greater. Thus, corn seems technically weaker.
4) Compared to corn, wheat futures are lower priced relative to the Loan, and also relative to last year's lows.
5) As the accompanying chart [Figure 47] of price differences suggests, the wheat/corn spreads appear to have leveled off after a steep decline, and this action now suggests that an upturn may be beginning.

This spread, it should be recalled again, is not one which has performed with utter regularity in the past. We are recommending it because we think fundamental and technical factors have shifted in wheat's favor.

Processor's Straddle

A common type of straddle involves a single commodity at different stages of processing. Soybeans are crushed to yield meal and oil. Fresh eggs are broken and then frozen. When futures contracts exist for two stages of processing, there is a vehicle for traders to interpret price difference.

The most popular processor's straddle is one between soybeans and its products, soybean meal and soybean oil.[7] It is a useful straddle for a variety of reasons. In the United States, nearly all soybeans harvested are

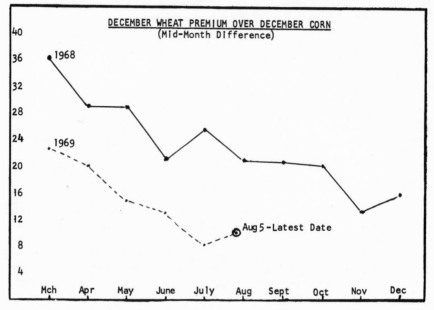

Fig. 47. (Courtesy of *Wheat and Corn—The Tortoise and the Hare*, Reynolds & Company, August 1969, p. 15.)

crushed. The value of by-products other than meal and oil is negligible, amounting to less than 5¢ per bushel.

Essentially, this straddle entails a long position in products (meal and oil) and a short in beans when it appears the processing margin will widen; and conversely, a short position in products (jointly) and long beans when a narrowing of the conversion spread is indicated.

The "board conversion" (processing margin) is the premium of meal and oil jointly over beans as computed from prevailing prices on the Chi-

7. One bushel of soybeans, weighing approximately 60 pounds, is crushed into 48 pounds of soybean meal and 11 pounds of soybean oil.

cago Board of Trade. To compare the difference, a formula is often used which approximately reflects the meal and oil content of a bushel of beans. The oil price is multiplied by 11, since there are 11 pounds of oil in each bushel. The meal price, quoted in dollars per ton, is first divided by 2,000 to convert it to a per-pound basis. It is then multiplied by 48 since there are 48 pounds of meal in each bushel of beans. The total is then multiplied by 100, since the result is desired in cents rather than in dollars. A combination of these steps calls for the dollar price of meal to be multiplied by 2.4. For example, if meal sells at $72.00 per ton, it is equal to about $1.73 per bushel—and if oil is at 9.00¢ per pound, it is worth 99¢ per bushel. If we combine the two we get a price of $2.72. We then measure this joint product value against the price of soybeans for the same delivery month, and see if there is a minus or a plus conversion difference.

Let us say we are comparing March products and March beans and we find that the "board conversion" is 5¢. We study past charts of this spread's behavior and find that March products have usually varied from 5¢ under March beans to 20¢ over, with some recurrent tendency (not very consistent) for this difference to widen in the last few months of the March contract's life.

Will that happen this year? The most important single consideration is the size of crushing capacity. If it is very large, then product margins over beans may remain small. On the other hand, if there is reason to anticipate heavy demand for products relative to crushing capacity, product margins can be very wide.

One of the most extraordinary changes in the soybean conversion spreads occurred in the 1969–1970 season when the premium of January products over January beans soared from 1 or 2¢ to 50¢. In this rare instance, the profit on a low margin and relatively low-risk straddle matched what one might happily contemplate on an outright position. In this instance, the spread widened to a unique degree because the demand for soybean products soared to a level which strained existing processing capacity.

At times, product demand may be especially keen for either meal or oil. Typically, demand for feed meal is most intense during the winter, particularly when weather conditions are unusually severe. Soybean meal is therefore highly dependent on livestock and poultry numbers, whereas oil requirements are especially sensitive to variations in supplies of competitive fats and oils. Beans themselves can come into temporary scarcity during late summer and fall. Shortages around harvest time can be brought about by a holding policy on the part of farmers, by a delayed harvest, or an extra-large export movement.

As the analyst often notes with some incredulity, the board conversion between beans and products is sometimes very small. On such occasions, the products appear to be worth less than the beans. Is this so? And if it is, how do processors stay solvent? There are several explanations. First of all, beans delivered to a Chicago elevator cost appreciably more than they do on a farm in central Illinois or Iowa, while the crusher buys from the lower-priced farm source. Secondly, the crusher obtains the small by-product value mentioned earlier. Thirdly, he is able to sell some meal at premium prices, due to higher protein content. And finally, the processor is often able to use futures to reduce his bean cost, or to improve his effective margin. For example, when "board margin" is high, the processor may sell product futures against his bean purchases to, in effect, "lock in" the higher profit margin.

For any trader initiating a conversion or processor's spread, it is desirable that the dollar amount of the products should about equal the dollar amount of beans. This is achieved minimally when one buys (or sells) one contract of beans versus the sale of one contract each of meal and oil. A more exact ratio entails 10 contracts of soybeans versus 9 contracts of oil and 12 contracts of meal.

Another straddle of this type is the fresh egg/frozen egg processor's straddle. It involves the following computation: 1 contract of fresh eggs contains 600 cases of 30 dozen each. Each case weighs about 40 pounds liquid equivalent. Therefore, the weight of the liquid egg in the contract is 24,000 pounds. A contract of frozen eggs contains 36,000 pounds of liquid eggs. So three contracts of fresh eggs contain 72,000 pounds and 2 contracts of frozen eggs also contain 72,000 pounds. The straddle is thus 3 contracts fresh versus 2 contracts frozen. The straddle may be done in either direction.

Since one case weighs 40 pounds and there are 30 dozen in the case, then 1 dozen weighs approximately 1.33 pounds. If we divide the price of a dozen fresh eggs by 1.33 we get the liquid per-pound equivalent. We then must account for about 2–4¢ per pound processing costs. The pure mathematics breaks down here. The eggs delivered on the contracts are not the same eggs broken. The fresh eggs delivered against short positions must be in warehouses (size graded) and must pass approximately 80 percent USDA grade A. The eggs broken for highest grade frozen eggs are brought directly from the farmer or producer ungraded and are broken at a nearby breaking plant. One must not be misled by the great difference in value existing between the liquid value of the fresh egg quotation for a given month and the frozen egg price. The important consideration is the price which farmers are getting from the breaking plants, not the price of fresh eggs delivered on the exchange. If these figures also show a discrepancy after the cost of processing is added, there may be reason for a straddle.

The reverse is also true. If it appears that the difference is too large, one may sell the fresh eggs and buy the frozen.

Other Straddle Plays

To straddle is to play one kind of futures game. To be a winner, one must play this game objectively, not impulsively, and with a full understanding of the rules. Often, the simple, straightforward approach is best. Now and then, a specialized type of straddle procedure may be justified.

Some people enter straddles by putting on "legs" at different times. In this way, they combine an outright position with a straddle. This may make sense if it is originally planned in this manner. Sometimes, however, a straddle is initiated with the notion of hedging a losing outright position. This is done to prevent a margin call, or to avoid the unpleasant necessity of taking a loss. Such a tactic is usually unsound. It will not revoke the loss—it will only initiate a new position. In general, a straddle should be chosen on its own merit or not at all.

A converse tactic may be still more imprudent. Some traders, having erred in their choice of a straddle and having established a "paper loss" will lift one leg, rather than liquidate both simultaneously and accept the loss. Here they are creating an outright position and a new risk. They are not erasing a loss. The appropriate question to ask is: Would I enter this straddle or outright position on its own merits if I were not faced with a prior losing commitment?

In general, markets are unkind to traders who will not let go of past errors and who seek to rectify them by wishful actions.

As we said before, the purpose of these straddles is to profit from more-or-less predictable changes in price difference. However, there is one type of straddle which is not concerned entirely with the possible gain from changing price differences. We refer to the so-called "tax straddles" which, in addition to providing the risks and profit possibilities of straddles in general, may provide specific tax advantages to certain investors. Typically, this type of straddle seeks to convert short-term into long-term capital gains and to defer the tax liability into the following year. In addition, certain straddle transactions may, as a corollary benefit, convert ordinary income into a capital gains category. And finally, a number of straddle techniques may be of significant interest to corporations, with respect to their particular tax situations. The specific application of these straddles comprises an appropriate subject for detailed discussion with one's commodity broker and tax counsel.

CHAPTER **17** **Commodity Put and
Call Options**

In commodities as in securities trading, a prime consideration in any speculative undertaking is the magnitude of risk involved. The successful speculator seeks to establish, with every market commitment, an acceptable and predetermined risk allowance. Any method of trading which limits risks while permitting a relatively unlimited profit potential merits close attention.

Commodity put and call options, traded primarily in London, provide the opportunity to speculate in fast-moving commodity markets with limited and predictable risks.

Experienced commodity operators recognize that the longer-term position trader is more apt to be successful than the short-term "in and out" speculator. A major problem facing the position trader, however, is that even when he is correct in his basic market position, he may be whipsawed out of the market by adverse short-term fluctuations, or by failure to promptly meet variation margin calls. Through the use of commodity options, an investor can initiate and maintain a net position in a high profit potential commodity market, with the following assurances.

1. His risk has a set limit (the option premium plus commission), whereas his profit potential is relatively unlimited.

2. He can maintain his basic net position (or "hedge" it when he deems it opportune) for an extended period of time; e.g., for up to 14 months, without the risk of margin calls, stop-loss closeouts, and whipsaw moves.

Although the use of put and call options by serious investors in the securities market is quite common, only very few of the more sophisticated commodity market operators are fully knowledgeable concerning option possibilities as they relate to commodity trading. Let's examine the technique of trading commodities through put and call options.

258

What Is a Commodity Put or Call Option?

1. A "call option" gives the holder the right to "call" (or buy) a specified quantity of the commodity future at a price specified in the option contract, on or before a specified date.

2. A "put option" gives the holder the right to "put" (or sell) a specified quantity of the commodity future at a price specified in the option contract, on or before a specified date.

3. A "double option" is a combination "put" and "call" on the same commodity. It permits the holder to either buy or sell (but not both) a specified quantity of the commodity future at a price specified in the option contract, on or before a specified date.

Where Are Commodity Options Traded?

Commodity options are traded primarily in London, as follows:

Cocoa: London Cocoa Terminal Market Association.
Coffee: London Coffee Terminal Market Association.
Metals: Directly between dealers.
Sugar: United Terminal Sugar Market Association.

What Are the Elements of a Put or Call Option?

THE "STRIKING PRICE" (BASIS PRICE)

This is the price at which the holder of a call option can "call" (buy) his futures contracts, or the price at which the holder of a put option can "put" (sell) his futures contracts. The striking price is, generally, the price at which the corresponding future is trading at the time the option is purchased, and it is specified on both the option contract and the broker's confirmation.

THE "PREMIUM"

This is the sum of money which the option buyer pays for the option privilege. Generally, the premium is governed by the life of the option; the longer the option life for a given commodity, the higher the premium. (Most commodity brokers can furnish current premium quotations on available options.)

THE "COMMISSION"

This is the broker's fee for handling the transaction. A commission is charged for each option purchased, with a second commission charged only if the option is declared (exercised).

THE "DECLARATION DATE" (EXPIRATION DATE)

As specified on both the option contract and the broker's confirmation, this states the exact date and hour that the option will expire. In order for the option to be "declared" (exercised), the broker must receive appropriate instructions prior to expiration of the option. Any option not declared prior to the declaration date is automatically "abandoned."

THE "BREAK-EVEN POINT"

This element of an option can be calculated by adding the premium and the round-turn commission to the "striking price" of a call option; or deducting the premium and the round-turn commission from the "striking price" of a put option. An option holder may find it advantageous to "declare" an option just prior to its expiration, if the price of the respective future is higher than the "striking price" of a call option, or lower than the "striking price" of a put option. Declaring the option will, at least, recover part of the costs.

What Is the Life of a Commodity Option?

Commodity Options are generally available for periods ranging from 2 to 14 months.

Who Writes Commodity Options?

Commodity Options are primarily written by trade firms engaged in the actuals (cash) commodity business (e.g., dealers, manufacturers, and processors). Certain large speculative commodity operators, at times, write options in conjunction with their basic trading program. The option premium paid by the "taker" (buyer) is credited to the account of the "granter" (seller), but is not actually paid out until the option has either been exercised or abandoned. The London Produce Clearing House, Limited, will pay interest to the "granter" on premiums held, at the then prevailing rate of interest.

Who Guarantees Commodity Options?

Options in London cocoa, coffee, and sugar are guaranteed by the London Produce Clearing House, Limited. Metals options are guaranteed by the writer of the option.

Trading Futures Against an Option Position

Why should one buy or sell futures against an option position? The purpose of this market action is simple, even if the technique appears complex at first sight. One trades against an option position in order to respond flexibly to changing judgment of the price outlook.

Let us say that you own a call option, and your confidence in the market's strength has faded; you feel that a downturn is likely. In this circumstance, you may sell futures against your essentially bullish call option. On the other hand, if you hold a put option and you begin to feel that the market is turning upwards, then you may purchase futures against this bearish put option.

What have you accomplished through this sophisticated hedge stratagem? First and foremost, you have reversed your market position as soon as it seemed timely, without creating a wide-open risk. Note that the turnabout in your position is complete. If you previously held a call option, on which you enjoyed unlimited profit potential on the upside and a specified loss limit on the downside, selling futures short versus the call creates an unlimited profit potential on the downside, with no loss possibility on the upside.

For example, let us assume that you had bought a call option on December silver at 1.71, and that the market had vindicated your bullish judgment, advancing to 1.92. Thus, you would now have a "paper" profit of $2,100 less the cost of the call itself. However, you have come to believe that a price downturn is likely, and you would like to reverse your position without jeopardizing your profit, or incurring any additional risk. You may achieve this by hedging your call option with the short sale of a December silver future. You have just succeeded in reversing your position. You now have no risk (no further profit potential, either) on the upside, with unlimited profit potential on the downside. Should the market advance further, the additional gain on your call option will be offset by the corresponding loss incurred on your short futures position. Nor can you lose any of the profit that was "locked into" your call option at $1.92, except for the commission charge on your short futures position.

It should be clear that, had the market originally fluctuated in a narrow range or had it failed to yield any initial profit on the call option, there would be no advantage to this trading technique. Sophisticated though this method is, it offers no automatic or guaranteed gain; only intriguing flexibility and protection.

In summary, then, this trading technique permits one to "lock in" a profit on an option position, and then to "reverse" one's trading position in the market while maintaining full protection against adverse market action. Thus, in trading against options, one can exercise market judgment within the framework of fully controlled risk.

Using Options to Protect a Profitable Futures Position

What can a trader do when his futures position shows a good profit, and yet he is uncertain whether the market will continue to move in his favor? If he liquidates the position, or hedges it with an offsetting position in a different future, he will be "locking in" the profit. However, he also will have eliminated the opportunity for further gain from a continuation of the prevailing move. Commodity options can be particularly useful in such situations.

Let us assume a trader, anticipating a bull move in sugar, initiates a long futures position. If he is right, and the market moves up, he will at some point be faced with an interesting dilemma. Assume that the market has reached his basic price objective, and he is now concerned with "locking in" or, at least, protecting his profits. He believes that the major trend is still upwards, and that if he sells out here he may miss a prolonged further rise. At the cost of the option premium he can buy put options, and thus achieve a double advantage. First, he preserves his "long" futures position and hence his ability to profit from a further price upswing. Second, he has at the same time protected himself from a market reversal. (If the price turns down, he can recover from his put option any profit lost on his long futures position.) In an analogous way, a profitable "short" position can be protected by means of the purchase of call options.

Converting a Call Option into a Put Option, and Vice Versa

Sometimes a trader wants to buy a particular option, but finds that, at that moment, only the opposite option is available. What alternative does he then have? He can either defer making the option commitment, and perhaps miss an appealing position, or else he can buy whichever option is readily available, and convert it into the opposite desired option. For example, if he wants to buy put options, and only calls are available, he can achieve his basic objective by buying the calls and simultaneously selling short a like quantity in the corresponding futures position. Just as if he had bought the puts, this "converted" position will afford him profits from any downwards move. Yet, in the event of an unexpected upturn, his risk is limited to the option premium. The disadvantage of this technique is the additional round-turn commission cost on the short futures position; however, that cost may be modest relative to the potential market gain. Similarly, a put option can be converted into a call through the purchase of the put option and the simultaneous purchase of the corresponding futures position.

Using Options to Make Long-Term Capital Gains on a Profitable Short Position

Based on existing United States tax laws, a profit on any short position (be it in commodities, commodity futures or securities) is treated as a short-term capital gain, regardless of its holding period. (By contrast, a profitable long position would be eligible for long-term capital gains treatment if it was held open for six months plus one day or longer.)

It may be possible, through proper employment of commodity options, to make long-term capital gains from a profitable "bearish" position. Let us assume a trader is bearish on silver, at a price of $2.05 for a year-off future. He correctly anticipates a major sell-off to around the $1.70 level. If he sells the future short at $2.05, not only does he risk margin calls and a virtually unlimited loss potential (if the market continues upwards), but also he can expect no better than a short-term capital gains tax on his profits, even though he may have remained short for 8 to 10, or even 12 months.

Instead of selling the future short, let us assume that he had purchased a 12-month put option and that, over the course of the next 12 months, the market had declined by 30¢ per ounce (equal to $3,000 per contract). What would be the most advantageous method of "realizing" his $3,000 (less expenses) profit? He could "declare" his put option (at the $2.05 "striking price") and simultaneously buy-in his newly created short position at the then-prevailing price of $1.75. However, the profit from this operation would be considered a short-term capital gain, and would be taxed accordingly. A more advantageous alternative would be to sell the put option back to the broker. (Before originally buying the option, it should be ascertained that the broker can handle such a transaction.) The proceeds from the sale of the option should equal the profit which would have resulted from the closeout of the futures position. However, since the option was sold after having been held for more than six months, the profit accruing from the sale would be taxed at long-term gain rates. (Similarly, the more-than-six-months holder of a profitable call option could, when "cashing in" his position, sell the option back to his broker, rather than "declare" it and simultaneously sell out the future.)

Using London Commodity Options as a Currency Hedge

From time to time an interesting "play" develops in international currency (foreign exchange) markets. Whereas one can, at times, capitalize on an adroit analysis of the international currency situation by properly trading futures, it is possible to further refine the operation (limited risk, etc.) by dealing in London commodity options. Assuming one anticipates a weakening and possible devaluation of the British pound sterling, it is possible to take advantage of such a currency realignment by buying call options on forward commodities in London. The London commodity will tend to advance over its New York counterpart by roughly the same percentage as the pound sterling is devalued; for example, a 14 percent devaluation would lead to approximately the same percentage advance in the price of London sugar over New York sugar. The purchase of appropriate call options in London commodities provides the investor with the normal profit potential versus modest risk of the call option, *plus* the added "kicker" of the devaluation percentage appreciation, should it occur.

EXAMPLES OF CALL OPTIONS*

Limited-Risk Speculation. Mr. A. is bullish on world sugar, and buys a one-year call option in London. His striking price is £43.50 per ton (equivalent to 4.20¢ per pound for New York sugar #11). The premium is £3.15 per ton (£157.50 or $378.00 per contract), and the round-turn commission is £15.00 ($36.00). Mr. A's break-even point is £46.95 (equivalent to 4.57¢ for New York sugar # 11), calculated as follows:

Premium	£157.50	$378.00
Commission (round-turn)	15.00	36.00
Total Cost	£172.50	$414.00
Striking Price	£43.50	4.20¢
Plus Cost	3.45**	.37¢
Break-even Point	£46.95	4.57¢

** Cost per ton.

To Replace a Long Futures Position. Mr. B. is long one contract (10,000 troy ounces) of distant silver futures. He decides to sell his futures commitment and replace the position with a call option. He sells

* All calculations are based on an exchange rate of $2.40.

the future at 76.5 pence per ounce (equivalent to $1.835 per ounce) and buys the same month London call option at the same striking price (76.5 pence). The premium cost is £354.00 ($849.60) and the round-turn commission is £19.00 ($45.60). Mr. B's break-even point is 80.2 pence ($1.925), calculated as follows:

Premium		£354.00	$849.60
Commission (round-turn)		19.00	45.60
	Total Cost	£373.00	$895.20
Striking Price		76.5 pence	$1.835
Plus Cost		3.7	.090
	Break-even Point	80.2 pence	$1.925

To Protect a Short Futures Position. Mr. C. is short world sugar futures (either in New York or London), and seeks to limit his risk. He initiates a protective hedge position by buying the same month London call option as he is short in futures. His striking price is £44.00 per ton (equivalent to 4.26¢ per pound for New York Sugar #11). The premium is £2.50 per ton (£125.00, or $300.00 per contract), and the round-turn commission is £15.00 ($36.00). Mr. C. has now limited the total risk on his short futures position to £140.00 ($336.00), from current levels, calculated as follows:

Premium		£125.00	$300.00
Commission (round-turn)		15.00	36.00
	Total Cost	£140.00	$336.00

Mr. C. can now maintain his basic short position, comfortably waiting to cover it at a time and price of his own choosing. Should Mr. C's bearish analysis prove wrong (and he can safely remain short during the entire life of the call option), he merely has to exercise his call option to liquidate his short futures position. Most commodity traders would be willing to initiate a short position in a bearish, fast-moving commodity, for up to 14 months, with their maximum loss limited to the premium and commission cost, and with a virtually unlimited profit potential.

To Add to an Existing Long Position, with Minimum Risk. Mr. D. is bullish on cocoa and is already long in a distant future. He would like to add to his basic long position, but does not want to commit additional funds to back up a larger futures position. Therefore, Mr. D. buys call options on distant months of London cocoa.[1] His striking price is 289/6 shillings per cwt. (equivalent to 31.02¢ per pound for New York cocoa). The premium is 23 shillings per cwt. (£115.00, or $276.00 per contract), and the round-turn commission is £12.00 ($28.80). Mr. D's total risk on

1. This illustration refers to a contract of London cocoa, which consists of 5 tons, as compared with the 13.4-ton contract for New York cocoa.

his additional long position is just £ 127.00 ($304.80), while his profit potential is virtually unlimited.

Premium	£115.00	$276.00
Commission (round-turn)	12.00	28.80
Total Cost	£127.00	$304.80

EXAMPLES OF PUT OPTIONS

Limited-Risk Speculation. Mr. E. is bearish on world cocoa, and buys a nine-month put option in London.[2] His striking price is 287 shillings per cwt. (equivalent to 30.75¢ per pound for New York cocoa). The premium is 21 shillings per cwt. (£ 105.00, or $252.00 per contract), and the round-turn commission is £ 12.00 ($28.80). Mr. E's break-even point is 263/6 shillings per cwt. (28.23¢ per pound), calculated as follows:

Premium	£105.00	$252.00
Commission (round-turn)	12.00	28.80
Total Cost	£117.00	$280.80
Striking Price	287/–	30.75¢
Less Cost	23/6	2.52
Break-even Point	263/6 (per cwt.)	28.23¢ (per pound)

To Replace a Short Futures Position. Mr. F. is short world sugar futures. He decides to limit his risk by covering his futures commitment and replacing it with put options. He covers his short position at 4.09¢ per pound (New York price) and simultaneously buys the same month London put option at the equivalent striking price of £ 42.42 per ton. The premium cost is £ 2.75 per ton ($330.00 per contract), and the round-turn commission is £ 15.00 ($36.00). Mr. F's break-even point is £ 39.37 per ton (3.76¢ per pound).

Premium	£137.50	$330.00
Commission (round-turn)	15.00	36.00
Total Cost	£152.50	$366.00
Striking Price	£42.42	4.09¢
Less Cost	3.05*	.33
Break-even Point	£39.37	3.76¢

* Cost per ton.

To Protect a Long Futures Position. Mr. G. is long silver futures (either in London or New York), and seeks to limit the risk on this position. He

2. *Ibid.*

initiates a protective hedge position by buying the same month London put option as his long future. The striking price on his put option is 75.7 pence per ounce (equivalent to New York silver at $1.817 per ounce). The premium cost is £270.80 ($650.00) and the round-turn commission is £19.00 ($45.60). Mr. G. has, by employing a protective put option, limited the total risk on his short silver position to £289.80 ($695.60) from current levels, calculated as follows:

		£270.80	$650.00
Premium		£270.80	$650.00
Commission (round-turn)		19.00	45.60
	Total Cost	£289.80	$695.60

Mr. G. can now maintain his basic long futures position, with the option of liquidating it whenever he chooses. If Mr. G's bullish market assessment proves wrong (and he can safely remain long during the entire life of the put option regardless of adverse price fluctuations), he can ultimately exercise his put option to offset his long futures position. From a trader's point of view, Mr. G. enjoys a most enviable position. He is long in a bullish silver market with his maximum potential loss limited to £289.80 ($695.60), and with an unlimited profit potential during the entire life of the option.

To Add to an Existing Short Position, with Minimum Risk. Mr. H. is bearish on world sugar, and is already short in a distant future. He would like to add to his basic short position, but cannot commit sufficient additional funds to adequately back up the larger futures commitment. As an alternative, Mr. H. buys put options on distant London sugar. His striking price is £44.10 per ton (equivalent to 4.27¢ per pound for New York sugar No. 11). The premium is £2.50 per ton ($300.00 per contract), and the round-turn commission is £15.00 ($36.00). Mr. H's total risk on his additional short commitment is just £140.00 ($336.00), calculated as follows:

		£125.00	$300.00
Premium		£125.00	$300.00
Commission (round-turn)		15.00	36.00
	Total Cost	£140.00	$336.00

THE DOUBLE OPTION

The double option offers the following possibilities:

1. It permits protected short-term trading within a broadly fluctuating market.

2. In the event that a trading-range market comes alive and commences a major move in either direction, the double-option-holder is assured of having a market position from the very inception of the move. Further-

more, he can safely maintain this position for a year or more, without the risk of margin calls, stop-loss orders or whipsaw moves.

Mr. J. notes that world sugar futures are locked within a broad trading range, with the likelihood that any significant breakout from this trading range will presage a move of substantial proportions. Ideally, Mr. J. would like to: (1) scalp the market while prices are locked within the broad trading range, (2) have a "holding" position as the market commences a major move.

As a means of accomplishing these diverse objectives, Mr. J. buys a 12-month double option in London sugar. His striking price is £43.90 per ton (equivalent to 4.25¢ per pound for New York sugar No. 11). The double-option premium is £5.25 per ton ($630.00 per contract), and the round-turn commission is £15.00 ($36.00). The entire cost of Mr. J's full-year double option operation is £277.50 ($666.00), calculated as follows:

Premium	£262.50	$630.00
Commission (round-turn)	15.00	36.00
Total Cost	£277.50	$666.00

If Mr. J. takes full advantage of the tactical possibilities afforded by the double option, by aggressively trading the market and ultimately participating in a major price move, his final results should be profitable.

PART VI

THE USE OF

FUTURES MARKETS

BY COMMERCIAL INTERESTS

CHAPTER **18**   **Futures as a Versatile Marketing Medium**

Our glimpse at the history of futures markets (Chapter 1) emphasized the fact that futures originated, basically, in response to an urgent and spontaneous need for a hedging medium—a marketing device for laying off unwanted price risks. This particular use of futures markets is examined in detail in this and the ensuing two chapters. As a prelude to these hedging chapters, however, let us broaden our focus to include futures' more universal possibilities. For it has evolved into a highly versatile pricing and marketing medium, one which offers diverse options and opportunities to both trade and industry.

Quite often, the organized commodity exchange of our time is remarkably close to being an ideal market. It is a free and open market, standardized as to contract and trading regulations, and providing virtually complete protection against default of either buyer or seller. Typically, the prices registered in futures trading become the preferred barometer providing, at any given moment, the most accurate value indicator available for every delivery month of the commodity in question.

The science of economics, in its purest sense, is concerned with the logic of choice. And the modern futures market, with its diverse possibilities, is ever ready to broaden the range of sensible and potentially profitable choices available to all who deal in commodities.

Futures as an Alternative Market

Imagine, for example, that you are a copper user contemplating the forward purchase of 100 tons of copper wire or bar. Let us assume that you consider the prevailing price attractive; you are willing to buy now to take advantage of this price, although you fully realize that copper prices could go up or down prior to the delivery date. What are your available

271

options? You may deal in the *cash market,* by buying a forward delivery commitment of actual copper from your regular refiner source. Alternatively, you may purchase similar coverage in the *futures market,* by buying eight copper futures contracts (each futures contract contains 12.5 tons of copper).

The economics of choice is relatively clear. If the actual copper offered by your refiner source is inexpensively priced relative to copper futures, or if the refiner is in a position to offer you the benefit of any price reduction prior to the physical delivery of the copper, then you may well buy this actual copper (it is assumed here that facilities exist for the proper storage, handling, and financing of the copper). If, on the other hand, after careful study of cash/futures price differences, you conclude that futures are a less expensive source of actual copper than the cash market (e.g., forward premiums on futures total less than the costs of carrying actuals, i.e., interest on capital, storage charges, handling fees, etc.), then you may elect to establish "long coverage" (a buying hedge) on the exchange.

In general, taking the latter option (the buying hedge in futures) means that you have temporarily substituted a futures contract for an actuals commitment. This transaction is referred to as a "temporary substitute" because you will, more than likely, ultimately sell out your long futures hedge position, simultaneously replacing it with the requisite actuals copper purchased from your regular supply source. If you are able to effect this "switch" at a time when the price of the actuals position has declined relative to the price of futures (remember, you are seeking to buy the actuals and sell the futures), then your use of futures has proved profitable and advantageous.

It should be clearly noted that hedging does not eliminate risks. Rather, by establishing a position in futures opposite to that committed in the cash market, hedging substitutes a "basis risk" for the ever-present (with net, nonhedged positions) speculative price risk. We may observe that, from the trade hedger's point of view, the basis risk is generally more tenable than is an outright price risk.

The following hypothetical example should clarify this discussion. Let us assume that, on January 1st, a manufacturer of electrical motors determines that he will need a specified type and quantity of actual copper for fabrication around June 1st. Assume further that, as of January 1st, his required actual copper is priced at 53¢ per pound, while the copper future (appropriate for his hedging purposes) is priced at 50¢ per pound. The manufacturer has, on January 1st, the following three options available:

1. He can do nothing until June 1st, when he will purchase from his regular supplier the required type and quantity of actual copper.

2. He can buy the specific type and quantity of actual copper, carrying it in inventory until June 1st, when it will be used in fabrication.
3. He can buy a long hedge in copper futures, maintaining this hedged position until June 1st, when he can switch it into actuals.

Option 1 is deemed too risky. Here the manufacturer would have to assume an outright speculative price risk with the potential loss should the copper market advance in price, being far out of proportion to the anticipated profits on the manufactured items.

Option 2 is considered. However, the manufacturer's analysis of the copper market indicates the likelihood of a decrease in the "basis," the premium of spot copper over futures. Accordingly, option 3 is selected.

Let us assume that the manufacturer's market forecast proves to be correct and that, as of June 1st, the following prices existed:

Spot copper	50¢ per pound
Future copper	48¢ per pound

Thus, in ultimately switching, on June 1st, out of the long futures hedge and into the actuals copper position, the manufacturer would have incurred a loss of 2¢ per pound; however, the actual copper had declined by 3¢ per pound during the same period. Thus, option 3 would have, in fact, yielded a profit of 1¢ per pound (we overlook, in this illustration, commission and other costs).

The selection of copper in the previous example was arbitrary and illustrative. Whatever (exchange-traded) commodity one's business entails, there exists an ever-present choice: take a market position in actuals, or take one in futures. That choice is reversible whenever changing price relationships render the switch advisable. If and when it appears timely to do so, one can readily liquidate a futures commitment and replace it with a position in actuals or, perhaps with somewhat less facility, switch an actuals position into futures.

The essence of the matter, for the alert trade firm, is that the futures market affords an alternate facility in which to buy or sell. This alternative may be entirely in lieu of a corresponding position in actuals (i.e., you can sell futures short and fulfill the contract by making delivery, or you can buy futures and then take delivery). More typically, a futures contract may be taken as a temporary substitute for a merchandising contract in actuals, either because the futures position offers a margin of price advantage, or because an actuals delivery position covering specific requirements may not be immediately available.

Commercial Uses of Futures Markets

Type of Use	Nature of Operation	Example
HEDGING	*Buy Hedge:* the purchase of futures against a forward sale of actuals.	A silverware manufacturer books orders for his product at a set price for delivery in six months. He may buy an equivalent silver futures position as a hedge, prior to actually purchasing the spot silver from a bullion dealer. When he ultimately does buy his actual silver, he will simultaneously sell out his long futures hedge position.
	Sell Hedge: the sale of futures against the ownership of actuals.	The operator of a country grain elevator buys soybeans from local farmers at harvest time. To protect himself against loss due to price decline in the period before he is able to sell these soybeans, the operator hedges by selling (short) Chicago soybean futures. When he ultimately sells his cash soybeans, he will simultaneously cover his short futures position.
QUASI-HEDGING OR PRICE SETTING	*Buy Versus Fixed Selling Price.* Buy futures to cover input requirements for a product whose selling price is fixed or relatively stable.	A bottler who uses sugar as an ingredient in the manufacture of a soft drink, sold for 10¢ per bottle, buys forward delivery domestic sugar futures when it affords him a reasonable cost-price basis for this sugar.
	Sell Versus Fixed Cost. Sell futures when it affords an attractive selling basis relative to fixed or relatively stable costs.	A farmer, who sees corn prices have risen sharply, sells new crop futures short, even before he plants his seed. This assures him an acceptable price basis on the corresponding portion of his forthcoming new crop.
		A plywood manufacturer sells plywood futures short, at wide premiums over actuals. He calculates that the existing selling basis provides a substantial "cushion" against foreseeable changes in his raw material costs.

FIXING THE "BASIS"	*Buy on the "Basis."* Establish an acceptable premium or discount for the purchase of a specified grade of actuals.	A chocolate manufacturer buys Ghana cocoa for December delivery, at 300 points (3¢ per pound) over the December future. When he considers the price opportune, the manufacturer will purchase December futures, thus fixing his cost basis for Ghana cocoa at the price of the December future plus 300 points.
	Sell on the "Basis." Establish an acceptable premium or discount for the sale of a specified grade of actuals.	A cocoa dealer sells a manufacturer actual cocoa for December delivery at 200 points above the December future, believing that, sometime prior to December, he will be able to purchase the Ghana cocoa for less than 200 points over December.
ADJUSTING INVENTORY ACCORDING TO A PARTICULAR VIEW OF THE MARKET (SPECULATING)	*Expanding Coverage.*	A foreign sugar user adds to his coverage in world sugar futures on a scale down basis when the price is below 2¢ per pound.
	Reducing Coverage.	A chocolate manufacturer, who built up his cocoa bean inventory when prices were low, sells futures against this inventory when the market advances above 40¢ per pound; in effect, reducing his net coverage.

Is It a Hedge or a Speculation?

The temporary "substitute position," in futures referred to above, may be initiated to offset an existing net long or short position in actuals. If so, it is usual to classify the futures transaction as a "hedge." On the other hand, the futures position may be initiated as a preferred way to establish the price for a particular transaction, whether on a forward purchase or a sale. In that case, the transaction may be essentially speculative, or it may be partially protective and partially speculative.[1]

Thus, in the above copper illustration, the initial purchase, whether it was effected in actuals or in futures, may have been made simply in the expectation of a price advance. Or, it may have been undertaken as a means of establishing the hedger's input cost against a relatively predictable output price. In this second case, we may assume that the copper user confidently expects to sell a copper-containing product at some time in the future, at a given price. On that assumption, he might prudently decide to buy forward-delivery copper against his anticipated future requirements, if and when the copper is available at a particular price.

Is this hedging? It perhaps falls short of meeting the formal requirements of a two-sided hedge operation because one side (the forward sale of product) has not yet been consummated. Yet, in essential concept, the copper user is utilizing a kind of "buy-hedge." His purchase has a clearly protective function; he reasonably expects that copper prices (and hence, the manufactured cost of the finished product) will rise and yet, due to competitive pressures within his industry, he cannot raise his selling prices to compensate for the increased costs.

We begin to appreciate the diverse possibilities available to industry and trade, in terms of using futures in a manner that helps to price their goods, reduce costs, eliminate unwanted price risks, or accept preferred risks in a selected manner. The outline on pages 274-275 may help to suggest the full range of commercial applications of futures.

In a broad, economic sense futures provide trade and industry with an alternative market in which to buy or sell; a market that is as flexible and adaptable as it is dependable. Thus, in addition to its value as a hedging facility:

1. Futures provide a dependable pricing medium to substitute for an ordinary merchandising contract.

1. In reality, hardly any hedge transactions are either completely protective or completely speculative. There exists an element of each, on every hedge transaction, with the emphasis on each trade dependent on the market approach and viewpoint of the hedger.

2. Futures provide a flexible medium for carrying inventory, which may be used to either expand or reduce coverage.
3. Futures enable a producer to sell his product whenever the price appears sufficiently attractive (including the sale of a product before it actually exists, e.g., a farmer selling new crop grain futures).
4. Futures enable a user to readily cover forward requirements at a price deemed attractive relative to his selling price.
5. Futures provide a speculative medium, par excellence, in which a properly margined individual or firm can readily take market positions, or liquidate positions, in accordance with their market views.

CHAPTER **19**   **Hedging for Insurance and Profit**

Introduction to Hedging

We have noted (in Chapter 18), that futures are a versatile marketing medium, offering useful pricing options to both trade and industry. Notwithstanding this diverse capability, futures have come into being and continue to exist, to a large extent, to provide hedging facilities for commercial interests. Experience has demonstrated that, as the need for hedging in a particular commodity decreases, activity in that futures market wanes. Thus, government activities which restrict price fluctuations have often resulted in reduced hedging and dwindling futures trading. For example, the demise of a once active butter futures market was associated with government purchases of butter for price support reasons.

A foretaste of the theory and practice of hedging has been given in earlier chapters (especially in Chapter 1 concerning the history of futures markets). From this and other sources, the reader has no doubt formed an impression of the essential nature of hedging. As a simple definition, we may say that: *To hedge is to take a position in futures opposite to that which one has assumed in actuals.* This kind of offset transaction reduces, or under ideal circumstances eliminates, the price risks that arise either from being long actuals (carrying unsold inventory), or from being short actuals (making forward sales without already owning the cash commodity).

Starting from this basic concept, the notion has arisen that hedging is undertaken simply with an eye to minimizing risk, to securing a form of insurance against the hazards of price fluctuation. In reality, hedging—as practiced by people in the commodity business—involves considerably more than risk avoidance. The hedge is a straddle in which one is simultaneously long and short different cash and futures positions in the same commodity. In a hedged position (as in a straddle) one's salient concern is the direction of change in price differences. The question is: Will one's position in actuals advance or decline more than the opposite position in futures? *The hedger has not eliminated risk; he has substituted for the extensive and often unpredictable price risk of an outright long or short position the oftentimes more acceptable risk of variation in price difference between actuals and a given futures position.* As we shall see later in this chapter, it is the hedger's special knowledge of price differences in his commodity that makes this hedging difference a sensible businessman's risk, highly preferable to the risk of speculative loss on an outright position. In fact, for many trade and industry people who deal in actual commodities, speculation in the outright long or short sense may be totally avoidable. On the other hand, speculation in price differences may be viewed as a reasonable part of their business operation, and an important element in their pursuit of profits.

Our study of hedging in this chapter has two main facets: First, we consider the nature of risk in commodity ownership and the role of hedging in reducing this risk. Second, we focus on the way in which hedging seeks to enhance opportunities for profit in the commodity business. In the following chapter, detailed examples are given to illustrate more advanced use of futures by commercial interests in hedging operations.

The Need for Hedging

As a first approximation, it is useful to think of hedging simply as risk avoidance. To understand the need for it, one must appreciate the nature of the risks involved in owning or dealing in commodities. One must study the commodity business and the activities of commercial interests who are among its principal participants.

It is, of course, basic that ownership of goods involves a variety of risks. Financial loss may arise from such hazards as fire or flood damage, deterioration, or theft. The businessman, understandably, contracts to transfer as many of his risks as possible to other parties who, for a financial consideration, undertake to assume them. Some forms of risk transference utilized by businessmen include commercial insurance (protection against loss caused by fire, flood, etc.); commercial bonding (protection against loss due to dishonesty on the part of employees); and sale of accounts receivable (protection against loss due to delay or nonpayment of accounts receivable).

There exists one substantial risk, however, for which no commercial insurance is available: the risk of adverse price change. Prices of agricultural and industrial commodities are constantly fluctuating. Those who deal in commodities are subject to losses due to a decline in the price of a commodity owned and not yet sold, or an advance in the price of a commodity sold ahead for future delivery but not yet owned. For this particular kind of risk, the extraordinary "insurance medium" which has evolved is the futures market.

To appreciate its significance, consider the character of the leading commercial interests who use futures. These firms may be country elevator operators (in the grain trade), shippers (whose function is to move the commodity from one terminal to another), terminal warehousemen, exporters, processors, or the very large merchants whose activities span all or most of these functions. Typically, these businesses operate in an extremely competitive environment, where a small price increment might mean the difference between a profitable or an unprofitable piece of business.

Because the commodity business is so highly competitive, commodity prices are usually more volatile than prices in large "follow-the-leader" manufacturing industries. In the case of industrial raw materials, severe price fluctuations may arise from mine strikes or other shutdowns, or from cyclical variations in demand. In the case of agricultural produce, drastic and largely unpredictable price changes often occur as a result of capricious weather and crop developments. The consequences of such price disturbances may be extremely damaging to large and small dealers alike.

Let us assume, for example, that a grain elevator operator is carrying an inventory position of 30 million bushels of grain (some of the larger grain elevator firms have in excess of 60 million bushels of storage space). This operator, like others in the industry, handles large quantities of grain at relatively low profit margins and, at times, owns substantial inventory both in transit and in store. A price fluctuation of just one cent per bushel on a 30 million bushel position would represent a total inventory value change of $300,000; and grain prices frequently fluctuate by more than one cent (per bushel) on any given day. The elevator operator must hedge his unsold inventory position—he just could not manage his business assuming such enormous price risks.

The tendency for commodity prices to fluctuate widely is enhanced by the fact that supply and demand for most commodities is typically inelastic. That is, price change has little effect on the size of production (especially in the short run) and also relatively little impact on consumption. Accordingly, if supplies are short in any one season, it may take a considerable price advance to curb consumption enough to restore the supply-demand balance.

Another characteristic of the commodity market which presents problems for the trade is the seasonality of crop production and marketing. It would be easier to synchronize purchases and sales and thus minimize price risks if production occurred more or less uniformly during the year. But nature wills it otherwise. Typically, marketing pressure is most intense over a period of two or three months; in this brief period millions of bushels of grain, hundreds of thousands of tons of cocoa, and millions of bales of cotton move into the market. While supplies come in bunches, demand is spaced more evenly throughout the year. For the most part, industry buyers are not in the business of storing commodities, and their warehouse space is usually limited. Normally, it is the dealers who will be heavily long actuals; that is, their purchases will far exceed the quantities they are immediately able to sell. In the absence of a hedging medium and in the face of considerable price uncertainties, dealers might be reluctant to buy much more than they could handle immediately. Yet, not to stock up during the harvest run—whether a hedging market exists or not—is to run the risk of being undersupplied later in quantity or quality, and perhaps of forfeiting business to a more enterprising competitor. Besides, profit margins are apt to be very narrow, and the only way a dealer can earn a respectable return on his investment is by conducting large volume operations. Yet, as we have seen, a large unhedged inventory position exposes the dealer to the possibility of a disastrous price decline.

Dealers may, at other times, be faced with a different kind of price risk. Late in the season, with inventories at relatively low levels and with both domestic and foreign buyers placing orders for new crop deliveries, the volume of goods sold ahead will, at times, exceed stocks on hand, leaving the dealers short actuals. They have sold for forward shipment at stipulated prices more of the commodity than they actually own. In this case, dealers now run the risk of a price rise between the time of their forward sale and the time that they "cover" this sale through a corresponding purchase. The dealer can, at his option, cover his short actuals position by buying spot or shipment positions in the cash market, or by going long futures contracts. The choice he makes—whether to purchase actuals or "hedge buy" in futures—will depend on the relationship between cash and futures prices (other factors being equal he will select the least costly of the two alternatives).

Whether the merchant is long or short actuals, it is clear that he would have no need of futures if he could immediately consummate an equal and opposite cash transaction on acceptable terms. The crucial fact is that often he must wait before he can attractively sell his long or cover his short actuals position and, in this interim, it is prudent for him to avoid price risk by offsetting his position in futures. *In nearly all cases, hedging is the use of a futures contract as a temporary substitute for a merchandising contract.*

In addition to reducing or eliminating speculative risks due to price fluctuations, hedging offers another major advantage to the trade firm—it facilitates large scale financing of inventory positions. Financial institutions will lend a greater percentage of inventory value if the goods have been properly hedged. In fact, some banks require that inventory be hedged as a condition of their providing major financing. In addition, the ability to finance inventory enables a trade firm to utilize its own funds for other constructive operating and capital purposes.

We have examined how price risk comes into being. Let us consider now how it can be reduced or eliminated through hedging in each of the two types of situations discussed above: (1) a situation in which one owns unsold actuals, and (2) a situation in which actuals have been sold ahead but "cover" against this sale has not been purchased.

Types of Hedge Transactions

There are two basic types of hedge transactions: (1) *The selling hedge,* where *the hedger is short futures* versus a long cash (actuals) position, and (2) *The buying hedge,* where *the hedger is long futures* versus a short cash (actuals) position.

THE SELLING HEDGE

Assume that a dealer in Chicago has bought 50,000 bushels of corn from an elevator operator. There are no offsetting sales on his books for this particular purchase, so the dealer is long the cash commodity (he owns the physical inventory). If the market declines between the time of this purchase and the time he negotiates a sale, the dealer stands to lose considerably more than the profit which he anticipated from a successful transaction. To eliminate this price risk (or, at least, to greatly reduce it) the dealer sells, as a hedge, an equivalent amount of corn futures on the Chicago Board of Trade. It should be noted that when the dealer sells the futures contracts, he does not necessarily contemplate meeting the contractual obligation by delivering the actual grain. In the main, he regards futures not as a delivery outlet but as a marketing medium as well as a means of protection in the event of an adverse price change. His premise is that any price decline in his actuals will be reflected commensurately in his futures position.[1] Once he finds a customer for his grain and consummates a sale, he will buy back his short futures position. Having sold his actuals, he no longer needs the protection of a short hedge position in futures.

The sequence of purchases and sales is summarized below:

1. This simplified illustration depicts the hedger as hoping merely to "break even" on the entire transaction. In reality, however, the hedger seeks to profit on his hedge through a favorable change in price differences.

THE SELLING HEDGE

	Cash Transaction	*Futures Transaction*
Sept. 15	Buys 50,000 bushels corn @ 1.46.	Sells 50,000 bushels May corn @ 1.53.
Jan. 15	Sells 50,000 bushels corn @ 1.41.	Buys 50,000 bushels May corn @ 1.47½.
	Loss 5¢ per bushel	*Profit* 5½¢ per bushel

Result: a gross profit of ½¢ per bushel before commissions and costs.

In the above illustration we have assumed that, after the dealer had bought and hedged his corn, the market declined. As a consequence, he lost 5¢ per bushel on the actuals portion of the hedge transaction. However, the short futures position brought him a 5½¢ per bushel profit, offsetting the loss in the cash account. Had the market, instead, advanced in price, the profit on the long cash position would have equalled or, hopefully, have exceeded the resultant loss on the short futures position.

THE BUYING HEDGE

Let us consider now the risk that prices may rise after a dealer has made forward sales commitments but before he owns the actual commodity. The dealer, in this case, is said to be short actuals. To protect himself from the risk of a price rise, he will initiate a buy-hedge in futures. That is, he will go long futures versus his short actuals position. If cash prices advance, he will be obliged to pay more for the actual commodity than the price at which he sold to his customer. But the loss incurred on this cash account should be offset by a gain in the long futures position, which presumably will also have advanced in price. Let us note again that, although the futures contract, if held to maturity, calls for and indeed compels accepting delivery of the actual commodity, *a hedge purchase of futures is rarely undertaken with an eye to accepting delivery.* The purpose, rather, is to obtain protection in the event cash prices advance. Ordinarily, once the dealer has purchased the cash commodity needed to fill his forward sales contract, he will liquidate his long futures position. An example of the buying hedge follows:

THE BUYING HEDGE

	Cash Transaction	Futures Transaction
Feb. 15	Sells 30,000 troy ounces silver bullion @ 174.50¢.	Buys 3 contracts September silver @ 182.90¢.
Jul. 15	Buys 30,000 troy ounces silver bullion @ 178.50¢.	Sells 3 contracts September silver @ 186.90¢.
	Loss 4¢ per ounce	*Profit* 4¢ per ounce

Result: break-even, before commissions and costs.

In the above illustration of the buying hedge, the market advanced 4¢ per ounce after the dealer committed himself to ship silver. However, this loss was offset by an equal profit on the long futures position.

Price Variations Between Cash and Futures Market: The Basis

So far, our hedging examples have been based on the simplifying assumption that cash and futures prices move together in parallel fashion. In reality, significant although usually modest price variations do occur between these two markets. To a hedger, these price variations are of crucial importance. *In fact, hedging is typically undertaken to profitably exploit changes in cash-versus-futures price differences, rather than to simply ensure protection against an overall price change.*

The Price Spread Between a Cash Commodity and a Related Future is Called the "Basis" (or "Cash Basis"). The basis expresses the premium or discount (stated in points or cents) at which a cash commodity of specified grade and location sells versus a particular future. For example, it might be said that the basis for No. 2 yellow soybeans at country terminals in southern Illinois is 5¢ under November futures. This simply means that No. 2 yellow cash soybeans at this location are selling at a 5¢ discount to the November future.

From the standpoint of the hedger, the basis is probably the most often used and most important technical term in the entire commodity lexicon.

Merchandising Profits and Risks and the Basis

Hedging eliminates major speculative risks stemming from price changes. However, hedging introduces another, perhaps more complex risk—the possibility that cash (actuals) prices will not move in parallel with futures prices. This risk is referred to simply as the "basis risk."

Suppose, for example, that in June a dealer buys a particular grade of cash soybeans at a point in southern Illinois (a major producing region) for $2.50 per bushel. The July future is then selling at $2.53 in Chicago. The dealer decides to hedge his cash purchase by selling July futures. Let us assume the market subsequently declines, with the cash price dropping to 2.40 and the futures price to 2.45. At that point, the short futures position shows a gain of 8¢; however, the cash position shows a loss of 10¢. If the dealer were to sell his cash beans and lift his hedge (cover his short futures position), the combined result would be a 2¢ loss. This is a considerably smaller loss than he would have suffered had he bought beans and not hedged. Expressed in basis terms, we would say that the hedge was put on when the basis was "3¢ under" and taken off when the basis was "5¢ under." In practice, if such a worsening of the basis had occurred, the dealer might have deferred selling his cash beans until the basis had improved. Or, he might have considered tendering his cash beans against his futures position when it became spot.

Let us see what this tells us about the source of merchant profits. Dealing in commodities must seem a provocatively difficult business. To take a large, unhedged cash position is obviously dangerous; however, it is quite difficult to synchronize cash purchases and sales, let alone to mesh them profitably. Buying cash commodities and selling futures as a hedge provides protection against major speculative price losses. However, hedging can seldom be done at a wide enough spread to assure profitable delivery on futures. Short of such delivery, there is an ever-present basis risk: the risk of the basis moving adversely between the time the hedge is put on and the time it is lifted.

Of course, it is also possible to profit on basis changes, and this understandably is the objective of the hedger. Suppose that in the foregoing example, when the cash price dropped to 2.40, futures had declined to 2.41. Again, there would be a 10¢ loss in the cash position, but in this case the short position in futures would have yielded a 12¢ profit. The combined result of the cash/futures transactions—the initiating and lifting of the hedge—would be a gross profit of 2¢ per bushel. Again, expressed in basis terms, we would say the hedge was initiated when the basis was 3¢ under (as in the previous example) and taken off when the basis was 1¢ under.

As we observed at the outset of this discussion, in any highly competitive undertaking, there can be no profit without a commensurate risk. In order to operate effectively, the responsible merchant must reduce or eliminate the risks associated with outright price speculation. He can then direct his efforts towards analyzing and projecting basis trends, where his specialized knowledge of cash market conditions provides him with a considerable market advantage. Commodity trade firms are, in reality, speculating at all times—but on the basis, not on outright trading. Basis risks are unhedgeable, and constitute an acceptable and, in fact, desirable element in cash market operations.

The Nature and Causes of Basis Changes

To further understand the tactics of the dealer-hedger, we must learn more about the nature and causes of basis variations.

Because a futures contract provides for physical delivery, the ultimate convergence of its price with that of the cash commodity, on contract terms, is assured. However, a futures market does enjoy a certain independence from the influence of cash prices even in its own terminal market. This independence is conferred upon it by virtue of the fact that physical delivery is not permitted until the last month of each contract's life. Prior thereto, futures may be much more responsive than cash to the changing expectations of speculative elements. Sometimes, speculative buying will strengthen futures relative to cash; at other times, speculative selling will cause futures to weaken relative to cash. One way or another, speculative activity contributes to the mutability of cash versus futures price spreads. Apart from speculative influences, the basis reflects a combination of three related factors: location, grade, and time element. A futures market is tied to a specific locality (a particular terminal market). The prices of future deliveries will therefore differ from location to location, depending on shipping cost differences and variations in supply and demand between terminals. The price of wheat in the East or at the Gulf will be at a premium to Chicago and, hence, to Chicago futures prices, because of the freight differential between these regions and Chicago. The precise amount of this premium, however, will vary depending upon the particular supply and demand conditions. For example, if demand from interior mills in the Central States is strong while European export interest is relatively weak, the premium will be smaller than if the reverse were true.

The basis also expresses the price difference between the so-called "basis grade" (the grade or grades deliverable against the futures contract at contract price) and other grades of the same commodity. Price differences between grades reflect their relative abundance or scarcity. For example, a short wheat crop may produce an unusually high percentage of high-protein wheat. Although wheat prices may rise sharply, the premium of the high-protein to the so-called ordinary wheat (deliverable against futures at par) may narrow.

Finally, the basis will tend to reflect the time discount or premium of the cash price to a specific future. In a carrying-charge market, the cash price in the deliverable position will be at a discount to all but an about-to-expire futures delivery; in an inverted market the cash price will be at a premium to all but the about-to-expire future. In the first instance, the basis will be quoted as the number of points under a particular future; in the latter as the number of points over a future.

Consider the example on p. 284–5. The dealer bought cash beans at a location in southern Illinois in June at 2.50 when the nearby July future was selling at 2.53. We would say, in this case, that the basis for No. 2 yellow soybeans was 3¢ under July. Since these cash soybeans represent the basis grade, the cash discount reflects one of two influences, or both—location and time discount. It is impossible to separate the two influences and to determine how much of the discount is attributable to one and how much to the other. All one can say confidently is that the cash price will not appreciably decline below a level that fully reflects both freight and carrying costs. If it did, spreading interests would find it profitable to buy cash beans and sell futures short. They would ultimately liquidate the position by delivering the cash soybeans against their short futures position. Because of competition for such opportunities, it is rare that the price discount of cash to futures is ever sufficient to permit a so-called "perfect" (riskless) hedge. There are invariably some large commercial operators who are willing to go long the basis (buy actuals versus sell futures) when futures are selling at less than a full carrying and freight premium to cash.

Anticipating Changes in the Basis

The most reliable and predictable change in the basis results from the gradual disappearance of the time premium (in a carrying-charge market) or discount (in an inverse market) of a future relative to the cash commodity, as the future approaches expiration. The dealer who purchases grain in Chicago (in a deliverable position) and sells futures at carrying-charge premiums is assured that he will earn carrying charges for his efforts as the basis gradually strengthens (cash advances in price relative to futures).

We have emphasized that speculative activity may have an important influence on basis variations, particularly in a high open interest situation. In a declining market, liquidation of long positions can, for a time, cause the futures market to assume an identity of its own, declining relative to the cash price, thus causing the basis to strengthen. The opposite situation may arise if speculative trading activity turns overwhelmingly bullish. In this situation, speculative buying may strengthen futures relative to cash, thus weakening the basis.

Strength may develop in an out-of-position locality relative to the terminal location where the futures market is located. For example, there have been occasions when corn prices in Pennsylvania, New York, and other eastern areas have been strong (based largely on export demand), while prices in the Midwest were relatively weak. If a cash commodity gains strength vis-à-vis futures in such so-called out-of-position locations, then cash prices in these locations will rise relative to futures, i.e., the eastern cash basis will strengthen. The limit of this price disparity will be the transportation differential. When it becomes feasible to profitably ship grain from the futures terminal to the out-of-position location, the basis will stabilize.

Despite an overall abundance of a particular commodity, some grades may temporarily be in relatively tight supply. For example, in July 1968, a bumper wheat crop was being harvested. Yet, during the early harvest run, the proportion of high-protein wheat relative to ordinary wheat was low. This resulted in a substantial premium on high-protein wheat relative to other grades and to the futures market. As the harvest moved northward into Kansas and Nebraska, high-protein wheat became somewhat more plentiful and the basis eased (i.e., premiums on this type of wheat declined).

As general conditions change from abundance to scarcity and vice versa, the price relationship between cash and futures (as well as between different futures) will change. When there are large supplies on hand, the price structure will tend towards carrying charges and the extent of carrying charges will depend on the degree of abundance. If and when spot supplies tighten, buyers must look harder for immediate coverage and nearbys begin to attract buying support which they had previously lacked. If cash demand really becomes aggressive, the cash price may even move to premiums over nearby futures. Gradually, the entire futures market may become inverted, with discounts on each successive future. Under these conditions the basis, by definition, is strengthening, though more for some grades than for others. Conversely when scarcity is relieved, nearby premiums will gradually disappear. For domestic crops, a return to normalcy generally means a return to a situation in which adequate supplies are carried throughout the year. Carrying charges will then tend to reappear, and the cash basis for all grades will weaken, with the basis for some grades reacting more than for others.

Basis Trading

In the previous example, a cash commodity was bought and a futures contract sold, establishing a short hedge. This transaction may be referred to as being "long the basis," i.e., long cash versus short futures. Such a hedge will be initiated if the dealer expects the basis to strengthen (i.e., he expects the cash price to gain relative to futures). If the cash price was initially at a discount to futures, a strengthening basis means that the discount will narrow (as was the case in the foregoing example) or disappear. If, on the other hand, the cash price was at a premium to futures, a strengthening basis implies that the cash premium will increase.

In the long hedge (as noted previously), a dealer sells cash forward and hedges this (short) actuals position by buying futures. This long hedge entails being "short the basis," that is, short actuals versus long futures. For the hedger to profit, futures must strengthen relative to cash which, in our new vernacular, means that the basis must weaken.

One predictive generalization concerning basis changes is that cash and futures prices must ultimately converge, on contract terms, as each future approaches expiration. Therefore, if cash is priced at a discount to futures, the basis must ultimately strengthen (on contract terms). Conversely, with cash selling at premiums, the basis must ultimately weaken (again, on contract terms). The term "ultimately," however, should be emphasized because—even in deliverable position—it is temporarily possible for cash and futures prices to diverge.

At locations remote from the futures terminal—the so-called out-of-position areas—there may be no predictable means of forecasting basis changes, even to the expiration of a future. For example, the cash basis of wheat in New York may widen or narrow rather independently of the cash basis of Chicago wheat, within the limits established by time and cost of shipping cash wheat between the two markets.

In his role as hedger, the dealer is not primarily concerned with the absolute level of prices or with the overall trend of the market. His vital interest is in relative price movements or, more specifically, the strength or weakness of cash prices relative to futures. Above all, the hedger thinks in basis terms. If he expects cash prices at a specific location to strengthen relative to a given future, he will go "long the basis," by buying the cash commodity and putting on a short hedge. If, on the other hand, he foresees a weakening in the basis for some grade in a particular location (i.e., he anticipates a cash decline relative to futures), he may go "short the basis," by selling cash ahead and buying futures.

When properly executed, hedging offers the trade firm the flexibility of several operating alternatives. The astute hedger enjoys the option of deciding when and how to close out all or just a portion of his hedge position. Depending upon relative prices and conditions underlying both cash and futures, he may deal with his "sell" hedge by:

1. Delivering his long actuals position against his short futures position.
2. Selling his actuals in the cash market and simultaneously covering his short futures position.

3. Rolling over his hedge position; that is, while holding his long actuals position, he covers his short futures position, maintaining the hedge by simultaneously selling a different future.

Perhaps the first decision the trade firm must make is how to deal with an existing inventory position in actuals, whether or not to hedge, in which market, and in which future. The following observations may be useful:

The Premium Market. Here the selling hedge is generally most effective. The higher the premiums on successive futures, the closer they will be to full carrying costs. As futures premiums approach full carrying costs it becomes progressively more profitable for a trade firm to buy actuals for their inventory position and hedge-sell in futures. Under such circumstances, the hedger stands to gain on the inevitable strengthening of the basis as each future approaches expiration.

The Inverted Market. In an inverted market, the buying hedge is generally most effective. Depending on the extent of price inversion, dealers will find it profitable to sell their actuals position in the cash market and hedge-buy in futures to replenish their inventory. While it may not be feasible for a trade firm to completely deplete its inventory, the astute dealer will maintain stocks at the absolute minimum level, depending on his buy-hedges as the source of needed actuals.

Which Market? In the event that more than one futures market exists for a given commodity (i.e., sugar and cocoa are traded both in New York and London, and wheat is traded in Chicago, Minneapolis, and Kansas City), the hedger must determine in which futures market to hedge. In general, he will find it advantageous to hedge in that futures market which most closely corresponds to his particular grade and type of actuals.

Which Future? The hedger is also concerned with the decision of which futures month to place his hedges. This determination will depend, to a great extent, on the purpose of the hedge. If it is a "carrying-cost hedge," he will select that deferred future offering him the highest relative premium. Here, the dealer's intimate knowledge of carrying-cost structure will prove invaluable. If, on the other hand, the hedge is intended as a short-term "operational hedge," he may find it advantageous to place his hedges in a nearby future, as it likely bears the closest price relationship to his actuals, hence offering the maximum risk protection.

Lifting Hedges. When lifting hedges, if an actuals position is sold to a trade firm which itself must hedge in futures, the (short) hedge position may be simultaneously transferred. This type of exchange of futures is quite common in the commodity trade. The exchange may be effected by the floor broker outside of the trading ring; hence the name, "ex-pit transaction."

Clearly, hedging is not the elementary, mechanical process portrayed in our simple risk-avoidance model, or in certain popular introductions to hedging. There, the dealer is seen as one who takes a position in actuals and immediately eliminates his risks by hedging. In practice, the dealer's emphasis is twofold: (1) to substitute a basis risk for a speculative price risk, and (2) to profit through a correct analysis and projection of basis changes, and the timely execution of these hedge transactions.

Hedging: Pitfalls and Proprieties

In general, hedging is a subtle and sophisticated operation, one which requires considerable expertise. Properly managed, hedging can help to protect profits or, indeed, make it possible for farmers, merchants, or processors to operate profitably. It is equally true, of course, that mismanaged hedging can undermine an otherwise sound business. Thus, a few words of caution may be in order.

It is especially important that a hedge be a hedge, and not a cover for a speculative position. In some instances, when markets seemed intriguing, individual businessmen have allowed themselves to dress speculative intentions in the reassuring cloak of the hedge. An oft-quoted example is the so-called "Texas hedge." This refers to the case in which some cattlemen—inspired by a period of consistent price advance—acquired the habit of buying futures regularly, as a kind of "cover" in anticipation of a price rise. Since they already owned the actual cattle they had, in effect, "doubled up" on the long side by buying futures. To be sure, their gains would multiply if prices moved up, but so too would their losses, given any marked price decline. This speculative trading approach is plainly inconsistent with sound, prudent business management. In short, speculation should be undertaken on its own merits, and not obscured under the veil of hedging.

The route to successful hedging has been outlined, to a large extent, in this chapter. The hedger's guiding star is a thorough knowledge of the price relationship between a particular commodity and its related futures market. The "road map" can handily be a chart showing changes in this price basis, or simply picturing simultaneous variations in the relevant cash and futures markets. By way of illustration, let us consider how a storage holder of frozen pork bellies in Chicago might interpret the cash and futures situation shown in Figure 48.

Let's start by examining the price relationship which existed in the summer of 1970. As is often the case at this time of year, belly production was seasonally low, and cash bellies commanded a wide premium over futures. In mid-July, cash bellies (12–14 pounds at Chicago) were priced around 44.00–46.00¢, while at the same time, August 1970, belly futures

4 — 8 — 71

PORK BELLIES (FROZEN) MAY 1971- CHI.
EACH HORIZONTAL LINE = 40 POINTS

Spot Pork Bellies (12-14 lbs.) Chi.

Commodity Chart Service, Commodity Research Bureau Inc.

Fig. 48.

were selling just under 40.00¢ and May 1971 futures were priced around 33.00¢. At that time, hedging cash bellies via short sales in futures was a questionable operation, because one would have had to sell futures at great discounts to actuals.

From the short hedger's standpoint, the cash versus futures price relationship was far more inviting by mid-September. By then, cash was 33.00¢ while May 1971 futures were about 35.00¢. At least, one could hedge-sell futures at a modest premium over cash. However, the seasoned belly trader knows that, in time, cash will often drop to much more than 2.00¢ under May. In this case, if he waits until mid-October, he finds a vastly more attractive hedging situation. Cash is now around 24.00¢, while May futures are still priced at 32.00¢. It now becomes particularly interesting to buy cash bellies, and hedge them at an 8.00¢ premium, wide enough to pay carrying charges and a profit besides.

Now look at Figure 48 two months later, in mid-January. May futures have fallen to 24.00¢ and cash to 20.00¢, with the price difference between the two narrowing to 4.00¢. Assume that at this point our trade firm sells its cash bellies and repurchases its May short position. In that case, the firm has—through its hedging operation and with limited risk—achieved a gross profit of 4.00¢ per pound. That is the difference between the 8.00¢ futures premium at the start of the hedge operation in October, and the 4.00¢ premium when the operation is completed in January.

In this instance, the sell hedge worked out especially well in a period of price weakness. However, the success of sell-hedging in futures does not depend on an ensuing market decline, but rather on the fact that futures are sold at a desirable level relative to cash. Consider Figure 49 based on the cattle market.

The time is late October 1970. A cattle feedlot operator, perhaps apprehensive of a market decline, sells April 1971 futures as a hedge against unsold cattle in his inventory. At this time, he is able to sell April 1971 futures at around 30.25¢, nearly ½¢ above the then-prevailing quote for cash steers (choice, average, Chicago). A few months later, at the end of February, the feedlot operator sells his cattle at the then-prevailing Chicago cash price of 33.00¢ and buys back his hedge at 32.00¢. In this instance, he has lost 1.75¢ per pound on the futures side of his hedge transaction, while the cash market has advanced by over 3.00¢.

Now, let us examine the same cash and futures prices from the standpoint of a prospective buyer, say a meat packer seeking to cover nearby requirements. In mid-February, Chicago cash steers and April 1971 live cattle futures are both priced at around 33.00¢. However, at the end of February, the meat packer may be in a position to take advantage of a late-month selloff in futures to purchase the April (Chicago) future at around 31.50¢, well below the 33.00¢ still quoted for cash steers.

CATTLE (LIVE BEEF) APRIL 1971-CHI.
EACH HORIZONTAL LINE = 20 POINTS

CASH STEERS CHICAGO—CHOICE, AVERAGE

Commodity Chart Service, Commodity Research Bureau Inc.

Fig. 49.

Thus far, our example has assumed that the feedlot owner or packer was handling Chicago cash steers, while at the same time dealing in Chicago live cattle futures. Consider now the case of a feedlot owner who is operating in an out-of-position location such as California, and marketing animals not quite comparable to Chicago choice steers. In order to use Chicago futures as a hedging medium, this California cattle feeder would have to take careful account of variations in the price of his specific cash animals relative to Chicago futures. It would be his task as a businessman-hedger to keep records of basis variations, to know what seasonal variations usually occur in this basis, and to always be keenly aware of the levels at which price differences might become singularly appealing from a hedging standpoint.

Hedging Recapitulation: General Observations

1. Futures markets exist largely as a medium to facilitate hedging. If and when the need for hedging in a particular commodity wanes, trading in that futures market is likely to wane, too.

2. The hedge is an offset transaction. It is a long or short position in futures equal and opposite to that assumed in actuals.

3. In general, hedging involves the temporary use of a futures position as a substitute for a merchandising contract. Although the futures contract provides for ultimate delivery or acceptance of actuals, hedge transactions in futures are not necessarily undertaken with the objective of making or accepting delivery. In most cases, the merchant will "even up" his actuals position in the cash market, simultaneously closing out his futures position with an offsetting futures trade.

4. The "basis" is probably the most important aspect of hedging to the trade firm. It can be defined as the price spread between a specific cash commodity and a related future.

5. Hedging is principally undertaken to profitably exploit changes in cash versus futures price differences, rather than to simply insure protection against an adverse price move. Hedging does not eliminate risk. Rather, it substitutes a basis risk, acceptable to the hedger, in place of the otherwise present speculative price risk.

6. Quite often, the twofold decision—whether to take an actuals position and to hedge it in futures—is a simultaneous one. The basis provides an incentive to do either both, or neither. In other words, a commercial operator may scale his interest in actuals depending on the availability of a hedge in futures at a desirable price difference.

7. The hedge is quite analogous to the straddle (discussed in Chapter 16) and, in general, is subject to similar analysis and interpretation.

Hedging Recapitulation: Specific Observations

Especially for the newly initiated, it may be helpful to keep several precepts in mind as a starting point for successful hedging:

1. Above all, know your own basis situation thoroughly. Keep full records of price relationships between the cash grades in which you deal, and the various delivery positions in futures.

2. Aided by your basis records, establish high and low ranges in which action may be warranted—either to initiate hedge positions, or to unwind established positions.

3. In particular, take advantage of any consistent seasonal basis variations.

4. The sell-hedge is most effective in a premium market. The buy-hedge is most effective in an inverse market.

5. The very best hedge is, of course, one in which a profit is "locked in." For example, at times it has been possible to buy cash silver, and hedge-sell futures at premiums which more than pay full carrying charges.

6. Avoid hedging when you are not clear concerning the basis, and when the contract traded in futures is not related in a fairly determinate way to the respective actuals. Shun the "Texas hedge," of course.

7. Finally, remember that there is no substitute for an intimate knowledge of the commodity in question, and the factors which ultimately govern changing cash versus futures price relationships.

CHAPTER 20 Case Histories of Trade Hedging

In Chapter 19, we discussed the need for hedging, the diverse objectives of trade hedgers, the principles of sound and proper hedging, and the various types of hedges. We noted that hedging neither eliminates risk entirely, nor does it assure profitable operations. While the hedger may profit, he may also lose—due either to an error or miscalculation in his operating estimates, or to an adverse change in his respective basis.

We now examine hedging from a more pragmatic point of view, utilizing five specific examples of trade hedging involving various commodities. We shall follow the mechanics involved in these diverse examples, referring back to the principles and tactics discussed in Chapter 19, and illustrating the importance of both astute basis trading and a proper sense of market timing.

The ABC Chocolate Company

The ABC Chocolate Company, located in Philadelphia, Pennsylvania, manufactures a diverse line of chocolate products, including eating and drinking chocolates, cocoa powder, baking chocolate, and candy coatings. The company sells its products direct to food processors, candy manufacturers, and large grocery chains.

ABC is, of course, in business to earn a profit from the efficient manufacture of its products. The company has neither the capital nor the inclination to speculate on cocoa price fluctuations. ABC would have little need to hedge in the futures market if all orders from customers were for nearby delivery, and if all grades and origins of cocoa beans required in the manufacturing process were available at dependable price differentials. Unfortunately, these two conditions are rarely present. In their absence,

ABC finds that the hedging facilities provided by the New York Cocoa Exchange, Inc., provide an essential supplement to its regular business operations.

Let us assume that, in January, one of ABC's major customers requests a quotation on 1 million pounds of X brand milk chocolate, for delivery during the fourth quarter of the current year. This order would require approximately 630,000 pounds of cocoa beans. ABC does not presently own these beans, but anticipates being able to purchase its entire requirements in the cash market by mid-June.

The problem facing ABC is that it must quote the customer a price, in January, for delivery of the finished order some 10 months hence (and some 5 months prior to its purchase of the actual cocoa beans required to produce the order). ABC does this by calculating its costs, based on a price for cocoa beans equivalent to December cocoa futures plus its estimate of the premium required to exchange its futures position for the actual cocoa beans at the appropriate time.

With the December future currently quoted around 31.50¢ per pound on the New York Cocoa Exchange, Inc. (stated as 31.50), ABC estimates that it will be able to buy 630,000 pounds of the precise blend of beans needed at a premium of approximately 115 points (1.15¢ per pound) over futures. It therefore "costs" its cocoa beans at 32.65¢ per pound, then adds the cost of other materials required in the production of X brand milk chocolate and the operating costs involved. After estimating his manufacturing cost, and then adding a margin for profit adjusted to competitive conditions, ABC's sales manager can now quote a price to his customer.

Upon receipt of the customer's order, ABC buys 21 contracts of December cocoa at 31.50¢ per pound on the New York Cocoa Exchange, Inc. In this way, ABC's short actuals position (actual cocoa sold ahead in the form of chocolate for future delivery) has been hedged through the purchase of the 21 contracts of futures and ABC has relieved itself of concern over fluctuations in the price of cocoa beans. The only significant factor to ABC now is the basis (differential between cash and futures prices) in effect at the time that it goes into the market to buy its cash beans. So long as this basis does not exceed 115 points (1.15¢ per pound), the hedge has been successful.

This hedging operation did not guarantee a profit, because ABC's cost estimates could have erred, or the basis change could have proved adverse. However, the hedge operation did substitute a basis risk for the much more substantial outright price risk, which would have been incurred had the firm sold chocolate without covering its bean requirements in the cash market.

Let us now examine the actual details of the hedge operation.

CASH MARKET	FUTURES MARKET

January ABC sells 1,000,000 pounds X brand milk chocolate based on a bean cost of 32.65¢ per pound (630,000 pounds of cocoa beans) Total Price $205,695

ABC buys 21 contracts (630,000 pounds) December cocoa @ 31.50¢ per pound

Total Cost $198,450

June ABC buys 630,000 pounds of cocoa beans at an average cost of 34.65¢ per pound *Loss on cash operation of $12,600*

ABC sells 21 contracts December cocoa @ 33.80¢ per pound *Profit on futures operation of $13,230* (gross profit of $14,490 less commission of $1,260)

Summarizing this hedge operation, ABC sustained a $12,600 loss on its cash transaction and a profit of $13,230 on the futures transaction, for a net $630 profit on the overall hedge. In basis terms, the hedge was initiated at a 115-point difference, and closed out at 85 points—for a gross profit of 30 points (30/100¢ per pound), amounting to $1,890. Needless to say, the basis in a hedge operation is subject to fluctuation, and the hedger will either turn a profit or incur a loss, depending on his skill (and good fortune) in anticipating and trading basis changes.

The Amalgamated Copper Corporation

The Amalgamated Copper Corporation (ACC) operates copper smelting and refining plants in New Jersey and Virginia. ACC's business largely consists of buying scrap copper from dealers throughout the country and fabricating it into industrial products, mostly in the form of electrolytic wire and bar. Most of ACC's orders come from manufacturers of consumer and industrial electrical appliances.

Each 200 tons of copper scrap produces approximately 175 tons of finished copper products at a cost of about 2.25¢ per fabricated pound. The typical processing period from scrap to finished product spans approximately 60 days. ACC, like most other industrial operators, seeks to profit from the efficient fabrication of its products, while eliminating—or at least, minimizing—the speculative risks of adverse copper price changes. The firm's policy of balancing scrap purchases with sales of finished products cannot always be attained; accordingly, ACC—as a routine part of its operations—hedges its net long or short actuals position in the futures market.

On a given day, ACC buys 275 tons of copper scrap at an average price of 41.50¢ per pound. The sales department has orders in hand for 53 tons of finished products, requiring approximately 60 tons of scrap copper. Of the remaining 215 tons held unsold, ACC decides to hedge 200 tons, being willing to hold a net 15-ton long position, based on the firm's bullish view of the market. The hedging operation, involving the 200 tons of scrap copper (equal to 175 tons of finished copper), works as follows.

	CASH MARKET	FUTURES MARKET
May	Holds 200 tons copper scrap valued @ 41.50¢ per pound	Sells 14 contracts (175 tons) December copper @ 50.90¢ per pound
	Cost $166,000	Total Value $178,150
	Fabricates 175 tons copper products @ cost of 2.25¢ per pound Fabrication cost $7,875	
	Total cost of fabricated copper $173,875	
August	Sells 175 tons fabricated copper @ 48.50¢ per pound Total Receipts $169,750 *Loss on cash operation of $4,125*	Buys 14 contracts December copper @ 48.10¢ per pound Total Cost $163,350 *Profit on futures operation of $9,296* (gross profit of $9,800 less commission of $504)

In this illustration, a loss in the cash operation, due to a decline in the price of copper, has been more than offset by a profit on the short hedge position in futures. Once again, it should be noted that there is no assurance that a net profit will result as per this example. However, the hedger may have good prospects of emerging profitably if his positions in cash and futures are initiated advantageously.

The Crispy Potato Chip Company

The Crispy Potato Chip Company (CPC) of New Haven, Connecticut, is a major producer of potato chips and potato snacks. Its packaged products (retailing for 15¢, 25¢, and 50¢), are sold through supermarkets and food chains in the United States and Canada. In September, CPC estimates that it will require approximately 10 million pounds of potatoes for processing during the first half of the coming year. Inasmuch as both wholesale and retail prices for its packaged products are relatively fixed, CPC must establish its raw material costs well in advance for such a large quantity of potatoes.

Allowing for processing and material costs, and given its presently established selling prices, CPC calculates that it must buy its cash potatoes at a price less than $1.55 per cwt., FOB Maine, in order to achieve a satisfactory profit margin. It seeks a reliable means of establishing its cost for the required quantity and grades of potatoes. In this instance, CPC finds that it can cover its forward requirements through the purchase of 200 contracts (equivalent to 10 million pounds) of May potato futures, then priced at $3.50 per cwt. on the New York Mercantile Exchange (some $2.00 per cwt. over the then-prevailing cash price of $1.50 FOB Maine). CPC views this buy-hedge as a substitute merchandising contract. It has no intention of standing for delivery on the long position, as its processing operation requires delivery, in New Haven, of specific quantities of various grades of potatoes. The protective long-hedge will be closed as soon as the company has bought its actuals requirements in the cash market.

To continue our illustration, let us assume that in this case the fall harvest proves disappointing; by January, cash potatoes FOB Maine have advanced from $1.50 in September to $3.15, while May futures have advanced to $5.30. CPC contracts to buy its required potatoes in the cash market, at an average price of $3.15 per cwt. FOB Maine. The long May futures position is simultaneously sold out, at an average price of $5.30. The operation can be summarized as follows.

CASH MARKET	FUTURES MARKET
September	CPC anticipates requirements of 10 million pounds in the first half of the coming year (To maintain fixed selling price, maximum acceptable potato cost is $1.55 per cwt. FOB Maine)	Buys 200 contracts (10 million pounds) May potatoes @ $3.50 per cwt.
January	Buys 10 million pounds potatoes @ $3.15 per cwt. FOB Maine	Sells 200 contracts May potatoes @ $5.30 per cwt. *Profit on futures operation* $1.80 per cwt.

While CPC paid $3.15 per cwt. for its cash potatoes, its buy-hedge in futures scored a profit of $1.80 per cwt. In effect, this profit, applied to the potato purchase cost, reduces CPC's effective purchase price to $1.35 per cwt. FOB Maine, plus commission costs. That is, by covering in futures when the price seemed right, CPC effectively established both an acceptable cost basis for its potato requirements and protection against a possible market price advance.

General Cotton Corporation

General Cotton Corporation, a large Atlanta cotton dealer, buys 2,000 bales of cotton from farmers during September, at an average price of 26.00¢ per pound (each 100 bales equals 50,000 pounds). Because the company is unwilling to assume the speculative price risk on such a large inventory position (each 1¢-per-pound price fluctuation represents a $10,000 change in inventory value) and because its banks will extend more liberal financing terms on properly hedged inventory, General Cotton hedges this position on the New York Cotton Exchange, Inc. It sells 2,000 bales (20 contracts) of March cotton at an average price of 26.35¢ per pound.

Having established its buying basis at 35 points discount (the cotton was purchased at 35 points under the short March hedge position), General Cotton now offers the cotton for sale at 20 points over the March future.

Muffy Puffy Mills of Birmingham, a manufacturer of cotton Muffy Puffys, likes the quality of General's cotton and would like to use it for spring production. However, Muffy Puffy has not yet booked any orders for this production, and is therefore reluctant to take on such a sizeable unhedged position, pending those orders. It therefore contracts with General Cotton to buy the 2,000 bales for "20 points over March, Buyer's Call." (In such an arrangement, the actual transaction price will be determined by the purchase of General Cotton's short March hedge position, with the price being fixed at 20 points over the price paid for the March future.)

In January, Muffy Puffy books orders for its popular all-cotton Muffy Puffys, at a price based on a cotton cost of 20 points over March, plus costs and profit. Muffy Puffy notifies General Cotton that it wishes to fix the price on its purchase of the 2,000 bales, and requests General Cotton to lift its hedge (buy in the short 20 March contracts).[1] General Cotton sends a confirmation of this transaction to Muffy Puffy, using it to establish the price for the original cash sale back in September. This double-hedge

1. Alternatively, General Cotton may authorize Muffy Puffy to lift the hedge (buy in the short 20 March futures) for the account of General Cotton, thereby fixing the transaction price for the sale of the actual cotton.

transaction, involving both General Cotton and Muffy Puffy, works as follows:

CASH MARKET	FUTURES MARKET

GENERAL COTTON CORPORATION

	CASH MARKET	FUTURES MARKET
September	Buys 2,000 bales cotton @ 26.00¢ per pound (35 points under March)	Sells 20 contracts (2,000 bales) March cotton @ 26.35¢ per pound
January	Sells 2,000 bales cotton @ 24.40¢ per pound (20 points over March)	Buys 20 contracts March cotton @ 24.20 per pound
	Loss on cash operation $16,000	*Profit on futures operation $21,500* (less $900 commissions)

MUFFY PUFFY MILLS

	CASH MARKET	FUTURES MARKET
September	Buys 2,000 bales cotton @ 20 points over March, Buyer's Call. (This price is subsequently established in January, at 24.40¢ per pound)	(General Cotton's sell-hedge, above, represents the hedge on this transaction)
January	Sells products utilizing 2,000 bales cotton based on cotton cost of 20 points over March (24.40¢ per pound) plus costs and profit	(General Cotton's buy-in of its short hedge, above, represents lifting of the hedge position)

In summary, General Cotton lost $16,000 on the cash transaction, but turned a $21,500 profit (less $900 commissions) on the futures transaction. In basis terms, it locked in a 55-point (55/100¢ per pound) profit, having bought the cash at 35 points under March, and sold it at 20 points over March. Muffy Puffy, on the other hand, fixed its raw materials cost well in advance of orders, yet retained the option of establishing its cotton buying price based on its ultimate product selling price. Muffy Puffy was relieved of the risk of adverse price fluctuations, depending for its profit on efficiency and expertise in the manufacture and marketing of Muffy Puffys.

General Farm Corporation

General Farm Corporation (GFC) owns and operates farms and live-stock herds throughout Illinois and Indiana, with corn accounting for three-quarters of its total grain output. The corn is planted around mid-May, and reaches maturity in late August. Harvest commences about October 15th, just after the first hard frost, and nears completion by the middle of November. Nearly 80 percent of GFC's corn crop is consumed as live-stock feed on the same farms where it is grown, while the balance is sold in the marketplace as "cash crop."

Let us assume that, during the first week of November, GFC's management decides to store 300,000 bushels of its newly harvested corn in bins located on its farms. The company intends to sell this corn in the market-place later in the season. The corn is to be hedged on the Chicago Board of Trade, with the dual objective of: (1) avoiding the speculative risk of loss due to a possible decline in corn prices, and (2) utilizing the futures market as a means of earning carrying costs plus a profit on the stored corn.

GFC's hedging manager, studying the then-prevailing cash versus futures price situation (the basis), notes that corn in his local cash market is then selling at 14½¢ under the Chicago December future, and at approximately 23½¢ under the May future. From past experience, as well as on the basis of charts and other technical studies, the hedging manager recognizes that the cash basis tends to be at its widest point during the height of the harvest movement, narrowing later in the season as cash marketings start to fall off. As a matter of fact, cash corn prices at country points usually approach the price of Chicago futures by late spring or early summer.

Anticipating that the 300,000 bushels of cash corn may not be sold until sometime in the spring, the hedging manager elects to place his short hedges in the May future, with the cash basis then 23½¢ off (discount to) May. The hedge operation would be handled as follows:

	CASH MARKET	FUTURES MARKET
November	Holds 300,000 bushels corn currently valued at $1.17 per bushel (23½¢ under May)	Sells 300,000 bushels May corn @ $1.40½ per bushel
May	Sells 300,000 bushels corn @ $1.33½ per bushel (3¢ under May)	Buys 300,000 bushels May corn @ $1.36½ per bushel
	Profit on cash operation 16½¢ per bushel (less cost of carrying corn)	*Profit on futures operation 4¢ per bushel* (less 5/8¢ commission)

In this instance, the combined cash-futures operation grossed GFC 20½ ¢ more per bushel than would have been obtained by simply selling the 300,000 bushels in November. From this gross profit, one must deduct commissions and carrying costs incurred during the November to May period. Measured in terms of the changing basis, the hedge sale of futures was initiated, with cash 23½ ¢ off (discount to) May, and closed out at 3¢ off; hence a profit of 20½ ¢ per bushel. This type of hedge—based on the quite consistent seasonal tendency of the cash corn basis to narrow from harvest time to late spring—represents one of the most popular and successful producer hedge operations.

It should be clear that the incentive to initiate such a hedge operation depends largely on the existence of what is judged to be an attractive basis at harvest time. If this basis happened, rather unusually, to be 3¢ in November rather than 23½ ¢ (referring again to the example above), GFC might have deemed it wiser to avoid basis uncertainties and commission costs, and sell its corn at once in the cash market.

APPENDIXES

APPENDIX A Commodity Trading Data

United States and Canada

Commodity:	BROILERS, ICED
Where traded:	Chicago Board of Trade, Chicago
Trading hours	
New York time:	10:15 A.M. to 2:05 P.M.
Chicago time:	9:15 A.M. to 1:05 P.M.
Contract size:	28,000 pounds
How price is quoted:	Cents per pound
Minimum fluctuation	
Per pound:	2½/100¢
Per contract:	$7.00
Value 1¢ move:	$280.00
Maximum trading limit	
From previous close:	2¢
Between daily high and low	4¢
Commission (round-turn)	
Regular:	$30.00
Straddle:	$36.00
Day trade:	$20.00

Commodity Chart Service, Commodity Research Bureau Inc.

Fig. A1.

Commodity:	CATTLE, LIVE BEEF
Where traded:	Chicago Mercantile Exchange, Chicago
Trading hours	
New York time:	10:05 A.M. to 1:40 P.M.
Chicago time:	9:05 A.M. to 12:40 P.M.
Contract size:	40,000 pounds
How price is quoted:	Cents per pound
Minimum fluctuation	
Per pound:	2½/100¢
Per contract:	$10.00
Value 1¢ move:	$400.00
Maximum trading limit	
From previous close:	1¢
Between daily high and low:	2¢
Commission (round-turn)	
Regular:	$40.00
Straddle:	$43.00
Day trade:	$25.00

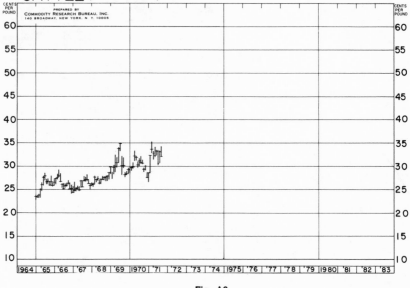

CATTLE (LIVE BEEF) CHI.MERC.EXCH. MONTHLY H,L,& C OF NEAREST FUTURES

Fig. A2.

Commodity:	COCOA
Where traded:	New York Cocoa Exchange, New York
Trading hours	
New York time:	10:00 A.M. to 3:00 P.M.
Contract size:	30,000 pounds
How price is quoted:	Cents per pound
Minimum fluctuation	
Per pound:	1/100¢
Per contract:	$3.00
Value 1¢ move:	$300.00
Maximum trading limit	
From previous close:	1¢
Between daily high	
and low:	2¢
Commission (round-turn)	
Regular:	$60.00
Straddle:	$70.00
Day trade:	$30.00

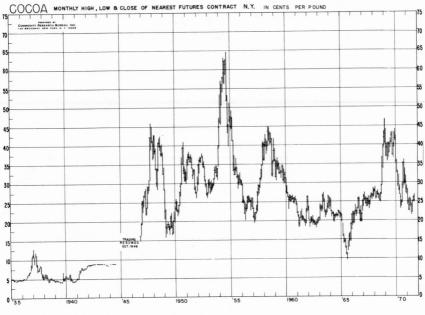

COCOA MONTHLY HIGH, LOW & CLOSE OF NEAREST FUTURES CONTRACT N.Y. IN CENTS PER POUND

Fig. A3.

Commodity: COPPER

Where traded: Commodity Exchange, Inc., New York

Trading hours
  New York time: 9:45 A.M. to 2:10 P.M.

Contract size: 25,000 pounds

How price is quoted: Cents per pound

Minimum fluctuation
  Per pound: 5/100¢
  Per contract: $12.50

Value 1¢ move: $250.00

Maximum trading limit
  From previous close: 2¢
  Between daily high
  and low: 4¢

Commission (round-turn)
  Regular: $36.50
  Straddle: $51.40
  Day trade: $18.50

Fig. A4.

Commodity:	CORN
Where traded:	Chicago Board of Trade, Chicago
Trading hours	
New York time:	10:30 A.M. to 2:15 P.M.
Chicago time:	9:30 A.M. to 1:15 P.M.
Contract size:	5,000 bushels
How price is quoted:	Dollars and cents per bushel
Minimum fluctuation	
Per bushel:	1/8¢
Per contract:	$6.25
Value 1¢ move:	$50.00
Maximum trading limit	
From previous close:	8¢
Between daily high and low:	16¢
Commission (round-turn)	
Regular:	$30.00
Straddle:	$36.00
Day trade:	$20.00

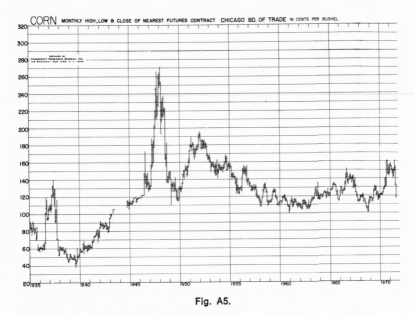

Fig. A5.

Commodity:	COTTON NO. 2
Where traded:	New York Cotton Exchange, New York
Trading hours New York time:	10:30 A.M. to 3:00 P.M.
Contract size:	50,000 pounds (100 bales)
How price is quoted:	Cents per pound
Minimum fluctuation Per pound: Per contract:	1/100¢ $5.00
Value 1¢ move:	$500.00
Maximum trading limit From previous close: Between daily high and low:	2¢ 4¢
Commission (round-turn)* Regular: Straddle: Day trade:	$45.00 $54.00 $19.00

* When price is 40¢ or less.

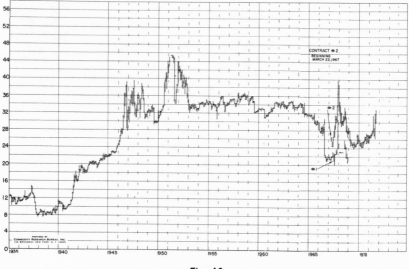

COTTON MONTHLY HIGH, LOW & CLOSE OF NEAREST FUTURES CONTRACT N.Y. COTTON EXCHANGE IN CENTS PER POUND

Fig. A6.

Commodity:	SHELL EGGS (Fresh)
Where traded:	Chicago Mercantile Exchange, Chicago

Trading hours
New York time:	10:15 A.M. to 1:45 P.M.
Chicago time:	9:15 A.M. to 12:45 P.M.

Contract size:	22,500 dozen
How price is quoted:	Cents per dozen

Minimum fluctuation
Per dozen:	5/100¢
Per contract:	$11.25

Value 1¢ move:	$225.00

Maximum trading limit
From previous close:	2¢
Between daily high and low:	4¢

Commission (round-turn)
Regular:	$40.00
Straddle:	$43.00
Day trade:	$25.00

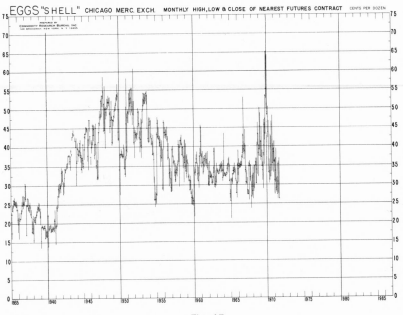

EGGS "SHELL" CHICAGO MERC. EXCH. MONTHLY HIGH,LOW & CLOSE OF NEAREST FUTURES CONTRACT CENTS PER DOZEN

Fig. A7.

Commodity:	FLAXSEED
Where traded:	Winnipeg Grain Exchange, Winnipeg
Trading hours	
New York time:	10:30 A.M. to 2:15 P.M.
Winnipeg time:	9:30 A.M. to 1:15 P.M.
Contract size:	1,000 bushels
How price is quoted:	Dollars and cents per bushel
Minimum fluctuation	
Per bushel:	1/8¢
Per contract:	$1.25
Value 1¢ move:	$10.00
Maximum trading limit	
From previous close:	10¢
Between daily high and low:	20¢
Commission (round-turn)	
Regular:	$5.00
Straddle:	$10.00
Day trade:	Full rate

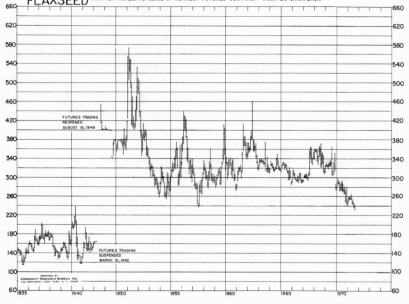

Fig. A8.

Commodity:	HOGS, LIVE
Where traded:	Chicago Mercantile Exchange, Chicago
Trading hours	
New York time:	10:20 A.M. to 1:50 P.M.
Chicago time:	9:20 A.M. to 12:50 P.M.
Contract size:	30,000 pounds
How price is quoted:	Cents per pound
Minimum fluctuation	
Per pound:	2½/100¢
Per contract:	$7.50
Value 1¢ move:	$300.00
Maximum trading limit	
From previous close:	1½¢
Between daily high	
and low:	3¢
Commission (round-turn)	
Regular:	$35.00
Straddle:	$38.00
Day trade:	$22.00

HOGS (LIVE)   Chi. Merc. Exch. (WEEKLY Hi, Lo, & Close OF NEAREST FUTURES)   CENTS PER POUND

Commodity Chart Service, Commodity Research Bureau Inc.

Fig. A9.

Commodity:	OATS
Where traded:	Chicago Board of Trade, Chicago
Trading hours	
New York time:	10:30 A.M. to 2:15 P.M.
Chicago time:	9:30 A.M. to 1:15 P.M.
Contract size:	5,000 bushels
How price is quoted:	Dollars and cents per bushel
Minimum fluctuation	
Per bushel:	1/8¢
Per contract:	$6.25
Value 1¢ move:	$50.00
Maximum trading limit	
From previous close:	6¢
Between daily high and low:	12¢
Commission (round-turn)	
Regular:	$25.00
Straddle:	$36.00
Day trade:	$17.00

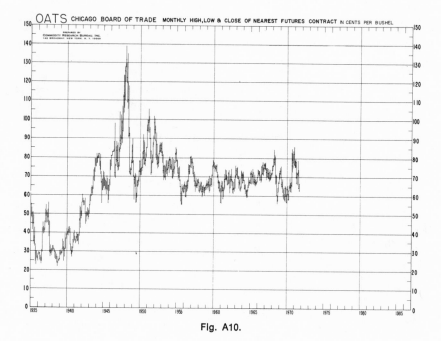

Fig. A10.

Commodity:	ORANGE JUICE (Frozen Concentrated)
Where traded:	Citrus Associates of New York Cotton Exchange, New York

Trading hours
  New York time: 10:15 A.M. to 2:45 P.M.

Contract size: 15,000 pounds

How price is quoted: Cents per pound

Minimum fluctuation
  Per pound: 5/100¢
  Per contract: $7.50

Value 1¢ move: $150.00

Maximum trading limit
  From previous close: 3¢
  Between daily high
  and low: 3¢

Commission (round-turn)
  Regular: $45.00
  Straddle: $54.00
  Day trade: $25.00

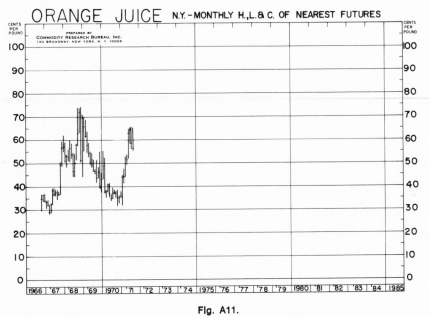

ORANGE JUICE N.Y.-MONTHLY H.,L.& C. OF NEAREST FUTURES

Fig. A11.

Commodity:	PALLADIUM
Where traded:	New York Mercantile Exchange, New York
Trading hours New York time:	10:20 A.M. to 12:55 P.M.
Contract size:	100 troy ounces
How price is quoted:	Dollars and cents per troy ounce
Minimum fluctuation	
Per ounce:	5¢
Per contract:	$5.00
Value $1.00 move:	$100.00
Maximum trading limit	
From previous close:	$2.50
Between daily high and low:	$5.00
Commission (round-turn)*	
Regular:	$42.00
Straddle:	$44.00
Day trade:	$21.00

* Price under $60.00

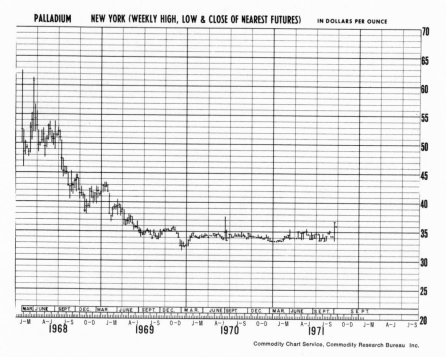

PALLADIUM   NEW YORK (WEEKLY HIGH, LOW & CLOSE OF NEAREST FUTURES)   IN DOLLARS PER OUNCE

Commodity Chart Service, Commodity Research Bureau Inc.

Fig. A12.

Commodity:	**PLATINUM**
Where traded:	New York Mercantile Exchange, New York

Trading hours
New York time: 9:45 A.M. to 1:30 P.M.

Contract size: 50 troy ounces

How price is quoted: Dollars and cents per troy ounce

Minimum fluctuation
Per ounce: 10¢
Per contract: $5.00

Value $1.00 move: $50.00

Maximum trading limit
From previous close: $10.00
Between daily high
and low: $10.00

Commission (round-turn)
Regular: $45.00
Straddle: $45.00
Day trade: $22.50

PLATINUM — New York (WEEKLY H., L., & C. OF NEAREST FUTURES)

DOLLARS PER OUNC

Commodity Chart Service, Commodity Research Bureau Inc.

Fig. A13.

Commodity:	PLYWOOD
Where traded:	Chicago Board of Trade, Chicago
Trading hours	
New York time:	11:00 A.M. to 2:05 P.M.
Chicago time:	10.00 A.M. to 1:05 P.M.
Contract size:	69,120 square feet (½" thick)
How price is quoted:	Dollars and cents per 1,000 square feet
Minimum fluctuation	
Per 1,000 square feet:	10¢
Per contract:	$6.912
Value $1.00 move:	$69.12
Maximum trading limit	
From previous close:	$7.00 per 1,000 square feet
Between daily high and low:	$14.00 per 1,000 square feet
Commission (round-turn)	
Regular:	$30.00
Straddle:	$40.00
Day trade:	$20.00

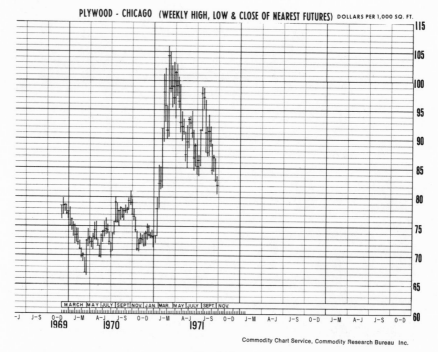

PLYWOOD - CHICAGO (WEEKLY HIGH, LOW & CLOSE OF NEAREST FUTURES) DOLLARS PER 1,000 SQ. FT.

Commodity Chart Service, Commodity Research Bureau Inc.

Fig. A14.

Commodity:	PORK BELLIES (Frozen)
Where traded:	Chicago Mercantile Exchange, Chicago

Trading hours
New York time: 10:30 A.M. to 2:00 P.M.
Chicago time: 9:30 A.M. to 1:00 P.M.

Contract size:	36,000 pounds
How price is quoted:	Cents per pound

Minimum fluctuation
Per pound: 2½/100¢
Per contract: $9.00

Value 1¢ move: $360.00

Maximum trading limit
From previous close: 1½¢
Between daily high
and low: 3¢

Commission (round-turn)
Regular: $45.00
Straddle: $48.00
Day trade: $27.00

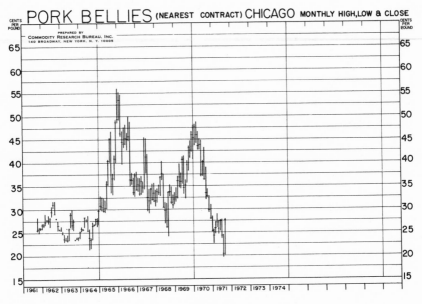

Fig. A15.

Commodity: POTATOES (Idaho)

Where traded: Chicago Mercantile Exchange, Chicago

Trading hours
  New York time: 10:00 A.M. to 1:50 P.M.
  Chicago time: 9:00 A.M. to 12:50 PM.

Contract size: 50,000 pounds

How price is quoted: Cents per pound

Minimum fluctuation
  Per pound: 1/100¢
  Per contract: $5.00

Value 1¢ move $500.00

Maximum trading limit
  From previous close: 35/100¢
  Between daily high
  and low: 70/100¢

Commission (round-turn)
  Regular: $30.00
  Straddle: $32.00
  Day trade: $15.00 per contract (two or more contracts)

Commodity:	POTATOES (Maine)
Where traded:	New York Mercantile Exchange, New York
Trading hours New York time:	10:00 A.M. to 2:00 P.M.
Contract size:	50,000 pounds
How price is quoted:	Cents per pound
Minimum fluctuation Per pound: Per contract:	1/100¢ $5.00
Value 1¢ move:	$500.00
Maximum trading limit From previous close: Between daily high and low:	35/100¢ 70/100¢
Commission (round-turn) Regular: Straddle: Day trade:	$30.00 $32.00 $15.00 per contract (two or more contracts)

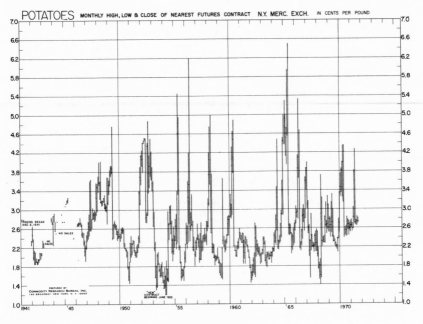

POTATOES MONTHLY HIGH, LOW & CLOSE OF NEAREST FUTURES CONTRACT N.Y. MERC. EXCH. IN CENTS PER POUND

Fig. A16.

Commodity:	RAPESEED
Where traded:	Winnepeg Grain Exchange, Winnipeg

Trading hours
New York time: 10:30 A.M. to 2:15 P.M.
Winnipeg time: 9:30 A.M. to 1:15 P.M.

Contract size: 1,000 bushels

How price is quoted: Dollars and cents per bushel

Minimum fluctuation
Per bushel: ⅛ ¢
Per contract: $1.25

Value 1¢ move: $10.00

Maximum trading limit
From previous close: 10¢
Between daily high
and low: 20¢

Commission (round-turn)
Regular: $5.00
Straddle: $10.00
Day trade: Full rate

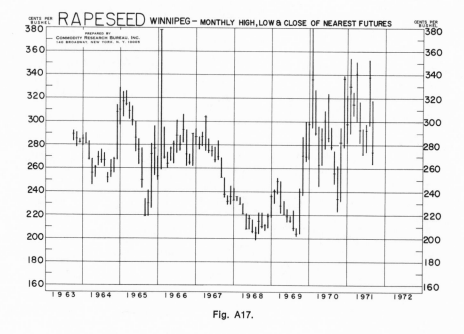

Fig. A17.

Commodity:	SILVER
Where traded:	Chicago Board of Trade, Chicago
Trading hours	
New York time:	10:00 A.M. to 2:25 P.M.
Chicago time:	9:00 A.M. to 1:25 P.M.
Contract size:	5,000 troy ounces
How price is quoted:	Dollars and cents per troy ounce
Minimum fluctuation	
Per ounce:	10/100¢
Per contract:	$5.00
Value 1¢ move:	$50.00
Maximum trading limit	
From previous close:	10¢ per ounce
Between daily high and low:	20¢ per ounce
Commission (round-turn)	
Regular:	$30.00
Straddle:	$32.00
Day trade:	$15.00

Commodity:	SILVER
Where traded:	Commodity Exchange, Inc., New York
Trading hours New York time:	9:30 A.M. to 2:15 P.M.
Contract size:	10,000 troy ounces
How price is quoted:	Dollars and cents per troy ounce
Minimum fluctuation Per ounce: Per contract:	10/100¢ $10.00
Value 1¢ move:	$100.00
Maximum trading limit From previous close: Between daily high and low:	10¢ 10¢
Commission (round-turn) Regular: Straddle: Day trade:	$45.50 $64.00 $23.00

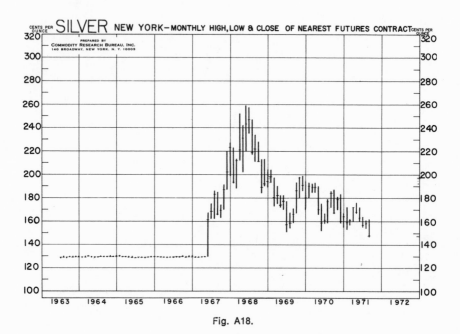

Fig. A18.

Commodity:	SILVER COINS (U.S.)
Where traded:	New York Mercantile Exchange, New York
Trading hours New York time:	9:25 A.M. to 2:15 P.M.
Contract size:	$10,000 face amount of U.S. silver coins (10 bags)
How price is quoted:	Dollars per bag
Minimum fluctuation Per bag: Per contract:	$1.00 $10.00
Maximum trading limit From previous close: Between daily high and low:	$100.00 per bag $200.00 per bag
Commission (round-turn) Regular: Straddle: Day trade:	$35.00 $35.00 $17.50 (two or more contracts)

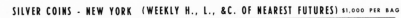

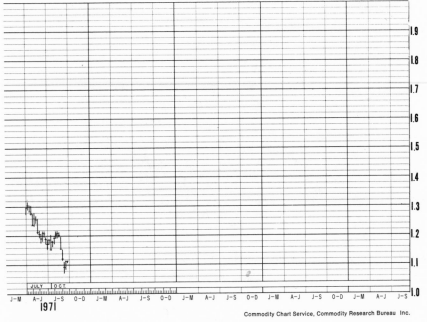

SILVER COINS - NEW YORK (WEEKLY H., L., &C. OF NEAREST FUTURES) $1,000 PER BAG

Commodity Chart Service, Commodity Research Bureau Inc.

Fig. A19.

Commodity:	SOYBEANS
Where traded:	Chicago Board of Trade, Chicago

Trading hours
New York time: 10:30 A.M. to 2:15 P.M.
Chicago time: 9:30 A.M. to 1:15 P.M.

Contract size:	5,000 bushels
How price is quoted:	Dollars and cents per bushel

Minimum fluctuation
Per bushel: ⅛ ¢
Per contract: $6.25

Value 1¢ move: $50.00

Maximum trading limit
From previous close: 10¢
Between daily high
and low: 20¢

Commission (round-turn)
Regular: $30.00
Straddle: $36.00
Day trade: $20.00

SOYBEANS MONTHLY HIGH, LOW & CLOSE OF NEAREST FUTURES CONTRACT CHIC. BD. OF TRADE IN CENTS PER BUSHEL

TRADING RESUMED JULY 7, 1947

TRADING SUSPENDED FEB. 19, 1943

PREPARED BY COMMODITY RESEARCH BUREAU, INC.

Fig. A20.

Commodity:	SOYBEAN MEAL
Where traded:	Chicago Board of Trade, Chicago
Trading hours	
New York time:	10:30 A.M. to 2:15 P.M.
Chicago time:	9:30 A.M. to 1:15 P.M.
Contract size:	100 tons
How price is quoted:	Dollars and cents per ton
Minimum fluctuation	
Per ton:	5¢
Per contract:	$5.00
Value $1.00 move:	$100.00
Maximum trading limit	
From previous close:	$5.00
Between daily high and low:	$10.00
Commission (round-turn)	
Regular:	$33.00
Straddle:	$44.00
Day trade:	$22.00

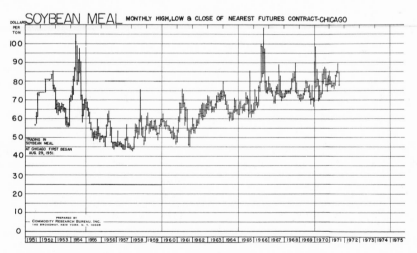

Fig. A21.

Commodity: SOYBEAN OIL

Where traded: Chicago Board of Trade, Chicago

Trading hours
New York time: 10:30 A.M. to 2:15 P.M.
Chicago time: 9:30 A.M. to 1:15 P.M.

Contract size: 60,000 pounds

How price is quoted: Cents per pound

Minimum fluctuation
Per pound: 1/100¢
Per contract: $6.00

Value 1¢ move: $600.00

Maximum trading limit
From previous close: 1¢
Between daily high
and low: 2¢

Commission (round-turn)
Regular: $33.00
Straddle: $44.00
Day trade: $22.00

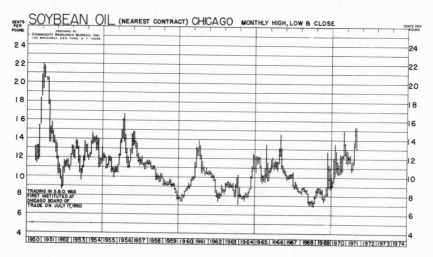

Fig. A22.

Commodity:	SUGAR No. 10 (Domestic)
Where traded:	New York Coffee and Sugar Exchange, New York

Trading hours
New York time: 10:00 A.M. to 2:50 P.M.

Contract size: 112,000 pounds (50 long tons)

How price is quoted: Cents per pound

Minimum fluctuation
Per pound: 1/100¢
Per contract: $11.20

Value 1¢ move: $1,120.00

Maximum trading limit
From previous close: ½ ¢
Between daily high
and low: 1¢

Commission (round-turn)

Regular: $42.00
Straddle: $42.00
Day trade: $21.00

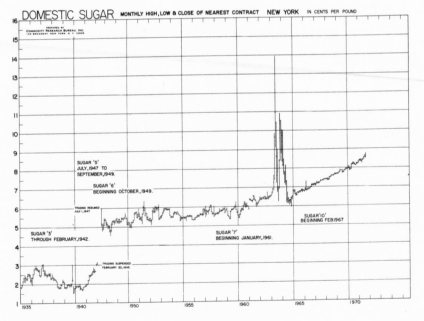

DOMESTIC SUGAR   MONTHLY HIGH, LOW & CLOSE OF NEAREST CONTRACT   NEW YORK   IN CENTS PER POUND

Fig. A23.

Commodity:	SUGAR No. 11 (World)
Where traded:	New York Coffee and Sugar Exchange, New York

Trading hours
   New York time: 10:00 A.M. to 3:00 P.M.

Contract size: 112,000 pounds (50 long tons)

How price is quoted: Cents per pound

Minimum fluctuation
   Per pound: 1/100¢
   Per contract $11.20

Value 1¢ move: $1,120.00

Maximum trading limit
   From previous close: ½¢
   Between daily high
   and low: 1¢

Commission (round-turn)	Price to 5.49	Price over 5.49
Regular:	$42.00	$62.00
Straddle:	$42.00	$62.00
Day trade:	$21.00	$31.00

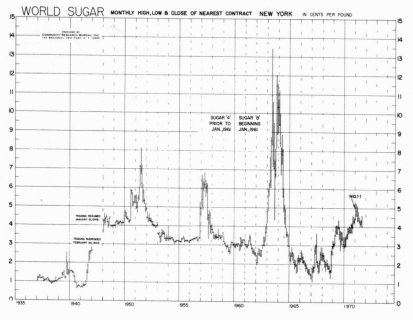

WORLD SUGAR MONTHLY HIGH, LOW & CLOSE OF NEAREST CONTRACT NEW YORK IN CENTS PER POUND

Fig. A24.

Commodity:	WHEAT
Where traded:	Chicago Board of Trade, Chicago

Trading hours	
New York time:	10:30 A.M. to 2:15 P.M.
Chicago time:	9:30 A.M. to 1:15 P.M.
Contract size:	5,000 bushels
How price is quoted:	Dollars and cents per bushel

Minimum fluctuation	
Per bushel:	⅛ ¢
Per contract:	$6.25
Value 1¢ move:	$50.00

Maximum trading limit	
From previous close:	10¢
Between daily high and low:	20¢

Commission (round-turn)	
Regular:	$30.00
Straddle:	$36.00
Day trade:	$20.00

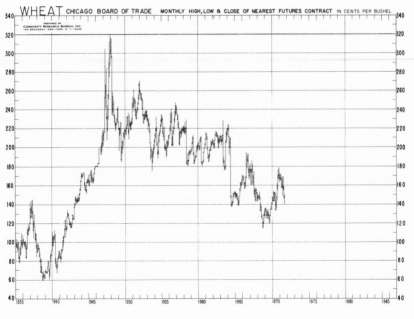

WHEAT CHICAGO BOARD OF TRADE   MONTHLY HIGH, LOW & CLOSE OF NEAREST FUTURES CONTRACT IN CENTS PER BUSHEL

PREPARED BY
COMMODITY RESEARCH BUREAU, INC.

Fig. A25.

Commodity:	WHEAT
Where traded:	Kansas City Board of Trade, Kansas City
Trading hours	
New York time:	10:30 A.M. to 2:15 P.M.
Kansas City time:	9:30 A.M. to 1:15 P.M.
Contract size:	5,000 bushels
How price is quoted:	Dollars and cents per bushel
Minimum fluctuation	
Per bushel:	⅛ ¢
Per contract:	$6.25
Value 1¢ move:	$50.00
Maximum trading limit	
From previous close:	10¢
Between daily high and low:	20¢
Commission (round-turn)	
Regular:	$22.00
Straddle:	$30.00
Day trade:	Full rate

Commodity:	WHEAT
Where traded:	Minneapolis Grain Exchange, Minneapolis
Trading hours	
New York time:	10:30 A.M. to 2:15 P.M.
Minneapolis time:	9:30 A.M. to 1:15 P.M.
Contract size:	5,000 bushels
How price is quoted:	Dollars and cents per bushel
Minimum fluctuation	
Per bushel:	⅛ ¢
Per contract:	$6.25
Value 1¢ move:	$50.00
Maximum trading limit	
From previous close:	10¢
Between daily high and low:	20¢
Commission (round-turn)	
Regular:	$30.00
Straddle:	$36.00
Day trade:	Full rate

Commodity:	WOOL (Grease)
Where traded:	Wool Associates of New York Cotton Exchange, New York
Trading hours New York time:	10:00 A.M. to 2:30 P.M.
Contract size:	6,000 pounds (clean basis)
How price is quoted:	Cents per pound
Minimum fluctuation Per pound:	1/10¢
Per contract:	$6.00
Value 1¢ move:	$60.00
Maximum trading limit From previous close:	5¢
Between daily high and low:	5¢
Commission (round-turn) Regular:	$50.00
Straddle:	$60.00
Day trade:	$27.00

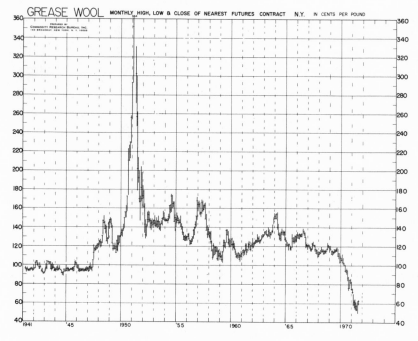

GREASE WOOL MONTHLY HIGH, LOW & CLOSE OF NEAREST FUTURES CONTRACT N.Y. IN CENTS PER POUND

Fig. A26.

United Kingdom

Commodity:	COCOA
Where traded:	London Cocoa Terminal Market Association
Positions traded:	Up to 15 months ahead, in March, May, July, September, and December

Trading hours	London time	New York time
Opening call:	10:00–unlimited	05:00–unlimited
Free trading:	–12:50	–07:50
Mid-day call:	12:50–13:00	07:50–08:00
Lunch break:	13:00–14:30	08:00–09:30
Unofficial call:	14:30	09:30
Free trading:	–15:30	–10:30
P.M. call:	15:30–unlimited	10:30–unlimited
Free trading:	–16:50	–11:50
Closing call:	16:50–17:00	11:50–12:00

Contract size:	5 long tons
How price is quoted:	Pound sterling per long ton
Minimum fluctuation	
Per ton:	50 pence
Per contract:	£2.50
Value £1.00 move:	£5.00
Maximum trading limit:	No limit for spot month. Other months £20.00 per ton above or below previous close. This is followed by a 30 minute recess. Thereafter, the market reopens with a special call and continues without limits, until the close of the day.
Commission (round-turn):	£12.00

Commodity:	COFFEE
Where traded:	London Coffee Terminal Market Association
Positions traded:	Up to 12 months ahead, in January, March, May, July, September, and November

Trading hours	London time	New York time
Opening call:	10:30–10:40	05:30–05:40
Free trading:	10:40–12:20	05:40–07:20
Mid-day call:	12:20–12:30	07:20–07:30
Lunch break:	12:30–14:30	07:30–09:30
P.M. call:	14:30–14:40	09:30–09:40
Free trading:	14:40–16:50	09:40–11:50
Closing call:	16:50–17:00	11:50–12:00

Contract size:	5 long tons
How price is quoted:	Pound-sterling per long ton
Minimum fluctuation	
Per ton:	50 pence
Per contract:	£2.50
Value £1.00 move:	£5.00
Maximum trading limit:	No limit for spot month. Other months, £20.00 per ton above or below previous close. This is followed by a 30 minute recess. Thereafter, the market reopens with a special call and continues without limits, until the close of the day.
Commission (round-turn):	£14.00

Commodity:	COPPER
Where traded:	London Metal Exchange
Positions traded:	Any single market date between current day (cash) and 3 months forward (3 months)

Trading hours	London time	New York time
Copper wirebars:	12:00–12:05	07:00–07:05
Copper wirebars:	12:35–12:40	07:35–07:40
Copper cathodes:	12:40–12:45	07:40–07:45
Kerb:	13:10–13:30	08:10–08:30
Copper:	15:45–15:50	10:45–10:50
Copper wirebars:	16:15–16:20	11:15–11:20
Copper cathodes:	16:20–16:25	11:20–11:25
Kerb:	16:35–16:50	11:35–11:50

Contract size:	25 long tons
How price is quoted:	Pound sterling per long ton
Minimum fluctuation	
Per ton:	50 pence
Per contract:	£12.50
Value £1.00 move:	£25.00
Maximum trading limit:	None
Commission (round-turn):	½% of value of initial transaction

Commodity:	LEAD
Where traded:	London Metal Exchange
Positions traded:	Any single market date between current day (cash) and 3 months forward (3 months)

Trading hours	London time	New York time
Trading:	12:15–12:20	07:15–07:20
Trading:	12:50–12:55	07:50–07:55
Kerb:	13:10–13:30	08:10–08:30
Trading:	15:40–15:45	10:40–10:45
Trading:	16:05–16:10	11:05–11:10
Kerb:	16:35–16:50	11:35–11:50

Contract size:	25 long tons
How price is quoted:	Pound sterling per long ton
Minimum fluctuation	
Per ton:	50 pence
Per contract:	£12.50
Value £1.00 move:	£25.00
Maximum trading limit:	None
Commission (round-turn):	½% of value of initial transaction

Commodity:	SILVER
Where traded:	London Bullion Dealer Market
Positions traded:	Any single market date up to 12 months ahead, as agreed between buyer and seller. As the official "fixing," prices are quoted for spot, 3 month, 6 month, and 12 month positions.
Trading hours:	Daily "fixing" at 12:30 P.M. (7:30 A.M. New York time). Dealings can be made at other times but are subject to negotiation.
Contract size:	5,000 troy ounces (minimum contract)
How price is quoted:	Pence per troy ounce
Minimum fluctuation Per ounce:	0.1 pence
Per contract:	£5.00 per 5,000 ounces
Value 1 pence move:	£50.00 per 5,000 ounces
Maximum trading limit:	None
Commission (round-turn):	Negotiated. Usually ¼% of value of transaction, when business is done at "fixing." Business done outside of the "fixing" is net of commissions.

Commodity:	SILVER
Where traded:	London Metal Exchange
Positions traded:	Any market date up to 7 months ahead, as agreed between buyer and seller. Prices are quoted for spot, 3 month and 7 month positions.

Trading hours	London time	New York time
Trading:	12:05–12:10	07:05–07:10
Official fixing:	12:25–12:35	07:25–07:35
Trading:	13:00–13:05	08:00–08:05
Kerb:	13:10–13:30	08:10–08:30
Trading:	15:55–16:00	10:55–11:00
Trading:	16:30–16:35	11:30–11:35
Kerb:	16:35–16:50	11:35–11:50

Contract size:	10,000 troy ounces
How price is quoted:	Pence per troy ounce
Minimum fluctuation	
Per ounce:	0.1 pence
Per contract:	£10.00
Value 1 pence move:	£100.00
Maximum trading limit:	None
Commission:	½ % of value of initial transaction

Commodity:	SUGAR
Where traded:	United Terminal Sugar Market Association
Positions traded:	Up to 15 months ahead, in March, May, August, October, and December

Trading hours	London time	New York time
A.M. Kerb:	10:00–10:40	05:00–05:40
Opening call:	10:40–10:55	05:40–05:55
L.D.P. fix:	11:00	06:00
Free trading:	11:00–12:30	06:00–07:30
Mid-day call:	12:30–12:45	07:30–07:45
Lunch break:	12:45–14:15	07:45–09:15
Unofficial call:	14:15	09:15
Free trading:	–15:30	–10:30
P.M. call:	15:30–15:45	10:30–10:45
Free trading	15:45–16:45	10:45–11:45
Closing call	16:45–17:00	11:45–12:00
Evening kerb:	17:00–20:00	12:00–15:00

| Contract size: | 5 long tons |
| How price is quoted: | Pound sterling per long ton |

Minimum fluctuation	
Per ton:	5 pence
Per contract:	£2.50

Value £1.00 move:	£50.00
Maximum trading limit:	No limit for spot month. Other months £5.00 per ton above or below the previous day's 12:45 official prices, until 12:45 the following day.
Commission (round-turn):	£15.00

Commodity:	TIN
Where traded:	London Metal Exchange
Positions traded:	Any single market date between current day (cash) and 3 months forward (3 months)

Trading hours	London time	New York time
Trading:	12:10–12:15	07:10–07:15
Trading:	12:45–12:50	07:45–07:50
Kerb:	13:10–13:30	08:10–08:30
Trading:	15:50–15:55	10:50–10:55
Trading:	16:25–16:30	11:25–11:30
Kerb:	16:35–16:50	11:35–11:50

| Contract size: | 5 long tons |
| How price is quoted: | Pound sterling per long ton |

Minimum fluctuation

| Per ton: | £1.00 |
| Per contract: | £5.00 |

Value £1.00 move:	£5.00
Maximum trading limit:	None
Commission (round-turn):	½% of value of initial transaction

Commodity:	ZINC
Where traded:	London Metal Exchange
Positions traded:	Any single market date between current day (cash) and 3 months forward (3 months)

Trading hours	London time	New York time
Trading:	12:20–12:25	07:20–07:25
Trading:	12:55–13:00	07:55–08:00
Kerb:	13:10–13:30	08:10–08:30
Trading:	15:40–15:45	10:40–10:45
Trading:	16:10–16:15	11:10–11:15
Kerb:	16:35–16:50	11:35–11:50

Contract size:	25 long tons
How price is quoted:	Pound sterling per long ton
Minimum fluctuation	
Per ton:	25 pence
Per contract:	£6.25
Value £1.00 move:	£25.00
Maximum trading limit:	None
Commission (round-turn):	½% of value of initial transaction

Seasonally Adjusted Open Interest and Volume Charts

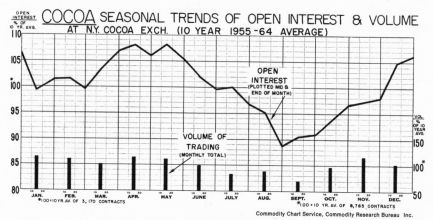

Fig. C1.

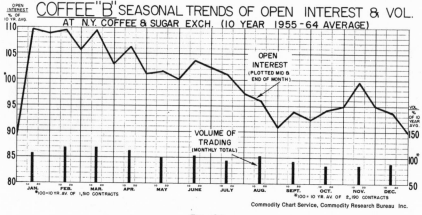

Fig. C2.

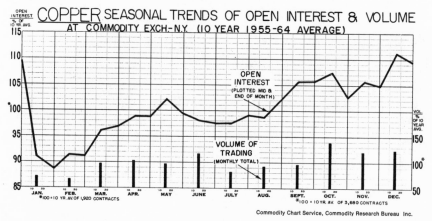

Fig. C3.

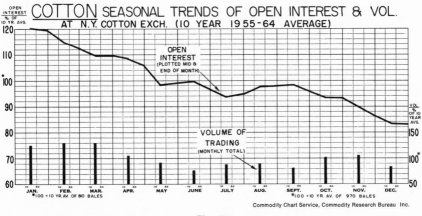

Fig. C4.

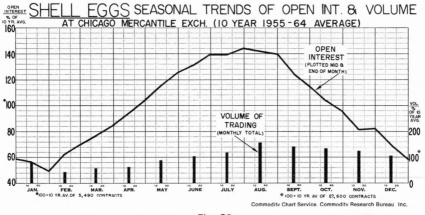

Fig. C5.

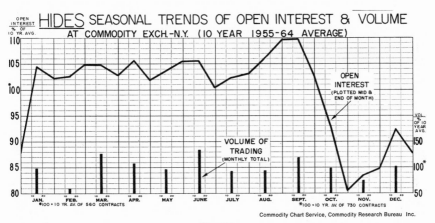

Fig. C6.

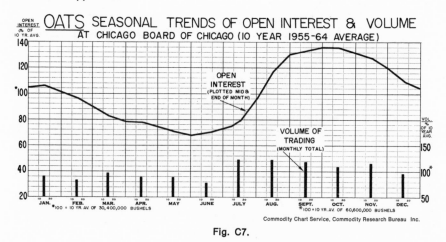

Fig. C7.

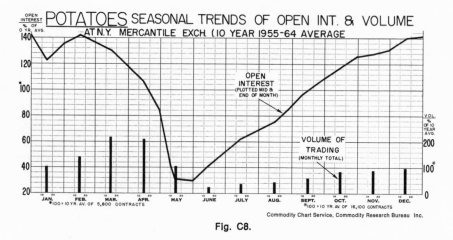

Fig. C8.

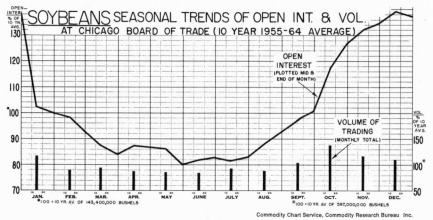

Fig. C9.

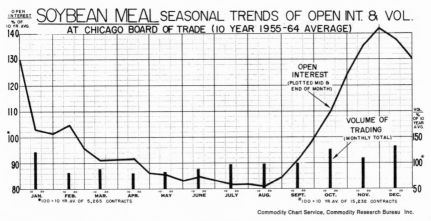

Fig. C10.

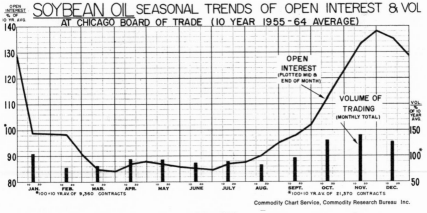

Fig. C11.

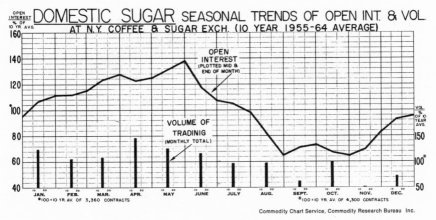

Fig. C12.

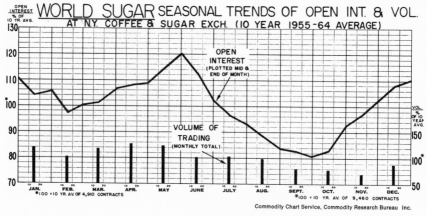

Fig. C13.

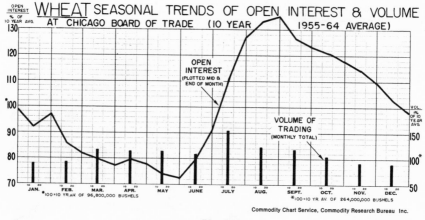

Fig. C14.

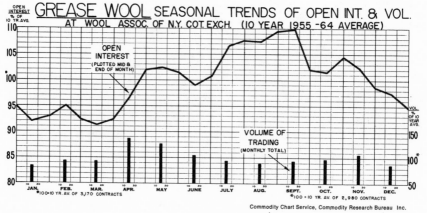

Fig. C15.

APPENDIX C

List of Commodity Exchanges

Chicago Board of Trade
    141 West Jackson Blvd., Chicago, Illinois
Chicago Mercantile Exchange
    110 North Franklin Street, Chicago, Illinois
Commodity Exchange, Inc.
    81 Broad Street, New York, New York
New York Cocoa Exchange, Inc.
    92 Beaver Street, New York, New York
New York Coffee and Sugar Exchange, Inc.
    79 Pine Street, New York, New York
New York Cotton Exchange, Inc.
    37 Wall Street, New York, New York
New York Mercantile Exchange
    6 Harrison Street, New York, New York
New York Produce Exchange, Inc.
    2 Broadway, New York, New York
West Coast Commodity Exchange, Inc.
    643 South Olive Street, Los Angeles, California

List of Commodity Trade Associations

Cocoa
  Cocoa Merchants Association of America, Inc.
Copper
  Copper Development Association
  National Association of Secondary Material Industries
Cotton
  American Textile Manufacturers Institute
  National Cotton Council of America
  Southern Cotton Association
  Texas Cotton Association
Grains
  Indiana Grain and Feed Dealers Association
  Iowa Grain and Feed Dealers Association
  Kansas Grain and Feed Dealers Association
  National Grain and Feed Association
Livestock
  American Meat Institute
Orange Juice
  Florida Canners Association
  Florida Citrus Mutual
Silver
  Silver Institute
  Silver Users Association
Soybeans
  American Soybean Association
  National Soybean Processors Association
Sugar
  The Sugar Association, Inc.

APPENDIX D   **Bibliography**

Baer, J. B., and O. G. Saxon. *Commodity Exchanges and Futures Trading.* New York: Harper & Row, 1947.

Baranyai, L., and J. C. Mills. *International Commodity Agreements.* Mexico: Centro de Estudios Monetarios Latinamericanos, 1963.

Belveal, L. D. *Charting Commodity Price Behaviour.* Chicago: Commodity Press, 1969.

———. *Commodity Speculation with Profits in Mind.* Wilmette, Ill.: The Commodities Press, 1968.

Board of Trade of the City of Chicago. *Commodity Trading Manual.* Chicago, 1971.

Cohen, A. W. *Point and Figure Stock Market Trading.* Larchmont, N.Y.: Chartcraft, Inc., 1968.

Commodity Research Bureau, Inc. *Commodity Year Book.* New York, published annually.

Cootner, P. H. (Ed.). *The Random Character of Stock Market Prices.* Cambridge, Mass., The M.I.T. Press, 1964.

Cox, H. *A Common Sense Approach to Commodity Futures Trading.* New York: Reynolds & Co., 1968.

Davis, J. S. *International Commodity Agreements: Hope, Illusion or Menace?* New York: Prepared for the Advisory Committee on Economics to the Committee on International Economic Policy in Cooperation with the Carnegie Endowment for International Peace, 1947, No. 12.

Dunn, D. D., and E. F. Hargitt. *Trader's Notebook.* Lafayette, Ind.: Dunn & Hargitt's Financial Services, Inc., 1970.

Ezekiel, M., and K. A. Fox. *Methods of Correlation and Regression Analysis.* New York: John Wiley & Sons, 1930, 1941, 1959.

Food and Agriculture Organization of the United Nations. *Commodity Review and Outlook.* Italy: FAO, annual issues.—*Monthly Bulletin of Agricultural Economics and Statistics.*

Foote, R. J. *Analytical Tools for Studying Demand and Price Structures.* Washington, D.C.: U.S. Department of Agriculture, 1958.

Fox, K. A. *The Analysis of Demand for Farm Products.* Technical Bulletin 1081, Washington, D.C.: U.S. Department of Agriculture, 1953.

Gold, G. *Modern Commodity Futures Trading,* 5th (rev.) ed. New York: Commodity Research Bureau, Inc., 1968.

Gray, R. W. "Fundamental Price Behavior Characteristics in Commodity Futures," *Futures Trading Seminar,* Vol. 3. Madison, Wisc.: Chicago Board of Trade, 1966.

Green, T. *The World of Gold.* New York: Walker and Company, 1968.

Horn, F. F. *Trading in Commodity Futures.* New York: Institute of Finance, 1969.

Irwin, H. S. *Evolution of Futures Trading.* Madison, Wisc.: Mimir Publishers, 1954.

Jiler, H., and G. B. Parker (Eds.). *Guide to Commodity Price Forecasting.* New York: Commodity Research Bureau, Inc., 1967.

Keltner, C. W. *How to Make Money in Commodities.* Kansas City, Mo.: The Keltner Statistical Service, 1950.

Larson, A. B. "Price Prediction on the Egg Futures Market," Proceedings of a Symposium on Price Effects of Speculation in Organized Commodity Markets. *Food Research Institute Studies.* Stanford, Calif.: Stanford University, Vol. 7, pp. 49–64, 1967.

Longstreet, R. W. *Viewpoints of a Commodity Trader.* New York: Frederick Fell, Inc., 1968.

Miller, N. C. *The Great Salad Oil Swindle.* New York: Coward McCann, 1965.

Schonberg, J. S. *The Grain Trade, How It Works.* Jericho, N.Y. Exposition Press, 1956.

Stewart, B. *An Analysis of Speculative Trading in Grain Futures.* Technical Bulletin No. 1001. Washington, D.C.: U.S. Department of Agriculture, Commodity Exchange Authority, October, 1949.

Teweles, R. J., C. V. Harlow, and H. L. Stone. *The Commodity Futures Trading Guide.* New York: McGraw-Hill, 1969.

Theil, C. C., Jr., and R. E. Davis. *Point and Figure Commodity Trading: A Computer Evaluation.* Lafayette, Ind.: Dunn & Hargitt's Financial Services, Inc., 1970.

Thomsen, F. L., and R. J. Foote. *Agricultural Prices.* New York: McGraw-Hill, 1936, 1952.

United Nations Conference on Trade and Development. *Commodity Survey.* New York: United Nations, annual issues.

Waugh, F. V. *Demand and Price Analysis.* Technical Bulletin 1316, Washington, D.C.: U. S. Department of Agriculture, 1949.

Wheelan, A. H. *Study Helps in Point and Figure Technique.* New York: Morgan, Rogers and Roberts, Inc., 1954.

Working, H. "New Concepts Concerning Futures Markets and Prices," *American Economic Review,* Vol. 51, No. 2, May 1961.

————. "A Theory of Anticipation Prices," *American Economic Review,* Vol. 48, No. 2, May, 1958.

————. "Theory of the Inverse Carrying Charge in Futures Markets," *Journal of Farm Economics,* Vol. 30, No. 1, February, 1948.

————. "Theory of Price of Storage," *American Economic Review,* Vol. 39, No. 6, December, 1949.

INDEX

75 10 9 8 7 6 5 4 3